$\mathcal{B}$ICYCLING
COAST $\tilde{to}$ COAST

BICYCLING COAST to COAST

A COMPLETE ROUTE GUIDE
VIRGINIA TO OREGON

DONNA LYNN IKENBERRY

THE
MOUNTAINEERS

To my dear friend Carol Kaufman

 Published by
The Mountaineers
1001 SW Klickitat Way, Suite 201
Seattle, Washington 98134

First printing 1996, second printing 2001

Published simultaneously in Great Britain by Cordee, 3a DeMontfort Street, Leicester, England, LE1 7HD

Manufactured in the United States of America

Edited by Sherri Schultz
Maps and book layout by Word Graphics
All photographs by Donna Lynn Ikenberry except as noted
Cover design by The Mountaineers Books
Book design and typography by The Mountaineers Books

Cover photographs: *Bicyclists near Philipsburg, Montana* Insets, left to right: *Virginia Creeper Trail, Virginia; Grand Teton National Park, Wyoming; Strawberry Hill, Oregon Coast*
Frontispiece: *Flowers and Dillon Reservoir from bike path between Breckenridge and Frisco, Colorado.*

Library of Congress Cataloging-in-Publication Data
Ikenberry, Donna Lynn.
    Bicycling coast to coast : a complete route guide, Virginia to Oregon / Donna Lynn Ikenberry.
       p. cm.
    Includes bibliographical references and index.
    ISBN 0-89886-468-2
    1. Bicycle touring—United States—Guidebooks. 2. Bicycle trails—United States—Guidebooks. 3. United States—Guidebooks. I. Title.
    GV1045.I54 1996
    796.6'4'0973—dc20
                                              95-42913
                                              CIP

CONTENTS

IDAHO

OREGON

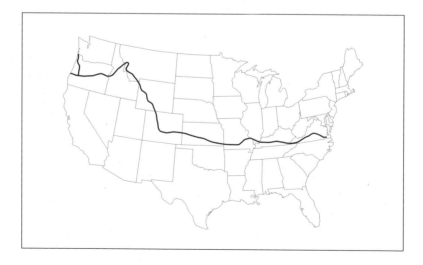

PREFACE

"Someday I'm going to ride the Oregon coast and the California coast, and then I'm going to ride clear across the country!"

I beamed those words the day after Christmas 1986. I had met my family for the holiday in Big Sur, California, and my brother Don had semi-surprised me with a ten-speed bicycle. By the next day my future plans for touring were set.

Less than a year passed before I was on my first tour, a semi-sagged affair down the Oregon coast. As I had once promised, the following year I rode California's coast. In 1991 I rode the Atlantic coast and wrote my first biking guidebook, *Bicycling the Atlantic Coast*.

As I rode the various coasts, my yearning for a cross-country ride never waned, so I was delighted when in 1993 Donna DeShazo of The Mountaineers Books wrote and asked if I still wanted to ride across the country. I literally ran to the telephone to tell her yes.

I wanted to do the ride for many reasons. First, I thoroughly enjoy touring, and a ride of several thousand miles sounded intriguing and challenging. Second, although I travel full-time, I had never seen most of the route I would be following, and I was anxious to see more of America. Third, I wanted to meet other bicyclists, enjoy the people of the small towns I would be passing through, and see some of the magnificent scenes the United States has to offer. And finally, I simply wanted to be able to say, "I bicycled across the USA!"

Although I didn't have a problem with riding alone, my family and friends expressed their concern on many occasions. Even strangers seemed concerned when told of my upcoming cross-country adventure. And I did have to admit that I would rather ride with someone than make the trek alone.

As a member of Adventure Cycling Association, I had often browsed through the "Companions Wanted" section of the group's magazine. Soon my own ad appeared, and within the next few months more than thirty people contacted me about my ride. I explained to everyone that I would be working during the ride— making images, transcribing notes at night, the usual guidebook stuff—and would therefore probably end up riding at a slower pace than most people, finishing in about four months. (I ended up finishing in three and a half months.)

I am grateful to everyone who called or wrote. Some people decided to take another route, others wanted to go faster; some wanted to ride in a large group, others just wanted to chat. However, by the time I landed in Virginia to begin my ride I had four men waiting for me, all of us strangers. And another couple was waiting for me midway, in Hutchinson, Kansas.

The ride began as planned, although it didn't take long to notice personality and riding differences. Loaded down with camera gear, I was definitely the slowest in the bunch. After one week my pals Dick Davis and Earl Norman, who were both over sixty years old, decided to go on at a faster pace. No hard feelings—the two were just into megamiles, and they wanted to move. Remarkably, they finished the ride about one month ahead of me! Gary Sears also decided to go ahead with the "Grumpy Old Men," as they called themselves, but headed for home upon reaching Kentucky via a combination of methods including pickup trucks, trains, planes, and a little more bike riding in Colorado.

Dan Mauro stayed with me off and on for the next month or so, but he went off route often. We finally said good-bye in Missouri and promised to meet up again in Wyoming. When Dan flagged me down in Grand Teton National Park he was driving a used car, his bicycle placed carefully in the back. Forced off the road twice, having cycled continuously since leaving New York on May 1, Dan had decided to quit riding in Wyoming and do some serious car touring instead.

I met Carol and Bill Kaufman in Hutchinson, Kansas. After they responded to my request in *Bike Report*, we had talked on the phone and written, making plans for Carol to ride with me from Hutchinson to perhaps Missoula, Montana. She had five weeks to cycle and wasn't in a hurry.

After taking a week off in Kansas (I left my gear at the Kaufmans' home and flew to Oregon to see my boyfriend), I rode through Kansas with Carol, and we became friends as fast as the wind blows across the prairie. Perfect riding companions, Carol and I blew through Kansas and on into Colorado, where Bill hooked up with us for a week and another new friend was made.

After my cross-country journey had ended, I often reflected on that memorable summer. I was thrilled to have pedaled more than 4,000 miles; I had seen lots of great scenes and met many interesting people. But most important of all, I made lasting friendships that I will always treasure.

ACKNOWLEDGMENTS

Although I bicycled across the country alone much of the time, I believe that I was never really "alone," for God was always with me. He was my constant source of support.

My family couldn't be there in the physical sense, but I felt their presence daily and welcomed their prayers and words of encouragement and love. My parents, Don and Beverly Ikenberry, secured a toll-free telephone number so I could call often, and along with my brothers, Don and Dave Ikenberry, made my mail drops just like Christmas. A number of very special friends added to the gifts with letters and prayers that I will always treasure. Barbara Bjerke did even more as she stockpiled the mail my parents forwarded to me, and mailed off packages of maps and gloves and other items to me at various points along the trail.

This book is dedicated to an exceptional person; avid bicyclist Carol Kaufman made the Kansas to Montana journey the best ride I have ever experienced.

I am grateful to all those who responded to my ad for cycling partners, including the four—Earl Norman, Dick Davis, Gary Sears, and Dan Mauro—who started the ride with me. I also appreciate the time and fun I had riding with several other bicyclists, including Donald Cochran, Jim Gallion, Steve Glockner, Randy Gonzales, Dan Hoffman, Bill Kaufman, Alan Thompson, and Mona Trekeld.

Several people made my nights more comfortable with offers of a shower and a bed or a place to pitch my tent. They include Bud and Mary Belden, Gene and Mary Everett, June Curry (the Cookie Lady), the Dusty Gilmore family, Bill and Carol Kaufman, Kathryn "Yodeling Katy" Lopeman, and the Ernest Margelot family.

In addition to all of those who provided information, gave me a lift when I needed to go off route for a bike part, or offered me a free pass to some point of interest, I must thank the people at Avocet for introducing me to the Avocet® Vertech, which I found highly dependable and a constant source of entertainment. Watching my daily elevation gain and loss made the miles zoom by!

And last, I must thank Donna DeShazo and the rest of the staff at The Mountaineers Books. Once again I am grateful to have been able to combine my work with the fun and learning of a cross-country trip.

Special note: I got married since my ride across the country so I'm happy to say Mike Vining rides with me now.

INTRODUCTION

Stretching from the historic town of Yorktown, Virginia, to the awesome beauty of Oregon's coast, the original TransAmerica Bicycle Trail embraces ten states, a potpourri of small American towns, and a multitude of landscapes.

Spanning more than 4,100 miles, the route snakes through the ruggedly steep hills of Virginia, embraces the rural countryside of Kentucky, roller coasters through the Missouri Ozarks, and bisects the nearly flat plains of Kansas. From there, it greets the Rocky Mountains and the Great Basin country of Colorado, follows the path of the pronghorn antelope in Wyoming, and explores the depths of Big Sky Montana. The route continues into Idaho, where it parallels one river after another before emerging into Oregon, where mountain climbs are common and the scenery is both beautiful and intense.

Heading west like the pioneers, you too can fulfill your dream of completing a cross-country journey, but without the hardships endured by the immigrants who followed the Oregon Trail. And like those pioneers, you can look forward to the grandeur of the Rocky Mountains, to moonlike scenes atop McKenzie Pass in Oregon's Cascade Mountains, and to that thrilling moment when you reach the Pacific Ocean.

Positive and Negative Aspects of Riding Across the Country

Bicycling across the country is not much more difficult than just getting on your bike and riding everyday. Of course, bicycling daily is a bit monotonous for some folks, there are camp chores to do after you've ridden 60 miles or so, and there's always dinner to be cooked. (If you aren't fond of cooking you can eat out, as I did.) In addition, braving the elements on a daily basis can grind you down, especially if rain or hail has been pounding your head for days, or the heat and humidity have you melting like Frosty the Snowman.

But for every negative aspect of riding across the country, there are many more positive ones. Perhaps the best thing about the journey is knowing that you have pedaled more miles than some people care to drive. If you can bicycle across America, you can do anything! Besides, camp chores aren't all that bad; after the ride is over some people deeply miss their tiny tent, cooking outdoors, and snuggling up inside their mummy bags. Strangely enough, some even miss sitting on their bike seat all day long!

Bicyclists at Yorktown Victory Monument, Yorktown, Virginia

In addition, touring is a great way to see the country at a slow pace. You're going fast enough to make fairly good time (you'll average in one day what most people do in an hour by car), and you can actually see, smell, and often hear the scenes before you. Also, it's a fantastic way to eat all of the food you care to and not gain a pound. Best of all, it's the best way to meet the local folks and perhaps make a lifelong friend or two.

Adventure Cycling Association

Once you begin looking for a route across America, you will find an endless number of possibilities. When I first started scanning maps, I decided that riding one of the routes designated by Adventure Cycling Association (originally called Bikecentennial) would be more to my liking.

The original TransAmerica Bicycle Trail, or TransAm Trail as it is commonly known, is one of three cross-country journeys selected by Adventure Cycling. The other two are the Northern Tier Route, which stretches from Washington state to Maine, and the Southern Tier Route, from California to Florida.

Inaugurated in 1976, when more than 4,000 riders from all over the world joined forces to celebrate the 200th year of our nation's existence with a cross-country bike ride, the TransAmerica Trail is still the most popular route across the country. In 1976, just over 2,000 cyclists rode the entire length of the trail. All fifty states and several foreign nations were represented; Holland alone boasted 200 riders. After the ride, the staff at Bikecentennial wrote, "Those who rode a TransAm trip in an average gear of 70 inches turned their cranks 1,239,550 times. At 10 miles per hour, Bikecentennial riders spent 1.1 million hours in the saddle, during 550,000 rider days, covering 11 million rider miles."

A twenty-fifth-anniversary TransAmerica ride may take place in the year 2001; you can get up-to-date information on this possibility from Adventure Cycling Association, today a nonprofit organization with 40,000 members. If you're not a member, I'd recommend joining. Membership dues are currently (in 2001) $30 for individuals, $37 for families, and $24 for students or seniors over sixty years of age. Lifetime memberships vary, but start at $475 for individuals. Write or call Adventure Cycling Association, P.O. Box 8308-ZE, Missoula, MT 59807; (800) 755-2453. Check the website at www. adventurecycling.org or email at info@adventurecycling.org.

Members of an Adventure Cycling Association TransAmerica tour. The group includes a minister, an engineer, a music teacher, a banker, a social worker, and a computer science student. Adventure Cycling photo by Greg Siple.

Rolling Right Along

The TransAmerica Trail explores ten states—Virginia, Kentucky, Illinois, Missouri, Kansas, Colorado, Wyoming, Montana, Idaho, and Oregon. This guidebook contains a section on each of these states, although the sections vary in length (for example, you'll spend thirteen days in Virginia and just three in Illinois). Because I didn't end each segment of the journey at state lines, however, some days will find you in one state in the morning and in another by the end of the day. Segments are always listed under the state where they end, not where they begin.

Although I adhered to the TransAmerica Trail almost exclusively, I did go off route on several occasions. I made my

Sign for TransAmerica Trail (often called "76 Bike Route"), Ordway, Colorado

own way twice in Virginia, once in Illinois, again in Montana, and for the last time in Oregon when I ended my ride in Florence, deemed the Alternate Route by Adventure Cycling. Their maps show the ride ending in Astoria, although they do acknowledge that westbound riders will no doubt end their ride in Florence.

My version of the TransAmerica Trail comprises a total of 4,136.4 miles, with a 238.5-mile alternate route available if you'd rather end the ride in Astoria. (If you end in Astoria you'll skip the Coburg to Florence segment, making your total ride 4,298.1 miles.) Total elevation gain for the main route is roughly 146,770 feet, with an additional 7,200 feet necessary if you end in Astoria. Of course, side trips add extra mileage and elevation gain.

The trip is divided into 77 daily segments or mileage logs (a total of 81 if you're aiming for Astoria), most of which end at a campground or city park where camping is allowed. (Campgrounds are noted on the maps in this book; however, parks without toilet facilities are listed in the text but not on the maps.) When campgrounds were nonexistent I ended the segment in the middle of a town. From that point you can decide if you'd rather get a motel room or ask a local family if you can pitch your tent in their backyard.

Although daily mileage varies from a low of 22.6 miles on your first day out to the 85.7-mile Buhler to Larned segment in Kansas, the average daily distance is under 54 miles. If you'd rather double up on some of the days, feel free to do so. And if you'd rather cut some of the days in half, you can do that too.

Do I Need to Ride Across the Entire Country in One Summer?

This guide was written for everyone: from people interested in nothing more than a day ride, to those self-contained individuals who think nothing of touring for weeks or months at a time.

The segments are guides to help you cross the country, but you needn't feel that you must conquer them all in one summer. Short of time? If you have only a month or so, why not divide the country in half and ride one half of the nation one summer, the other half the next? Or you can emulate Carol Kaufman, who rode from Hutchinson, Kansas, to Yorktown, Virginia, in 1989 and then did the Hutchinson to Missoula portion with me in 1994. Sometime within the next couple of years she'll finish her cross-country jaunt with a trip from Missoula to the Oregon coast. If you have even less free time, you can always cross one state at a time.

Why East to West?

I had a tough time deciding which way to cross the country. Oh, it wasn't difficult at first; I presumed that I would ride west to east, just like the prevailing winds.

But doubt entered my mind soon after speaking with Michael "Mac" McCoy of the Adventure Cycling Association. Mac continually tried to talk me into starting in the East. There were several reasons. For one, nearly all of their tours started in the East, and they had proved to be more successful than those that started in the West.

Mac said most people like traveling west, just like the pioneers. And everyone seems to look forward to the drier climate and the magnificent mountains of the more arid West. Also, the wind switches around halfway through the country, so very few riders sneak across without fighting some headwinds, and prevailing southerly winds always feel like a headwind no matter which direction you're headed!

I decided to ride from east to west and it's a decision I have never regretted. I found the wind almost nonexistent in the East. In fact, there were times when I nearly begged for a breeze just to cool off. Upon reaching Kansas I did encounter some wind, but I lucked out and flew through the state, a brisk tailwind pushing me along. During the time I cranked through Kansas and Colorado and even into Wyoming, I met several eastbounders who had done nothing but fight the wind for miles and miles. (Some westbound riders braved severe winds in Kansas, Colorado, and Wyoming that made them vow to ride west to east the next time around.)

My luck continued into northern Colorado, where a severe sidewind made life exciting and miserable for just over a day. But after entering Wyoming, I literally breezed through the state and on into Montana, where once again the wind was at my back. Oregon offered the most troublesome headwinds of my entire journey, but I avoided most of them by cycling early in the day and quitting around the time the wind came up in midafternoon.

Overall, the wind was not nearly as awful as I had imagined. Others reported lots of tough headwinds, though, so be prepared for some difficult days. If the wind doesn't come up, you'll feel nothing but joy.

Maps and Other Information

Adventure Cycling Association produces excellent maps that I found indispensable. Although this book includes maps of the area you'll be cycling through, I strongly recommend that you purchase Adventure Cycling maps as well. They fit perfectly inside your map holder and, most importantly, are highly detailed sources of data including route information, campgrounds, markets, and a brief history of the area you'll be riding through. In addition, there are elevation profile maps for the western states. An order form is enclosed with this guidebook.

You'll also find a listing of maps in *The Cyclists' Yellow Pages*, a directory for bicycle-trip planning available from Adventure Cycling. It lists organizations providing state maps and bicycling-related information for both the United States and Canada as well as many overseas destinations. Other listings include cycling periodicals; general information for women cyclists; bicycle-related videos, films, and books; airlines; and bike shops and bike clubs. Tour operators, international hostelling information, and touring tips are also included.

Maps and other types of information are available from several other sources, including the American Automobile Association (AAA). For information regarding specific cities, write to the local chamber of commerce, using the city, state, and zip code for each specific town. For specific biking information, write to the various agencies listed at the end of the introduction to each state.

Accommodations

Although I tried to end each day at a campground or a free city park, this guide was not written specifically for the self-contained

Bicyclists camped at Wytheville KOA, Wytheville, Virginia

tourist. Those who prefer hostels, bed-and-breakfast inns, or motel rooms will find the availability of such lodgings noted. Further, this guidebook offers information on the services available in every town you'll pass through. When you read that a town offers "all services" or "all facilities," this means you'll find at least one market, one café, and one motel. If the town is serviced by bus, train, or airplane transportation, that is noted as well. Bike shops and Laundromats are also mentioned.

Campgrounds are always noted, along with information about the available facilities. "All services" or "all amenities" means you'll find rest rooms, showers, and water. If groceries, a Laundromat, or some other amenity is also available it will be listed separately. If facilities are limited, specific conveniences will be listed. Campground fees are not listed unless camping is free. (It's free to camp at all of the city parks listed.) Unless otherwise specified, all campgrounds are privately owned and operated.

If you enjoy meeting other touring bicyclists, you can always add your name to the "Touring Cyclists' Hospitality Directory," established in 1977. It's a listing of people who volunteer to provide a place to sleep and a shower to bicyclists passing through their area. In exchange for their hospitality, you must also volunteer to host cyclists. Once listed, you will receive a directory of approximately 500 members. For more information, contact John Mosley, 2800 E. Observatory Rd., Los Angeles, CA 90027.

When Is the Best Time to Ride?

The best time to ride from Virginia to Oregon is May through September, since weather in the Rockies turns cold early and you'll want to avoid snowstorms. If you're opting for an Oregon to Virginia journey, leave in late May at the earliest, although mid-June is probably best. Expect hot humid weather in the East, particularly if you are in the region during midsummer. Expect heat and blowing winds in Kansas. And prepare for both hot and cold weather in the West.

Touring and Safety

Before you begin your ride, be sure to get in shape. Whether starting from the East or the West, you'll be climbing hills, and lots of them, within a few days.

Next, you'll want to examine your bike carefully and perhaps take it in for an overhaul. I'm not much of a mechanic, so I always take mine in for a checkup, and I usually start each trip with new or nearly new tires. I've had a few blowouts in recent years, so I always carry a spare just in case! Other essentials include a tire repair kit, spare tubes, a tire pump, chain lube, water bottles (four are handy for some of the more remote areas), a helmet, and a bike lock. An orange safety triangle, vest, or flag is also recommended. I also use a bike mirror (an item I wouldn't ride without), and I carry a small bike tool kit.

In regards to panniers and other touring equipment, I recommend reading a book on touring. For an extensive list of helpful publications, contact Adventure Cycling Association. For a brief list, see the Recommended Reading section of this book.

Although the TransAmerica Trail is a designated bicycle route across the country, it is not a bike lane shared with other bicyclists and pedestrians. Instead, it is a series of paved roadways—some uncrowded, some not, some secondary roads, some major highways—which you'll have to share with cars, trucks, and recreational vehicles (RVs).

Riding defensively is your best bet when you're out on the road. In other words, always be aware of your surroundings; if you get into a tight situation, plan what to do in an emergency. If you see a vehicle coming up behind you, never assume that it will get over for you. Watch it closely; if you have to, pull off to the side of the road and stop in order to allow it to pass.

Bicyclists must obey the same laws as those written for motorists, which means stopping for red lights and stop signs, pulling over for emergency vehicles, and riding single file.

Unfortunately, dogs and their owners do not always obey the law, especially in Kentucky, which is notable for its large number of stray dogs. I found pepper spray a much-needed weapon against these ferocious animals, who had nothing better to do than chase bicyclists all day long.

Minor inconveniences aside, there is nothing like the freedom of seeing this country by bicycle. Regardless of when or where you ride, remember to use caution, and most of all, have one heck of a good time!

A Note About Safety

Safety is an important concern in all outdoor activities. No guidebook can alert you to every hazard or anticipate the limitations of every reader. Therefore, the descriptions of roads, trails, routes, and natural features in this book are not representations that a particular place or excursion will be safe for your party. When you follow any of the routes described in this book, you assume responsibility for your own safety. Under normal conditions, such excursions require the usual attention to traffic, road and trail conditions, weather, terrain, the capabilities of your party, and other factors. Keeping informed on current conditions and exercising common sense are the keys to a safe, enjoyable outing.

The Mountaineers

Map Legend

Symbol	Description	Symbol	Description
)(	pass or summit	95	interstate
O	city/town	20	US highway
△	tourist attraction	156	state highway
▲	campground	652	county road
↑	hostel		

Monticello, home of Thomas Jefferson, Charlottesville, Virginia

VIRGINIA

The original TransAmerica Trail begins (or ends, if you are heading east instead of west) in Virginia, a state some bicyclists claim is both the prettiest and the most difficult of the entire 4,000-plus-mile route.

Although naming a "prettiest" state is tough to do when you're cycling through ten of the most beautiful states in the nation, Virginia is no doubt special. From the Atlantic Ocean to the Kentucky border, Virginia is a potpourri of quiet back roads, magnificent plantations, scenic valleys, rolling hills, steep mountains, and a lushness that gives everything a special green hue.

Except for the famous national parks of Yellowstone and Grand Teton, I probably saw more animal life in Virginia than anywhere else. Snapping turtles were common in the eastern part of the state, while box turtles seemed prevalent later on. I don't know how many times I stopped and got off my bike, prodding and pushing the hard-shelled creatures to the other side of the road. Unfortunately, I came across a lot of pancake-flat turtles that had perished before I happened along.

I saw some deer as well, although not nearly as many as I had expected. A variety of birds, including blue jays, added to the fun. Other critters included a variety of snakes in a rainbow of colors.

Virginia is more than just creatures and beautiful scenes. Eight U.S. presidents were born in this southern state, nicknamed the "Mother of Presidents." The list includes four of the first five presidents—George Washington, Thomas Jefferson, James Madison, and James Monroe. Others were William Henry Harrison, John Tyler, Zachary Taylor, and Woodrow Wilson.

One of four states officially called commonwealths (the others are Kentucky, Massachusetts, and Pennsylvania), Virginia also has the nickname "Mother of States." All or a portion of eight other states—Illinois, Indiana, Kentucky, Michigan, Minnesota, Ohio, West Virginia, and Wisconsin—were formed from western territory once claimed by Virginia.

The route officially begins at Victory Monument in Yorktown, Virginia. If you're headed west, Yorktown will mark the beginning of your journey. More importantly, it denotes the end of the American War for Independence. In 1781, Lord Cornwallis, the British commander, and his men surrendered, and after seven long years the Revolutionary War was over.

The Virginia segment of the ride consists of more miles than any other state's total mileage and ends nearly 600 miles later at

Farm scene off US 11, west of Wytheville, Virginia

Breaks Interstate Park. A must-see natural attraction, the park offers a variety of activities—hiking, horseback riding, and whitewater rafting—that may entice you.

I've divided Virginia's 595.2 miles into thirteen daily segments, some of which are short-mileage days due to the number of things to see and do. I also opted for shorter days in the beginning because many bicyclists (me included) are not in tip-top shape at the beginning of a ride. If you're getting into shape during the ride, I'd recommend low-mileage days for the first week or so. If you're in shape, however, and you'd rather double up on some of the days, feel free to do so.

There are several means of getting yourself and your loaded touring bike to Yorktown. Options include having a friend or family member drive you directly to the monument; or taking Amtrak or Greyhound, both of which provide direct service to Williamsburg.

Those arriving by airplane will have to assemble their bikes at the airport and ride from there, or take a bus or cab to Yorktown. The nearest airport, Newport News/Williamsburg Airport, is about 10 miles south, although you should check to see if your bike can travel with you. Many of the airlines service the area with small commuter planes, and boxed bikes are not permitted. However, some airlines provide both jet and commuter service. Check with your airline for more information.

The closest international airports are Norfolk International, about 30 miles southeast of Yorktown, and Richmond International, about 64 miles northwest of Yorktown. I flew into Norfolk, taxied to Newport News (bikes are prohibited on the Hampton Roads Bridge-Tunnel), assembled my bike at a motel, and pedaled to Yorktown the next day to begin my ride.

Another bicyclist flew into Newport News, but instead of packing his bike along with him, he shipped it the week before via UPS. A local bike shop accepted the bike for him, and he assembled it himself. Some bicyclists told of having their bikes assembled by bike shop employees; others had theirs disassembled and packed by the shop when returning home. Both are good choices.

Although the roads rarely, if ever, sport a shoulder, this won't be too great a concern, since most of the roads you'll be traveling consist of quiet lanes where you'll have time to smell the flowers and watch the turtles cross the road. You will also be touring along some busy roads, however, so always use caution. Note that riding is prohibited on most interstates.

Virginia's weather can be pleasant or miserable—very hot and humid. Expect rain, cold, heat, and sun, and you won't be disappointed. April and May see highs near 70 degrees and lows in the middle 40s; midsummer is hot and sticky with highs in the mid- to upper 80s and lows above 60 degrees.

For more information regarding biking in the state of Virginia, including a "Historic Triangle Bike Map" and/or a "Bicycling on Virginia Roads Map," contact State Bicycle Coordinator, Virginia Department of Transportation, 1401 E. Broad St., Richmond, VA 23219; (800) 835-1203; email: vabiking@vdot.state.va.us.

Yorktown to Jamestown (22.6 miles)

Regardless of whether you pedal across America from east to west or west to east, today's segment will be a significant one: either you'll be dipping your front tire into the York River to signify the end of your long journey, or you'll be dipping your rear tire into the water and dreaming of the day two to three months from now when you'll reach the Pacific.

History abounds on this first (or last) day as you explore York-town, Williamsburg, and Jamestown, also known as Virginia's Historic Triangle. This segment is a low-mileage day to allow for making images, reflecting, and enjoying what is the Tidewater region of Virginia. (If you'd rather ride more miles, feel free to combine this day with the Jamestown to Glendale segment for a total of 61.8 miles and an elevation gain of roughly 770 feet.)

The original TransAmerica Trail begins at Victory Monument in Yorktown, part of Colonial National Historical Park, which also includes Jamestown, the 23-mile Colonial Pkwy., and Cape Henry Memorial in Virginia Beach.

There are two ways to quickly learn about the region; one is free and one is not. The free one is Colonial National Historical Park Visitor Center, operated by the National Park Service, which offers a museum and a film. You can also walk around the battlefield. An admission fee is required to enter Yorktown Victory Center, which chronicles America's struggle for independence through film, thematic exhibits, and living history in which costumed interpreters demonstrate weapons, prepare meals, and so on in a Continental Army encampment and eighteenth-century farm.

Colonial Williamsburg is the largest restored eighteenth-century town in the world, a 173-acre potpourri of historic buildings and gardens where costumed folks describe and reenact Colonial life for visitors. In addition, there are militia exhibitions, concerts, lectures, and theatrical performances.

Just down the road, at historic Jamestown, visitors can see the remains of the first permanent English settlement in North America. Facilities include a visitor center with a museum, film presentation, and gift shop. There's also a glasshouse with daily glassblowing demonstrations.

Jamestown Festival Park is located near the entrance station. Here, visitors are delighted by the reconstructed James Fort and full-scale replicas of the three tiny English ships—*Susan Constant, Godspeed,* and *Discovery*—that brought the first settlers to the New World in 1607.

From Yorktown to Jamestown, you'll pedal along rolling plains (perfect terrain for those just beginning their ride) via the scenic Colonial Pkwy. Traffic can be heavy at times, so use caution.

MILEAGE LOG

0.0 The TransAmerica Bicycle Trail begins at Yorktown Victory Monument in the quaint town of Yorktown. After picture taking, exit the monument and make a right turn onto Compte De Grasse St. **SIDE TRIP:** If the Yorktown Visitor Center (located 0.5 mile away) is on your agenda, ride left on Compte De Grasse, left on Main St., staying to the right as Main turns

Bicyclist dipping rear tire in the York River at Yorktown, Virginia

into Zweybrucken Rd. Make a left on the Colonial Pkwy., following the signs to the visitor center.

0.1 Go left on Water St., pedaling along the York River and past a pub, which serves good, reasonably priced food. (There's a motel on Water St.)

0.5 Pass under the Hwy. 17 bridge. As you exit town you'll pass Yorktown Victory Center.

0.8 Water St. merges onto old Hwy. 238 West.

1.0 Turn right onto road signed "76 Bike Route," which parallels the York River.

1.4 Make a right onto the newly resurfaced Colonial Pkwy., which was reopened in 1994. Designated shoulders are non-existent, but the roadway is fairly wide and truck traffic is prohibited. Riding the parkway is a wonderful tree-lined treat as you continue to hug the York River for the next few miles, crossing or passing over Brackens Pond and Indian Field Creek en route.

5.1 Bellfield Plantation on the left.

5.9 Cross Felgates Creek.

6.1 Kingfield Picnic Area on the right.

7.0 Cross Kings Creek.

9.3 Cross Jones Mill Pond.

12.8 Fork; head left. **SIDE TRIP:** If you'd like to obtain information on things to see and do in Colonial Williamsburg, head
right for 0.2 mile to the visitor center. You can also buy tickets
for various tours and inquire regarding the many lodgings
and campgrounds. There are two bike shops in Williamsburg.
Amtrak and Greyhound provide service to and from the city.

12.9 Cross under the Lafayette St. bridge and make a right on the
first unsigned road.

13.0 Make a left on the unsigned road, which is closed to motor
vehicles; then make an immediate right, riding past the
Governor's Palace and curving to the left. This is downtown
Colonial Williamsburg, where history and snack shops
abound.

13.2 Make a right on Prince George St. If you miss this street you'll
reach a dead end in 0.1 mile at Duke of Gloucester St. If you
make a wrong turn, however, you can head right to S. Henry
St. and pick up the route from there.

13.4 Turn left on S. Henry St. (Sign states N. Henry because N.
Henry begins here.)

13.8 Turn left on Newport Ave.

13.9 Turn right onto the Colonial Pkwy. to Jamestown. As you
continue, you'll cross several creeks, including Halfway, College, and Powhatan.

16.9 Reach the James River. It's a lovely ride once again as the
roadway embraces the river.

22.4 Fork; go right on unsigned Hwy. 359 toward sign for ferry
and campgrounds. Both Jamestown Settlement and Jamestown Festival Park are a short distance to the left.

22.6 Cross Hwy. 31 and enter Jamestown Beach Campground,
"home" for the night; all services, including a pool, limited
groceries; snack bar open Memorial Day through Labor Day.
SPECIAL NOTE: After crossing Hwy. 31, but before entering
the campground, notice CR 614. This is where you'll make a
right and continue on route in the morning.

Jamestown to Glendale (39.2 miles)

If two words could describe the ride from Jamestown to Glendale, they would be "awesome plantations" because Hwy. 5 passes
one plantation paradise after another.

There are plenty of prominent plantations in the South, but I
never realized the density of those off Hwy. 5 until I bicycled past
them one cool spring day. Even by bicycle they seemed close together, with four plantations—Sherwood Forest, Evelynton, Berkeley, and Shirley—within a 14-mile stretch of highway.

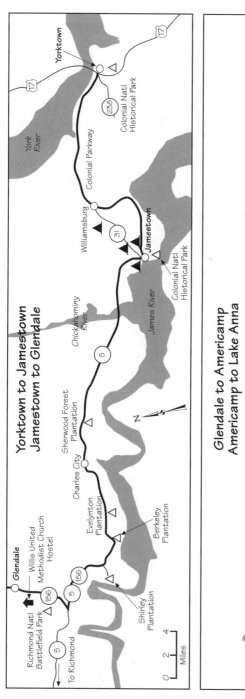

Yorktown to Jamestown
Jamestown to Glendale

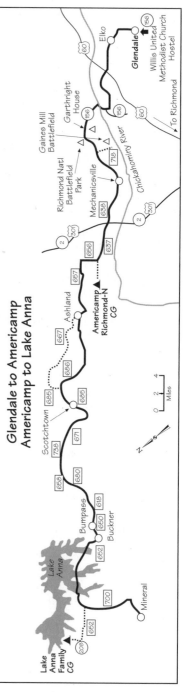

Glendale to Americamp
Americamp to Lake Anna

Sherwood Forest is the only plantation that was owned by two U.S. presidents. (William Henry Harrison inherited it in the late 1700s, and John Tyler lived there from 1842 to 1862.) The house, circa 1730, is 300 feet long, making it the longest frame dwelling in America. It comes complete with a 68-foot ballroom designed for dancing the Virginia reel.

The Evelynton Plantation was the site of several Civil War conflicts in 1862. During one skirmish, the original house and outbuildings were burned. The residence seen today was designed in 1937. Like others mentioned here, it is listed on the National Register of Historic Places.

Berkeley Plantation claims to be "Virginia's most historic plantation." The early Georgian mansion was the birthplace of Benjamin Harrison, son of the original builder and a signer of the Declaration of Independence. The first bourbon whiskey in America was made here from 1621 to 1622, and "Taps" was composed here in 1862, during the Civil War, while Union forces were encamped at the plantation.

The oldest plantation is the Shirley Plantation, founded six years after the settlement of Jamestown. Established in 1613, the Shirley Plantation was a supply center for the Continental Army during the Revolution. The present mansion was finished in 1738 and is recognized as an "architectural treasure." Perhaps its most notable feature is the three-story carved-walnut staircase, which ascends heavenward without visible means of support. It is the only one of its kind in America.

Even without the plantations, the ride to Glendale is a pleasant one through the Piedmont region of rural Virginia. Hills continue to roll gently (except for one steeper climb near the end of the day), the scenes are lovely, and the fragrance of honeysuckle saturates the air. Unfortunately, there is a downside—heavy truck traffic can be a problem, so be careful.

Several "76 Bike Route" signs lead to day's end at the Willis United Methodist Church Hostel, a roomy place with a kitchen, toilets, and sinks. Although it's free to stay at the hostel, a donation is much appreciated.

MILEAGE LOG

0.0 Jamestown Beach Campground entrance and junction CR 614 and Hwy. 31. If you're coming from the campground, turn left on CR 614. (If you're approaching the campground, make a right.)

2.2 Head left on Hwy. 5. There's a narrow shoulder as you head through lush trees and into open farmland.

6.7 Cross the Chickahominy River. **SPECIAL NOTE:** Use extreme care when crossing this long, narrow bridge. The bridge sports a steel-ridged surface that can grab bike tires. It is also slippery when dry and scarier than heck when wet. (No cause for panic, but be careful.)

13.1 Sandy Point Superette on the left; groceries. Owners also allow bicyclists to camp in back of their store.

16.9 Sherwood Forest Plantation exit on the left. **SIDE TRIP:** A gravel road leads 0.1 mile to parking area.

As you continue, Hwy. 5 sports an intermittent shoulder; be aware of trucks and buses.

19.6 Parrish Hill Creek crossing.

19.9 Country store on the left.

20.3 Junction Hwy. 155. Continue straight on Hwy. 5. Market and eatery located just before the junction.

22.7 Junction: CR 618 is to the left; just ahead it takes off to the right. There's a tavern/dining area at the junction.

24.6 Bed-and-breakfast inn on the right.

25.5 Turnoff to Evelynton Plantation on the left.

27.3 Bed-and-breakfast inn on the left.

27.5 Junction Herring Creek Rd. **SIDE TRIP:** Reach Berkeley Plantation by turning left on Herring Creek Rd. You'll pass

Cannons at Malvern Hill, Richmond National Battlefield Park, Virginia

a market in 0.1 mile (the owners allow bicyclists to camp here) before the paved road turns to gravel. After another mile reach the parking area for the plantation.

28.2 Junction CR 658 on the right.

30.0 Junction Hwy. 106 and Hwy. 156; keep straight on bike route.

30.7 Turnoff to Shirley Plantation on the left at the union of CR 608 and Shirley Plantation Rd. **SIDE TRIP:** The plantation is about 1.5 miles away via Shirley Plantation Rd.

36.3 Junction Hwy. 156 North (Willis Church Rd.); head right, following bike route signs.

37.4 A sign for Malvern Hill marks the top of the steepest climb to date. Cannons and interpretive signs also mark this portion of Richmond National Battlefield Park, a series of ten park units offering insight into the Civil War.

39.2 Willis United Methodist Church Hostel on the left; excellent accommodations. Make reservations by calling the pastor in advance at (804) 795-1895. If you need groceries or other supplies, see the Glendale to Americamp segment. There's a mini-market 0.9 mile away.

Glendale to Americamp (near Ashland) (31.6 miles)

The rolling history lesson resumes as you pedal past a network of Richmond National Battlefield sites en route to Ashland. A devastating attack known as the Battle of Cold Harbor took place here. General Ulysses S. Grant and his forces, numbering 50,000 strong, failed miserably against the strongly entrenched Confederate lines. When it was finally over, the Federal army had suffered 12,000 men killed, wounded, missing, or captured, while the Confederates agonized over nearly 4,000 casualties.

In addition to Civil War signs, bike signs for the 76 Route continue. The sweet smell of honeysuckle continues to perfume the roadway, perhaps making up for the skimpy shoulders and moderate traffic.

Hilly terrain is more abundant as you cycle through rural Virginia, where farms seem to be everywhere. If you're having trouble with the hills, just think of them as training sessions for the Blue Ridge Mountains up ahead.

MILEAGE LOG

0.0 Willis United Methodist Church Hostel. Continue north on Willis Church Rd.

0.8 Turn right onto Hwy. 156 North (Charles City Rd.), which changes to Elko Rd. en route.

0.9 Mini-market on the right.

6.6 Junction Hwy. 380 on the left.

7.1 Ride across US 60 onto Meadow Rd.

9.8 Turn right on Grapevine Rd.

11.3 Keep right on Old Hanover Rd. when Grapevine Rd. ends.

11.4 Back onto Hwy. 156 North; go right.

11.7 Cross the Chickahominy River.

12.3 Mini-market.

15.2 Junction CR 619 and CR 633; keep left on Hwy. 156.

15.6 Turnoff to the Garthright House. During the June 1864 Battle of Cold Harbor, the Union turned this middle-class plantation into a field hospital. It must have been a horrifying time for the residents, who were obliged to move into the basement, where they observed blood oozing down between the floorboards.

15.7 Cold Harbor National Cemetery on the right. More than 2,000 Union soldiers are buried in this small cemetery; sadly, more than 1,300 are unknown soldiers.

16.2 Cold Harbor Exhibit Shelter. One of ten sections in Richmond National Battlefield Park, this self-guided unit provides maps and information about the Battle of Cold Harbor.

16.4 Turnoff on the left to Gaines' Mill Battlefield via CR 718. The site is less than a mile south.

18.2 Junction CR 615; keep straight on Hwy. 156.

20.6 Cross over I-295.

21.6 Mechanicsville; post office, restaurants, assorted shops, market, and a Laundromat.

21.8 Junction US 360.

21.9 Cross Mechanicsville Turnpike and head straight on Atlee Rd./CR 638. Hwy. 156 ends at this point.

23.7 Junction CR 627; mini-market.

24.3 Cross over I-295.

26.0 Turn left on Hwy. 2/US 301; restaurant and groceries at the junction.

26.1 Cross under a set of railroad tracks and make a right on CR 637 in 0.1 mile.

30.1 Junction CR 656 (Sliding Hill Rd.); there's a grocery store, restaurants, and various other shops at the junction. Make a right to continue on route. **SIDE TRIP:** You'll have to go off route to reach Americamp Richmond-North Campground. From the junction, head straight instead of turning right. Be prepared for heavy traffic. After 1.3 miles go left on CR 809

Garthright House, used by the Union army as a field hospital during the battle of Cold Harbor, Richmond National Battlefield Park, Virginia

for 0.2 mile. Make a right and ride into the campground. In addition to the usual services, you'll find a store and Laundromat.

Americamp to Lake Anna (51.8 miles)

The ride from Americamp to Lake Anna once again provides bicyclists with the finest of rural Virginia. Lush green fields dominate the scene, and in the spring, purple flowers are abundant.

Exploring the railroad town of Ashland can add to the day's experience. You can pick up a self-guided tour map at the visitor center and walk, or pedal, to your heart's content. If you're visiting the first Saturday in June, be sure to attend the Strawberry Faire, where there are dozens of strawberry treasures and handmade crafts. If you arrive the first weekend in August, there's an annual native American powwow with dancing, drumming, crafts, and food.

You're still pedaling in terrain that continues to roll, but each day adds more elevation gain, with this being the first day that you'll gain more than 1,000 feet in elevation. Shoulders continue to be rare; traffic is usually moderate.

Lake Anna, one of Virginia's most popular lakes, is the destination for the night. Because the sites are located in the trees, they aren't the most scenic, but there are showers (for an extra charge), and it's the closest place to camp to the main route. **SPECIAL NOTE:** Upon reaching Ashland I found the main bike route closed due to bridge construction. Ashland Cycles owners Dani and Ron gave me up-to-date information regarding the closure and offered to do the same for other interested bicyclists. The bike shop is located at 302A England Stand. If you'd rather ride the Adventure Cycling route, refer to Map 147, mileage log "11.5 (19) Ashland" to "21 (35) Turn right following CR 685."

MILEAGE LOG

0.0 Americamp Richmond-North Campground. Head back on route to junction CR 637/CR 656.

1.5 Junction of CR 637 and CR 656 (Sliding Hill Rd.). Go northeast (left) on Sliding Hill Rd.

2.8 Junction CR 656 and CR 643; keep left at the fork on CR 656.

3.9 Make a left on CR 657 (Ashcake Rd.).

6.9 Cross over I-95.

8.2 Junction S. Washington Hwy. (US 1) in Ashland. Look for a Laundromat, mini-market, and restaurant at the corner. Most of the other facilities in this all-service town are to the right or north of here.

9.0 Just before the railroad tracks, turn right on S. Center St., a one-way street that leads past some nice old homes. You'll also pedal alongside the tracks that were so important to this community.

10.0 Junction Hwy. 54 in the center of town. An impressive visitor center is nearby, housed in a depot that was abandoned by the railroad in 1967 and donated to the town in 1983. The building is an architectural jewel, designed by Ashland native and well-known architect W. Duncan Lee. **ALTERNATE ROUTE:** From this point the original TransAmerica Trail (which is now the alternate route) stays straight. To reach Ashland Cycles turn right on Hwy. 54 for 2 blocks.

To follow the detour Ron recommended, the one that is now the main route, go left on Hwy. 54. Expect some traffic.

13.8 Turn right onto CR 686, and begin pedaling a series of quiet roads through rolling hills.

17.3 Road T's; turn right on CR 795/CR 686.

17.8 Road merges back to plain old CR 686; head left. At this point CR 795 continues, then ends.

18.5 Back to the main route at junction CR 685; go straight toward Scotchtown.

21.0 Home of Patrick Henry on the right. Built circa 1719, it is thought to be one of the oldest of Virginia's plantation houses. It was home to Patrick Henry during his most active political years; in fact, he lived here when he rode to St. John's Church in Richmond, where he made his famous "Liberty or Death" speech on March 23, 1775. The home has been restored and is furnished with eighteenth-century antiques.

If you're around Scotchtown for Memorial Day weekend, be sure to attend the annual Central Virginia Scottish Festival and Games.

21.2 Turn right on CR 671.

26.1 Junction CR 631. If you want groceries, head right 0.2 mile to a country store.

26.2 Turn left on CR 738.

28.2 On the left you'll see CR 658, a gravel road. Don't turn here; instead, continue to paved CR 658.

28.5 Paved CR 658; make a left.

30.6 Cross CR 715.

31.9 Turn left on CR 680.

33.1 Turn right on CR 618.

33.3 Store and gas on the right.

37.5 Bumpass Post Office on the right.

Bicyclists riding along Hwy. 54 northwest of Ashland, Virginia

38.6 Turn right onto CR 650. There's a mini-market just prior to the turn.

40.5 Turn left onto CR 652.

40.8 Cross over the first of several arms over Lake Anna.

43.9 Mini-market on the right.

46.9 Cross portions of Lake Anna several more times en route to junction CR 700. The main route continues to the left toward Mineral. **SIDE TRIP** to Lake Anna Family Campground. Keep straight on CR 652 for 3.3 miles, then turn right on Hwy. 208 East. Reach the campground in 1.6 miles. There's an extra charge for showers, and groceries are in limited supply.

Lake Anna to Charlottesville (66.1 miles)

Grades steepen and leg muscles tighten as you climb nearly 3,000 feet through Virginia's Piedmont region. It's a roller-coaster-like day to Charlottesville, with heavy traffic a problem as you near the city via shoulderless CR 795 and Hwy. 53.

En route you'll pass several historic sites—Ash Lawn Highland, Monticello, and Michie Tavern and Museum. Ash Lawn Highland was the home of James Monroe, fifth president of the United States. On the authentic early-nineteenth-century working farm, visitors see restored slave quarters and an overseer's cottage, gardens, and even peacocks. Special events include concerts, operas, and Colonial craft demonstrations.

Just beyond Ash Lawn Highland is Monticello, a hilltop masterpiece surrounded by orchards. Home of our third president, Thomas Jefferson, Monticello was designed by the president, who described it as his "essay in architecture."

Tours of the home offer a peek into a variety of rooms, including one of the most intriguing, the library, or "book room," where Jefferson housed most of his nearly 7,000 volumes. An avid reader of seven languages, Jefferson wrote to John Adams claiming, "I cannot live without books."

From Monticello you'll zoom down the hill toward Charlottesville, passing Michie Tavern along the way. If you'd like to see early tavern life, be sure to stop for a tour through this eighteenth-century tavern, originally located on a well-traveled stagecoach route. (In 1927, the Colonial inn was painstakingly relocated piece by piece and moved to this area some 17 miles from the original site.)

In addition to one of the largest and finest collections of eighteenth-century furniture and artifacts, you'll find Colonial-type meals at "The Ordinary," a 200-year-old converted log house.

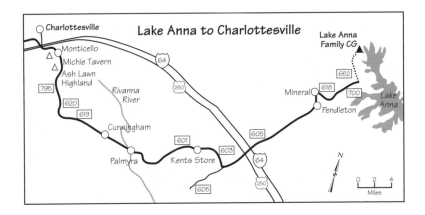

The day ends at the all-service town of Charlottesville, the largest city on the TransAmerica Trail east of the Mississippi River. If you want to explore this city of 45,000, head downtown to the pedestrian mall. The mall is the central feature of downtown, boasting the atmosphere and closed street of a European market square.

There are many motels to choose from in town; campgrounds are located out of town. The Charlottesville KOA is about 7 miles south via US 20 and Hwy. 708. See mileage log at the 64.6-mile mark for more information.

Amtrak also provides service for those interested in starting or stopping their ride in Charlottesville.

MILEAGE LOG

0.0 Lake Anna. Head back to the main route the same way you rode in.

4.9 Junction CR 700 and CR 652. If you're cycling from Lake Anna, make a right on CR 700; if you decided to make the last segment a longer day, make a left on CR 700.

9.7 Junction CR 618; turn right onto CR 618.

11.9 Junction US 522 and Hwy. 208; ride straight onto the highway and head over the railroad tracks into Mineral, an all-service town.

12.0 Junction. Turn left on US 522. There's a mini-market and Laundromat at the corner; look for a restaurant to the right 0.3 mile via Hwy. 208.

13.5 Junction CR 700 on the left.

13.7 Pendleton.

14.3 Keep straight, now riding CR 605.

15.9 Cross US 33.

20.9 Junction CR 646.

25.2 Cross over I-64.

25.8 Cross US 250.

27.8 Turn right on CR 603.

30.8 Make a left on CR 601.

32.6 Enter Kents Store; head left at the fork, staying on CR 601; post office.

37.8 Go left on CR 608, then make an immediate right on CR 601, which leads to Palmyra.

42.0 Junction US 15 in downtown Palmyra, where you'll find a post office, a country store, and a café; go left. Near the junction is an old stone jail museum built in 1828 and open to the public during the summer.

42.3 Cross the Rivanna River.

42.5 Make a right on Hwy. 53. There's a mini-market and pizza place on the right.

45.8 Turn left on CR 660, which leads to CR 619, where you'll make a right. (If you need groceries, continue north on Hwy. 53 for a short distance to Cunningham, where you'll find a mini-market.)

51.8 Turn right on CR 620.

53.6 Mini-market on the right.

56.1 Country store on the right.

57.9 Road changes from CR 620 to CR 795.

60.6 Ash Lawn Highland on the left.

61.4 Turn left on Hwy. 53.

63.0 Entrance to Monticello on the right. **SIDE TRIP:** Ride 0.2 mile to the entrance where you can purchase tickets, use the rest room, and so on. A bus will transport you to Monticello. As you descend from Monticello, look for Michie Tavern on the left.

64.6 Turn right on Hwy. 20 North. There's a visitor center just ahead on the left. Check here for motel and campground accommodations, bike shop locations, and so on in this all-service town. **SIDE TRIP:** To reach the Charlottesville KOA, the closest campground to town, head about 7 miles south via US 20. Make a right (go west) on Hwy. 708 (Red Hill Rd.) and continue a little more than a mile to the campground, where you'll find a Laundromat and a store in addition to the usual stuff.

65.1 Pass under I-64. Continue up Hwy. 20 (Monticello Ave.) to Elliott Ave. From this point to the end of the day you'll ride through Charlottesville's residential and business districts, where there are steep ups and downs.

65.6 Turn left on Elliott Ave.

66.3 Elliott Ave. changes to Cherry Ave.

68.2 Make a right on Cleveland Ave.

68.4 Go right on Jefferson Park Ave.

68.9 Junction Fontaine Ave. (Jefferson Park Ave. takes off to the right.) Head straight on Maury Ave., which changes to Alderman Rd. along the way.

70.2 Junction US 250 Business (Ivy Rd.); make a left on Ivy Rd.

71.0 Junction US 250/US 29 Bypass. Today's segment ends here; tomorrow's day starts here.

Charlottesville to Tye River Gap (57.9 miles)

June Curry, better known to cyclists as the Cookie Lady and a legend on the TransAmerica Trail, lives in Afton, the approximate halfway point in today's ride. She's the highlight of the day for most bicyclists.

From Afton, you'll ride the Blue Ridge Pkwy., a tree-lined, 469-mile route that parallels the crest of the Appalachian Mountain chain from Virginia to North Carolina. Often called "America's favorite drive," it boasts wide, sweeping vistas, brilliant rhododendron and mountain laurel blossoms come springtime, an orange and red maze of foliage in autumn, and one challenging climb after another. Although the road is shoulderless, it is closed to commercial vehicles and extremely pleasant to ride.

There are several hundred miles of hiking trails accessible from the parkway, including the Appalachian Trail, which stretches 2,144 miles from Georgia to Maine. No doubt you'll meet some "through-hikers" (hikers who are hiking not just a portion of the trail, but all of it) as you enter the parkway, since the trail crosses the parkway at Rockfish Gap.

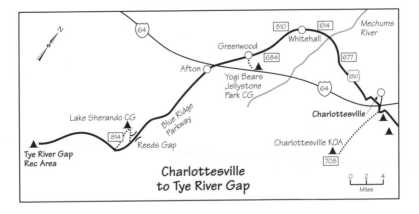

Charlottesville to Tye River Gap

Look for a variety of wildlife along the parkway: white-tailed deer, raccoon, skunk, the rarely seen black bear, and more than 100 bird species. Most of today's ride is a quiet one along country lanes where fragrant spring scents permeate the air; however, you should expect some traffic on the Blue Ridge Pkwy.

Unfortunately, the grades become steep here—steeper than the Rocky Mountains! The climb to Afton is particularly tough.

After gaining about 5,000 feet in elevation during the day, this segment ends with a speedy downhill (the steepest, longest descent of the entire cross-country journey) to Tye River Gap Recreation Area.

MILEAGE LOG

0.0 Junction US 29 Bypass and US 250 West; no shoulder for the most part; expect some traffic. Continue west on US 250.

1.8 Turn right on CR 677, an uncrowded country road through residential areas and woods. As you continue, the hills are roller-coaster-like but mostly moderate in intensity.

5.4 Turn right on CR 676.

6.0 Make a left onto CR 839.

7.1 Road T's at CR 614; go left.

7.2 Cross the Mechums River.

8.0 You'll climb to this point, where there is a good view of farmland and mountains.

11.3 Turn left onto CR 810 in downtown Whitehall, where there is a post office, community center, and Wyant's Store. Currently owned by Larry Wyant, the store has been owned and managed by the same family for more than 100 years. Cyclists can camp across the street at the community center.

14.9 CR 810 branches off to the left; stay to the right fork and merge onto CR 789.

15.6 Road T's; turn right on CR 788.

15.9 Make a left on CR 684.

17.1 Turn right on CR 691.

19.7 Turn right on CR 690. This is Greenwood, where you'll find a post office. **SIDE TRIP:** Yogi Bear's Jellystone Park Campground is located a mile southeast on CR 690, then a mile east on US 250. In addition to the usual services, you'll find a pool, Laundromat, and groceries.

21.8 Cross under I-64. Before and after this crossing, some steep hills make life more challenging.

23.1 Road T's; turn right on CR 796.

23.5 Road T's; go right on US 250 West. Climb again.

24.1 Turn left on CR 750, which is just past a country store that sells gifts, snacks, fudge, and cold drinks. (If you need a restaurant,

Bicyclist enjoying the view from 20-Minute Cliff, Blue Ridge Parkway, Virginia

motel, campground, or deli, continue about 0.5 mile west on US 250.) Continue to climb; it's a steep uphill.

26.2 Junction; Afton. Make a right on Hwy. 6. There's a post office and a couple of antique shops in the area. No other services sans June Curry, the Cookie Lady, who lives 0.1 mile ahead on the right.

26.8 Road T's; turn left on US 250 West. Continue climbing.

27.1 Antique shop on the left.

28.1 Turn right onto ramp leading to the Blue Ridge Pkwy. at Rockfish Gap, northern entrance to the parkway. Two hotels, a restaurant, and an information center are nearby.

28.4 Afton Overlook. Continue climbing and descending; you'll definitely ascend more than drop.

31.2 Shenandoah Valley on the right; unfortunately, the dense trees make you work for the view.

34.1 Humpback Rocks Visitor Center, where you'll find a small museum, a gift shop, rest rooms, and water. The reconstructed mountain farmstead is also worth a look.

37.0 Road on left leads to picnic area and rest rooms.

37.2 Reach the top of the hill at this point and level off for a while.

37.4 Greenstone Overlook on the right.

39.0 Rock Point Overlook—elevation 3,115 feet.

41.9 Three Ridges Mountains on the left.

42.4 Junction CR 664 at Reeds Gap—elevation 2,637 feet—crest of the Blue Ridge. CR 664 sports a very steep grade (downhill) to Lake Sherando, a Forest Service camp with hot showers. (If you want to camp here, you can drop down to the lake from this point and exit via Forest Road 91 and CR 814, which is not as steep. Directions are listed at the 45.0-mile mark below.)

45.0 Junction CR 814 on the right. Lake Sherando is about 4 miles via this road, then approximately 2 miles southwest on paved Forest Road 91.

47.9 Twenty-minute Cliff Overlook. An interpretive sign describes the history behind the name: "In June and July during corn-chopping time this cliff serves the folks in White Rock Community as a time place. Twenty minutes after sunlight strikes the rock face dusk falls on the valley below."

48.9 Flacks Overlook on the right. As with many of the overlooks, it's tough to see due to dense trees. Begin climbing a long hill.

50.8 Top of hill, then continue cycling up-and-down terrain.

51.3 Bald Mountain Overlook on the right. Pass two more overlooks in the next 4 miles.

56.4 Turn left at the Hwy. 56 offramp, then make a right on Hwy. 56 West.

57.9 Slow down for the turnoff to Tye River Gap Recreation Area on the left, since you'll be zooming down the steepest grade of your journey. The campground is about 100 yards away via a paved road. The all-service camp boasts a Laundromat, pool, game room, and limited groceries. Owner Robert Stull does not offer a special rate for bicyclists, but he'll work out some sort of deal if you ask him.

JUNE CURRY—THE COOKIE LADY

Of all the good samaritans on the TransAmerica Trail, certainly the most well known is June Curry, the Cookie Lady.

In the summer of 1994, June welcomed cyclist number 10,000 to her Blue Ridge Mountain home in Afton, Virginia. Although I wasn't the 10,000th, when I visited with June last summer I found her just as eager as ever to welcome new cyclists to her home.

June greets each one with a sweet grin and an assortment of cookies, soft drinks, juices, and other snacks. In addition, she offers lodging (for a small donation) in the "Bike House," a quaint cottage virtually wallpapered with cards and letters and other biking memorabilia. Most of the remembrances come from bicyclists who have stayed in touch with June over the years.

Bicyclists taking a break with June Curry, "the Cookie Lady," Afton, Virginia

June and her father, Harold "Dad" Haven, first began offering water to thirsty cyclists in the summer of 1976. As the first group of TransAmerica riders passed through town, riding directly by the Curry home, word soon spread of June and Harold's hospitality. June became the legendary Cookie Lady later, when June revived a tired, hungry bicyclist with fresh cookies.

June says she's been called "crazy and weird" because she helps strangers. Although she doesn't ride a bike and hates to cook, she thoroughly enjoys helping the bicyclists who ride through Afton. "They are a fantastic group of people," she says. "Very caring and very appreciative of just a drink of mountain water."

It's obvious that June does receive something in return for her kindness; she travels through others. "I have always wanted to *travel and since I can't, it has been a great experience to let the world come to my door."*

June has greeted people from all fifty states and at least twenty-eight foreign countries, including India, Holland, Portugal, South Africa, El Salvador, Venezuela, and Malaysia.

Tye River Gap to Natural Bridge (41.4 miles)

Tye River to Natural Bridge is a beautiful ride through some of the best of rural America. There's lots of fairly level riding, although you'll still gain about 3,000 feet in elevation. Some of the climbs are steep, but you can always stop for a while to watch the turtles along the roadway. (Note: Snapping turtles are lightning fast, and they bite hard; box turtles are gentle and sometimes even friendly.)

Historic Lexington is a must-stay-and-explore town. Located in Virginia's beautiful Shenandoah Valley, it's a nice town for walking or biking. Highlights include Stonewall Jackson's house, the

Lexington, Virginia

Virginia Military Institute, the Washington and Lee University (established in 1749), and the George C. Marshall Museum.

Natural Bridge, an unusual formation that connects one side of a chasm with the other, is a must-see even for those who shun typical tourist attractions. Located in Rockbridge County, this Virginia landmark (to which the county owes its name) was owned by the English crown, later deeded to Thomas Jefferson, and surveyed by George Washington.

In earlier times, visitors came by horseback and later by stagecoach to witness this natural phenomenon. Today, they come on foot to walk under the bridge, with Cedar Creek their musical companion to trail's end at Lace Waterfall. After browsing through the gift shop, visitors descend via a path along Cascade Creek to Cedar Creek, which is responsible for the natural beauty seen here. Cedar Creek labored for millions of years, carving through limestone, to form the precipitous walls that rise at near-vertical angles toward the heavens.

The day is a relatively short one, leaving you time to explore. If you'd rather ride, however, feel free to combine this segment with the next. Total miles—69.7; elevation gain—more than 5,000 feet.

MILEAGE LOG

0.0 Tye River Gap Recreation Area. Continue steep downhill.

2.5 Enter Vesuvius, where there's a market, fresh sandwiches, and a post office. Turn left on CR 608 and climb a few more hills before entering a long valley where the highway parallels the South River and the fishing is reported to be fine.

11.8 Mallard Duck Campground on the right. Shaded sites with the usual amenities; special rates for bicyclists.

12.5 Junction CR 603 on the left.

13.4 Country store on the left.

16.3 Road T's at junction CR 631; make a right. A market is on the corner. Cross over South River and begin another climb.

16.9 Turn left and continue riding CR 631 (Old RV Rd.); CR 706 stays straight. Climb for another mile, then it's roller-coaster-like as you proceed.

19.2 Cross under I-81.

20.8 Turn left on US 11.

21.0 Cross bridge over the Maury River and enter Lexington. US 11 is now called Main St. As you enter downtown, Main splits into two one-way roads. Southbound US 11 is Jefferson; northbound US 11 is Main St. (There's a bike shop on Main and another on Washington.)

22.0 Junction Washington St. **SIDE TRIP:** To reach the visitor center, go left on Washington St. It's 0.2 mile away.

22.1 Cross US 60.

22.4 Road T's; turn left on White.

22.5 Turn right on US 11 South.

23.4 Go right on Hwy. 251.

25.1 Make a left on CR 764.

26.2 Turn right on CR 610. CR 610 forks after a while and follows the banks of Broad Creek now and again during your journey.

33.6 Junction CR 690 on the left.

36.8 Turn left on CR 692.

38.4 Cross under I-81/US 11 and turn right (only if you opt against visiting Natural Bridge) on CR 609.

39.4 **SIDE TRIP:** Turn left on US 11 North to reach Natural Bridge and home for the night; or, if you're combining this segment with the next, make a right.

41.1 Junction US 11/Hwy. 130 at Natural Bridge. There are two motels and a restaurant here; several campgrounds are an additional 2 to 5 miles off route. The Natural Bridge complex consists of a gift shop, snack shop, wax museum, the bridge, and a tour of the caverns, which are about 0.2 mile up US 11 North. Check at the center for information regarding tours and prices.

Natural Bridge, Virginia

Natural Bridge to Troutville (28.3 miles)

This segment is typical of recent days, with quite a few climbs (although only a few steep ones), some lightning-fast downhills, and relatively little traffic. Except for a few jaunts onto US 11, the route is nearly traffic-free, even on Memorial Day weekend.

Camp at Troutville Park, Troutville, Virginia

You'll probably notice that this segment is a low-mileage day. I've kept some of the days short on purpose, taking the amount of elevation gain into consideration. For instance, this segment calls for 1,900 feet of elevation gain. If you combine it with the previous segment, you would ride 69.7 miles and climb more than 5,000 feet. You'll climb a similar amount if you combine this segment with the next one, and your total mileage would be 78.8 miles.

The day ends at Troutville Park, a nice, free retreat with shade *ramadas*, water, and rest rooms. If the park is your destination, please call ahead at 992-4401 (closed Mondays), or call park caretaker A. R. Poluin at 992-1910.

MILEAGE LOG

0.0 Natural Bridge; junction US 11/Hwy. 130. Head back to the main route.

1.7 Back at the US 11/CR 609 junction. Keep straight on what is now Hwy. F-055. US 11 joins I-81 at this point; F-055 parallels US 11/I-81. A mini-market is on the corner.

6.1 Turn right on CR 623, cross over US 11/I-81 and make a left on CR 623, which immediately swings to the right. Exit CR 623 and continue straight on Hwy. F-054.

10.2 Cross under I-81 and merge onto US 11, which is now a separate roadway.

10.6 Enter Buchanan, established in 1811.

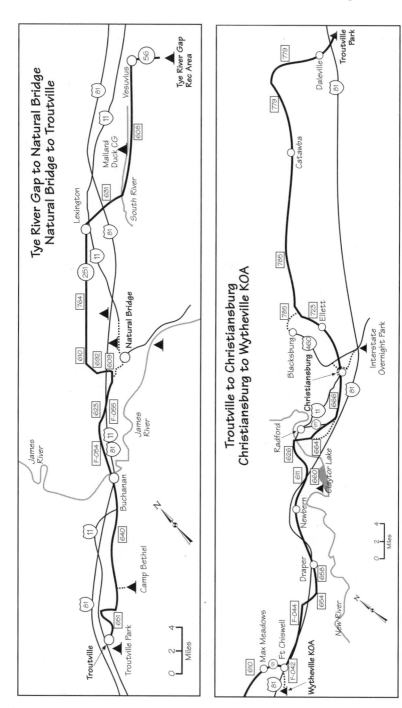

Tye River Gap to Natural Bridge
Natural Bridge to Troutville

Troutville to Christiansburg
Christiansburg to Wytheville KOA

11.4 Junction Hwy. 43 North is off to the right just before you cross the James River. After the crossing you'll see junction Hwy. 43 South. Buchanan has a Laundromat, two restaurants, a post office, market, and pharmacy.

14.0 Turn left on CR 640.

18.7 Junction CR 645 on the left.

20.5 Turnoff to Camp Bethel. **SIDE TRIP:** If you'd like a quiet, secluded camp, turn left and cross the bridge via CR 606. A gravel road leads to the camp in 0.4 mile. Rates are reasonable and include showers. **SPECIAL NOTE:** The camp is closed to cyclists from mid-June through mid-August because it is filled to capacity by children's groups.

22.9 Turn left and head across the railroad tracks, then make an immediate right, continuing on CR 640.

24.2 Turn left on US 11 South, a four-lane road; mini-market on the corner.

24.8 Pass a restaurant just before turning left on CR 651.

28.2 Turn left on signed Lee Hwy. North (unsigned US 11). (There's a grill and bar just prior to the junction.)

28.3 Troutville Park on the left; picnic facilities, water, rest rooms, no showers. A grocery store is nearby; a post office is at the other end of town.

Troutville to Christiansburg (50.5 miles)

Some might think pedaling along quiet lanes through rural Virginia monotonous, but this kind of routine is tough to whine about, since the scenery continues to be awe-inspiring. The virtually car-free country lanes remain uncrowded even during the holidays.

There's no doubt that Virginia's steep grades are a challenge to cycle, though. In fact, while the local people I met continually expressed their deep love for their state, they admitted that many bicyclists, after crossing the country from west to east, had exclaimed, "Virginia is the prettiest and the toughest state of all!" Expect some short, steep climbs combined with a roller-coaster-like ride to the campground at Christiansburg. The grade levels off a bit as you head toward town from the CR 723/CR 785 junction. Before reaching Christiansburg, you'll head out of the beautiful Catawba Valley via a long, but not too steep, climb—until you reach E. Main St, often called "Danger Hill" by cyclists, which is unbelievably steep, especially for those riding loaded bikes.

After attempting Danger Hill and failing (I was going so slow—1.5 mph—I just tipped over), I decided to ask others if they had had similar problems. I found that everyone was grumbling about "the climb"; some had barely made it to the top, while others had gone around it.

Snapping turtles have large heads and powerful jaws. Found mainly in the eastern half of the country, they can inflict a serious bite.

I contacted the local tourism department to check on alternate routes. A local bicycling advocate, Michael Abraham, wrote me back: "Yes, as you discovered, the East Main route is the climb from hell, plotted surely by masochists who never turned a crankset in their lives. Why they would have chosen this impossible route is a complete mystery to me. Our area is frighteningly corrugated to begin with, with hills to climb even in the flattest 'valleys.'"

If you'd rather avoid Danger Hill, you'll find alternate directions below.

MILEAGE LOG

0.0 Troutville Park. Head out onto US 11, a four-lane highway.

1.0 Turn right on CR 779, a country road with lots of ups and downs. Ride under I-81 in about 0.5 mile.

2.5 Road T's; turn right on US 220 in Daleville, then make a left on CR 779 in 0.1 mile and continue northwest. All food services, including restaurants, are near the US 220/I-81 junction about 2 miles south.

7.6 Market and snack bar on the left.

18.6 Junction Hwy. 320 North.

19.4 Junction Hwy. 311/CR 698. This is the town of Catawba; mini-market, post office, and a restaurant with limited hours. Ride left on CR 698, then make a quick right on Hwy. 311.

19.5 Restaurant on the left; limited hours and delicious food served family-style.

19.9 Turn left on CR 785.

37.2 Fork at junction CR 723/CR 785. Keep left on CR 723 and continue moderate roller-coaster ride. **SIDE TRIP:** CR 785 forks to the right and leads 3.7 steep miles to Blacksburg, a college town with all services, including two bike shops.

41.1 Junction CR 603 in Ellett; mini-market.

43.2 Begin uphill climb into Christiansburg.

45.1 Cross under US 460 and level off somewhat. Enter Christiansburg corporate limits just after. CR 723 is now called Ellett Rd.

45.6 Turn left on Cambria St. (Hwy. 111).

45.9 Road curves left and merges onto what is now Depot St. At this point you'll see the Christiansburg Depot, erected in 1848. **ALTERNATE ROUTE:** If you're going to stay in town instead of riding out to Interstate Overnight Park to spend the night, turn right on Depot St. and follow it past Franklin St. and Radford St., merging back on route at College St. about 2 miles from this point. If you'd like to take the alternate route but still visit the town, you can turn left and head into town via N. Franklin St.

46.1 Turn right on E. Main St., the toughest but shortest steep climb on the route. **ALTERNATE ROUTE:** Another alternate is available by staying on Depot St. until it merges with US 11/US 460 at the 48.0-mile mark. It's both easier and shorter.

46.2 Top of High St. and E. Main St.

46.8 Junction Roanoke St. (US 11/US 460) at bottom of hill, where there's a light. The 76 Route continues straight through downtown Christiansburg, where there are all services, including Greyhound bus service. There are some motels on the route, but no campgrounds. **SIDE TRIP:** To reach the campground, make a left on US 11/US 460 and read on.

47.4 Market.

48.0 Junction Roanoke St. and Depot St. (Hwy. 111). Continue straight on US 11, where you'll pass numerous motels and restaurants.

50.5 Interstate Overnight Park on the right; all services, including a Laundromat and showers.

Christiansburg to Wytheville KOA (51.4 miles)

Fine Virginia countryside continues, although the route parallels I-81 for some of the day, so you'll experience moderate noise pollution. If you're traveling in the spring, though, there's bound to be an abundance of wonderful scents to compensate for any noise.

You may also spot some big, black, nonpoisonous snakes lounging on the pavement.

If you'd rather get off the pavement, why not try bicycling the New River Trail, which winds more than 50 nearly flat miles through several counties? Best of all, it parallels the New River, the second-oldest river in the world and one of only a few that flow from south to north.

Once no more than a railroad-track bed, New River Trail State Park is Virginia's only linear state park. Although the railroad and trail are obviously man-made, part of the majesty of the park lies in its natural beauty. Fortunately for the people who bike, hike, or ride horses along the trail, much of the native land has been left untouched.

If the trail sounds inviting to you and you are touring on a road bike, you can either unload your bike and ride it without your gear, or rent a mountain bike at New River Bicycles in Draper. Owner Lanny Sparks, who says he recently increased his inventory to accommodate cross-country cyclists, will be happy to set you up.

Today you'll again climb more than 2,000 feet as you ride from Christiansburg to Wytheville. However, the easy-to-moderate rollers make the day a pleasant one. Be prepared, however, for a few short, steep climbs.

I went off route toward the end of the day because the Wytheville KOA sounded good to me and my fellow cyclists. After a long, hot day, there's nothing finer than a nice shower. If you'd rather camp at a city park, however, check with the community center in Wytheville, 228-2313, which allows camping at Elizabeth Brown Memorial Park.

Below I offer an alternate route to the 76, or main route. If you'd rather follow the main route, refer to your Adventure Cycling map.

MILEAGE LOG

0.0 Interstate Overnight Park/US 11 junction. Head back into Christiansburg.

3.4 Roanoke St./Main St. junction. Head left on W. Main St., traveling through downtown Christiansburg. You'll pass a motel and market en route.

3.8 Make a right on Radford St. (US 11 South). Before this turn you'll pass Depot St. on the right, a better alternative to steep E. Main St.

3.9 Turn left on College St., a wonderful, uncrowded frontage road that parallels I-81.

4.8 College St. turns into CR 666. Rolling hills continue with an occasional steep short climb.

9.7 CR 666 ends and merges onto CR 600, which goes straight and to the right; continue straight.

10.2 Turn right on Hwy. 177 North; a mini-market is across the street.

10.4 Turn left on CR 664. **ALTERNATE ROUTE:** The turnoff for CR 787 is someplace between this point and Radford city limits at the 12.7-mile mark. I missed the 76 Route turnoff for CR 787; it's at the bottom of a downhill, and I accidentally zoomed by it and entered Radford via CR 664. Although CR 664 is more direct, CR 787 is an easier grade. It merges onto Rock Rd. (CR 611) about a mile east of CR 664 at the 13.8-mile mark.

12.7 Enter Radford and start a long uphill climb.

13.1 Top of hill.

13.8 Road T's at Rock Rd.; head left. (If you take the 76 Route via CR 787, you'll merge back with the alternate route at this point.)

14.3 Turn right on Wadsworth St. and head through a residential area.

14.5 Market on the right.

15.6 Make a right on 1st St. You'll head through downtown, where there are all services. There's also a bike shop in town.

16.1 Make a left on US 11 and cross the New River.

16.5 Turn left on CR 626. A motel and restaurant are just ahead. Rolling hills continue.

20.6 Stop sign at junction CR 611; make a right on CR 611 and begin paralleling I-81 once again.

25.6 Road T's; keep left on CR 611 and ride over I-81. Nearby are motels and restaurants. About this time you should see CR 660, which leads to Claytor Lake State Park. (I must admit I missed this turnoff; if you do the same, ask for directions at one of the local businesses.) There are several campgrounds, all 1 to 3 miles off route. State park cabins are also rented on a weekly basis.

26.1 Enter the quaint town of Newbern, which consists of a post office and a number of antique shops.

26.3 An old jail still stands near this spot, the previous site of a courthouse that was in operation from 1839 to 1893. The Wilderness Road Regional Museum is nearby.

26.9 At the stop sign, turn left on the unsigned frontage road.

28.3 Road on left leads to Claytor Lake Marina area.

28.7 Mini-market on the left.

30.5 Junction Hwy. 99; keep straight on the frontage road.

30.7 Motel and restaurant on the right.

32.5 CR 658 curves to the left near Draper Elementary. Merge onto CR 658.

33.1 A must-stop market on the right: I've heard the owners have expanded their food line, offering "enough grub to pump 50 miles plus." Cost? About $2.

New River Bicycles offers a nice assortment of mountain bikes (for sale or rent) and accessories, and owners Lanny and Nancy Sparks offer shuttle service for the New River Trail. In addition, they will custom-plan trips that can include lunch, canoeing, camping, fishing, and biking. If you'd like to ride the trail and need to spend an extra day or two in the area, there are several options: a bed-and-breakfast inn about a mile away, and an all-facility campground with a pool and reasonable prices. Check with the Sparks for directions, including a shortcut to the campground.

If you'd rather camp for free, pitch your tent at Dick Moose Farm, about 0.5 mile west of the bike shop and store. Dick is a hiker, biker, and general outdoorsman who offers primitive camping on his land.

34.3 When CR 658 takes off to the left, keep straight, now riding CR 654.

36.5 Cross Hwy. 100.

39.2 Stop sign at Hwy. F-047. Cross the street and continue on Old Baltimore Rd.

39.4 Cross over I-81. Make a left on Hwy. F-044 (Honaker Rd.).

39.7 Junction Service Road 618; motel, restaurants, and market in area.

41.7 Motel on the left; several more up ahead.

44.5 Carter Wayside, a beautiful rest area with rest rooms and picnic tables.

47.3 Turn right on Hwy. 121 to continue 76 Route to Max Meadows and on to Wytheville. It's about 9 miles to Wytheville via Hwy. 121 and CR 610. **ALTERNATE ROUTE:** I went off route to end the day at the Wytheville KOA, where showers and a Laundromat made a hot day all the more tolerable. There are restaurants, motels, and a market near the junction of Hwy. F-044 and Hwy. 121. From this point go off route by making a left and crossing over I-81.

47.7 Head right on Hwy. F-042, a frontage road paralleling I-81.

50.4 Restaurant and mini-market.

50.8 Head left on CR 758; a sign points the way to the KOA.

51.1 Turn right on CR 776.

51.3 Enter the campground via a gravel road that begins here.

51.4 Wytheville Campground; all services, including a Laundromat.

Wytheville KOA to Damascus ("The Place") (63.8 miles)

Today's ride is the easiest in days, although you should expect some hills, more than 3,000 feet of elevation gain, and just a few steep grades.

The day begins with a ride through the all-service town of Wytheville. Here in the southwestern part of the Shenandoah Valley of Virginia, nestled by both the Blue Ridge and Allegheny mountains, summers are filled with carnivals and fairs. If you visit during the third week of June, be sure to attend the Chautauqua (pronounced Shah-TAW-kwah) Festival, an annual nine-day event.

History buffs, especially those captivated by unique architecture, are bound to enjoy downtown Wytheville's walking tour; ask for a free self-guided map at the visitor center.

Nature lovers will appreciate the hiking trails of Mount Rogers National Recreation Area. Managed by the Jefferson National Forest, Mount Rogers National Recreation Area was named for Virginia's highest peak and comprises more than 115,000 acres of national forest land. Trails are many and include access to the Appalachian Trail. Because there are so many things to see and do here, you may want to divide the day in two, camping midway through the segment at Raccoon Branch Campground.

The route parallels I-81 for the first quarter of the ride, so traffic is usually light. The road also winds along Straight Branch Creek, an excellent fishing area stocked with trout. You'll pedal tree-lined back roads past homes and farms, springtime flowers, and tiny towns. You may hear townfolk talking about the Tour Dupont; some of their steep side roads made the 1994 itinerary.

At the end of your day you'll no doubt share "The Place," a Damascus hostel frequented by Appalachian hikers, most of whom have interesting stories to tell.

MILEAGE LOG

0.0 Wytheville KOA. Head back to the frontage road.

0.6 Junction Hwy. F-042; make a left and once again ride parallel to I-81.

3.9 Turnoff on the right leads across E. Main St. (US 11) to a variety of motels and restaurants.

4.5 Hwy. F-042 ends at the junction of E. Marshall St. and Chapman Rd. Make a right on E. Marshall St., then a left on E. Main St. (US 11), a four-lane highway with no shoulders. You'll pass a market, motels, and restaurants en route.

5.4 Junction US 11 North leads to I-77 and I-81; keep straight on US 11 South and head through downtown.

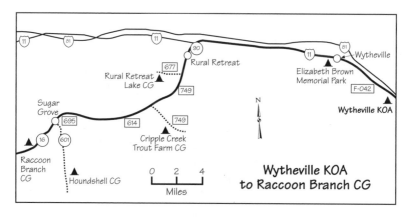

Wytheville KOA
to Raccoon Branch CG

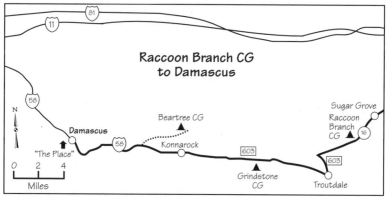

Raccoon Branch CG
to Damascus

5.7 Turn right on 1st St.

5.8 Go left on Monroe St. (Now you're back on the 76 Route.) There's a visitor center at the corner.

6.3 Turn right on N. 12th St. (US 11 South), a four-lane highway without shoulders. There are restaurants and a Laundromat in the area.

7.7 Jefferson National Forest Ranger Station on the left. Stop here to obtain information for Mount Rogers National Recreation Area. There's a motel just ahead.

8.1 Small grocery store on the right.

17.1 Turn left on Hwy. 90 East.

17.8 Enter Rural Retreat at the top of the hill. Hwy. 90 becomes Main St. as you drop down a hill to a restaurant and downtown Rural Retreat, then pedal uphill to a post office, a market, and a Laundromat in another 0.6 mile.

19.0 Reach the top of the hill just outside of town; Main St. turns into CR 749.

20.1 **SIDE TRIP:** Junction CR 677 on the right leads about 2 miles to Rural Retreat Lake and campground. It's an all-service campground with a pool, limited groceries, and bass fishing at the lake.

22.7 **SIDE TRIP:** Junction CR 749 on the left; road leads 4.5 miles to Cripple Creek Trout Farm Campground.

23.4 Make a right on CR 614.

31.2 T-junction; turn left on CR 695.

31.9 Junction Hwy. 16 and the town of Sugar Grove; turn left. Sugar Grove offers a deli-market, a post office, and an excellent diner with great, home-cooked food and fair prices.

32.2 **SIDE TRIP:** Junction CR 601 on the left leads to the Houndshell Campground about 4 miles away.

34.1 Enter Mount Rogers National Recreation Area.

34.3 Turnoff on the right to Raccoon Branch Campground, where two trout streams meander through camp. In addition, there are picnic facilities, water, and flush toilets. Two trails—the Dickey Knob Trail and Bobbys Trail—connect to the Appalachian Trail.

Continue climbing via Hwy. 16.

38.0 Top of hill—elevation 3,180 feet.

39.7 Make a right on CR 603 and begin another relatively easy climb; mini-market on the corner. **SIDE TRIP:** Continue straight on Hwy. 16 for 0.3 mile to Troutdale, where there is a country store and restaurant. If you need a post office, continue south from the restaurant on CR 603 for 0.1 mile.

42.6 Fairway Livery (horse and wagon rentals) on the left.

43.5 Cross the Virginia Highlands Horse Trail. There's a horse camp on the right with picnic tables and chemical toilets.

43.7 Appalachian Trail Trailhead.

44.6 Lews Fork Trailhead on the left.

45.4 Top of hill at 3,500 feet.

45.8 Grindstone Campground on the left. Tucked away in the trees, this all-service camp offers weekend programs at the amphitheater. At the camp, located at the base of the Lewis Fork Wilderness Area, there's a trail leading to the top of Mount Rogers. (Look for the trailhead near the registration site.)

From the campground, continue dropping, passing the Laurel Valley Community Church before you reach CR 600. This interesting log church boasts log pews and a log outhouse.

50.3 Turn left on CR 600, which joins the route and then leaves it a mere 0.1 mile later; continue on CR 603. A market and café are at the junction.

52.1 Enter Konnarock; mini-market.

53.0 Continue straight on US 58 West.

Church in Laurel Valley, east of Konnarock, Virginia

53.8 Look for the Virginia Creeper Trail on the left via CR 728. This 34-mile Rails-to-Trails path is now a National Recreation Trail dedicated in June 1987. A multipurpose trail, it was designed for biking, hiking, cross-country skiing, and horseback riding. It extends from Abingdon and continues to the North Carolina state line. If you'd rather ride the trail, it leads to the hostel in Damascus.

55.7 Top of hill after a gradual climb for the last couple of miles.

55.9 **SIDE TRIP:** Road on the right leads about 4 miles to the all-service Beartree Campground. It's 1.3 miles to the lake and a day use area where there are rest rooms and picnic areas.

Continue downhill along Straight Branch Creek for several miles.

59.6 Parking area for the Virginia Creeper Trail.

62.7 Appalachian Trail crosses the road.

63.5 Enter Damascus; market and Laundromat on the right as you enter town.

63.6 US 58 West (Laurel St.) takes off to the left. **SIDE TRIP:** To reach the hostel, ride off route by pedaling left on Laurel St.

63.8 "The Place" is located behind the Damascus United Methodist Church at the corner of Laurel and White. There are all services in addition to bunk beds. If you'd prefer sleeping in your tent, however, you can pitch it on the lawn. Restaurants include Quincy's Pizza, which makes the best and biggest turnovers you've ever seen. Some through-hikers claim Quincy's makes the best food along the entire trail.

Bridge on the Virginia Creeper Trail

Damascus ("The Place") to Elk Garden Hostel (35.6 miles)

I've made this segment a short one due to its numerous ups and downs. The hills are moderate in intensity until Hayters Gap, where there is a 4-mile climb. Feel free to join this segment with the next if you like, and you'll finish with 80.7 miles—but be warned that the total elevation gain is well over 5,000 feet.

Heavy traffic sometimes plagues Highways 91 and 80, so use caution. A fast, fun downhill leads to a market for dinner supplies and the Elk Garden Methodist Church Hostel for a good night's sleep.

MILEAGE LOG

0.0 From "The Place," head back to the main route.
0.2 Junction Laurel St. and Hwy. 91; make a left on Hwy. 91 North.
1.6 Ketron Corner; small grocery store.
3.0 Cross South Fork Holston River.
5.1 Junction CR 708 on the left.

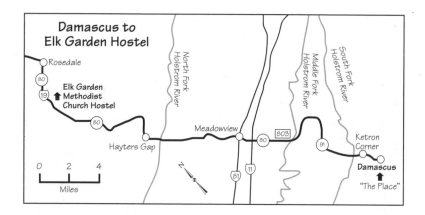

Damascus to Elk Garden Hostel

Rosedale

Elk Garden Methodist Church Hostel

Hayters Gap

Meadowview

North Fork Holstrom River

Middle Fork Holstrom River

South Fork Holstrom River

Ketron Corner

Damascus

"The Place"

0   2   4
Miles

6.2 Junction CR 722 on the left.

7.5 Make a left on CR 803. A sign points the way to Meadowview.

7.8 Keep left on CR 803 as the road passes between a church and a cemetery.

10.0 At the junction of CR 709, a "76 Bike Route" sign points to the left. *This was done in error.* Keep straight on CR 803.

10.2 Cross Middle Fork Holston River.

14.1 Junction US 11; at this point CR 803 becomes Hwy. 80. Keep straight on Hwy. 80. At the corner you'll find Quincy's Pizza, a Laundromat, and two mini-markets.

14.8 Cross under I-81. The roller-coaster stuff continues.

15.1 T-junction; turn left on Hwy. 80/CR 609 and ride through downtown Meadowview, a virtual ghost town.

15.3 Make a right on Hwy. 80 West. There's a diner here.

20.1 Junction CR 700.

22.0 Cross North Fork Holston River; soon after, pass the junction for CR 611. You'll reach this point after a long descent.

23.2 Hayters Gap Community Center.

25.4 Junction CR 613. Keep left on Hwy. 80 West and begin a long uphill, climbing about 1,500 feet in 4 miles.

29.5 Top of hill; begin fun downhill. **SPECIAL NOTE:** Watch for the super-tight hairpin turn in less than a mile. I almost missed it!

31.3 Hairpin turn! Be careful if westbound!

31.9 Junction CR 619 on the right.

32.1 Small market on the right offers food, antiques, and some camping supplies. Resume climbing and descending; occasionally there's a short, steep grade.

33.6 Junction CR 656 on the left.

35.6 Elk Garden Methodist Church Hostel, on the right. In addition to a place to throw down your sleeping bag, there are rest rooms (no showers) and kitchen facilities.

"The Place"—United Methodist Church Hostel, Damascus, Virginia

Elk Garden Hostel to Breaks Interstate Park (45.1 miles)

For the first time in my journey across the country, I suffered from bicyclist abuse through and around the cities of Honaker and Council. Perhaps it was due to the heavy traffic in the area. The abuse wasn't aimed just at me; the three others I was riding with (in separate groups of two) were clobbered with the same comments. Some people yelled at us, "Get off the road!" Others screamed, "Get a car!!!" Still others drove by as close as they could to us, then turned around to laugh and see if they had scared us. It was a pity to realize that this was probably the highlight of their day.

In all fairness, however, I must say that bicyclists who rode through on subsequent days and then caught up with me had good things to say about the people. In fact, after one guy crashed on the hill leading down to the hostel at Elk Garden (no, not on the hairpin turn), a Honaker resident drove him about 50 miles to a bike shop to drop off his bike, gave the bicyclist and his friend a place to stay for several days while the bike was being repaired, and then drove them back to the shop to pick up the bike.

Nice or ornery, I suppose you'll find both kinds of people in every town around the globe. Luckily, such incidents were rare, and

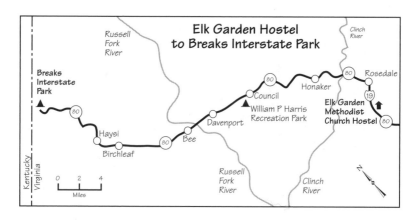

things improved as I headed west. The scenes remained mostly rural, and the people were friendly once again. The only hardship was the increase in mountain grades. Those with fairly light loads pulled the hills without any problems; others felt like dropping out. Some people ended up walking the steepest grades, while one person hitched a ride north and took Amtrak to Colorado. A 45-mile day is plenty to contend with when it includes these kinds of grades!

The day ends at Breaks Interstate Park, which straddles Virginia and Kentucky. It's a great spot for a layover day spent hiking, rafting, horseback riding, or just plain relaxing.

Thought to be one of the most scenic spots in either of the two state park systems, the 4,600-acre preserve offers a lake for fishing, an Olympic-size swimming pool, a 600-person amphitheater, picnic areas, and a campground in addition to motel rooms, cottages, a restaurant, and a visitor center.

It's easy to sit for hours enjoying the view at Breaks Gorge, a geological wonder. In the fall, brilliant colors add to the scene; in the spring, a rainbow of wildflowers and shrubs will delight you. In addition, more than sixty species of trees decorate the park, and the ground is blanketed with moss, fungi, and ferns.

The Russell Fork of Big Sandy River cuts through the gorge, providing one heck of a whitewater experience for those interested in plying the Grand Canyon of the South, as it is known. But you'll have to watch for rocks: the floor of the gorge is littered with millions of them, some small as an egg, others big as a house.

Also available are horseback riding, caving expeditions into the Pine Mountains, and hiking trips custom-fitted to your needs. Or you can hike on your own using the 12 miles of maintained trails within the park. For more information, contact Appalachian Expeditions, Inc., P.O. Box 766, Elkhorn City, KY 41522; (606) 754-8274.

MILEAGE LOG

0.0 Elk Garden Hostel; continue north on Hwy. 80.

0.2 T-junction; turn right on Hwy. 80 (US 19 North joins the route here), a four-lane highway. The highway is typical of other Virginia roads—shoulderless.

2.8 Turn left on Hwy. 80 West. US 19 continues straight. There's a motel, restaurant, and mini-market at the junction. Other necessities are ahead on US 19 in the all-service town of Rosedale.

5.3 Junction CR 640.

5.6 Cross over Clinch River, then begin climbing.

7.0 Top of hill.

7.4 Junction Hwy. 67 North; continue on Hwy. 80.

8.3 Enter downtown Honaker. You'll pass mini-markets, Laundromat, pharmacy, post office, and a few restaurants as you continue.

9.2 Restaurant on the left.

12.9 Small grocery store on the right.

15.1 Top of hill.

17.9 Enter Council; grocery store on the left.

18.4 Entrance to William P. Harris Recreation Park, where camping is permitted; swimming pool too. (Contact Betty Bostic at 859-2631 or 859-9319 for more information.) There's another entrance at the 18.8-mile mark, but it's at the top of a hill.

23.2 Enter Davenport and junction CR 600. There's a market and post office nearby.

23.8 Café on the left.

24.9 Cross the Russell Fork River. At the crossing is a tiny grocery store.

25.9 Enter Bee.

28.9 Market/deli on the left.

33.6 Enter Birchleaf, where you'll find a restaurant, a store, and a post office.

35.9 Hwy. 83 joins Hwy. 80 in downtown Haysi, where you'll find shops, markets, eating establishments, and a post office.

37.5 Junction Hwy. 83 takes off to the right; keep left, cranking up a steep hill via Hwy. 80.

38.7 Top of steep hill.

39.7 Junction CR 611 (Cumberland Gap Route) on the left.

42.3 Top of hill.

43.9 Enter Breaks Interstate Park.

44.6 Mill Rock Point Overlook on the left.

44.8 Entrance to Breaks Interstate Park on the left; no entrance fee for out-of-town bicyclists.

The author at Breaks Interstate Park, Virginia

45.1 Junction to the visitor center, restaurant, motel, and campground. Follow the signs to the campground registration booth in about a mile.

Lincoln Homestead State Park, Kentucky

KENTUCKY

To most folks Kentucky is a land rich in tobacco, coal, and champion thoroughbreds. Unfortunately, to bicyclists Kentucky also means dogs, dogs, and more dogs.

Stray dogs aside, Kentucky can be pleasant for cycling if you carry a can of dog repellent, keep your guard up, and take the time to enjoy the beautiful scenes of the Bluegrass State. To the east, Kentucky borders the Appalachian Mountains; about 350 miles to the west, the state touches the Mississippi River. In between, forests cover more than half of the land, and Kentucky boasts more miles of running water than any other state except Alaska.

Your 536.6-mile, ten-day journey through Kentucky offers the chance to enjoy some of the state's greatest treasures, including Berea, Harrodsburg, and my personal favorite, Bardstown. More than just a quaint town, it's also the site of My Old Kentucky Home State Park.

Other state highlights include the Abraham Lincoln Birthplace National Historic Site and Lincoln Homestead State Park. Abraham Lincoln was born in Kentucky in 1809 and lived there until 1816. Ironically, President Lincoln was born less than 100 miles from Jefferson Davis, president of the Confederacy during the Civil War.

Natural treasures are abundant as you continue through and then emerge from the Appalachians, the largest chain of mountains east of the Mississippi River. As you continue west you'll pedal the Cumberland Plateau and enter bluegrass country, where the grades lessen for the most part and you can enjoy some relatively flat terrain. Along the way you'll see ferns and an assortment of wildflowers.

Early spring is the best time to view *Poa pratensis*, the famed Kentucky bluegrass. Some Kentuckians claim they've never seen the grass when it is blue; others claim it is blue all year. It certainly wasn't blue when I passed through in June.

The name "bluegrass" covers approximately 200 kinds of grasses. Originally brought over from Europe and Asia by early North American settlers, bluegrass is often used in pastures today because it is nourishing for animals and can withstand frequent grazing. It is also the most popular grass for lawns and golf courses in the northern United States.

The Bluegrass State is also home to a variety of animal life: turtles, minks, foxes, raccoons, and woodchucks, to name a few.

The many bird species include egrets, blue and white herons, crows, grouse, kingfishers, ducks and geese, woodpeckers, and cardinals. Those interested in angling should note that more than 200 kinds of fish swim in Kentucky's waters.

A few back roads of Kentucky include shoulders; however, you should generally expect to ride narrow, shoulderless roads throughout the state. Fortunately, traffic is usually at a minimum, although you will encounter stretches of moderate to heavy coal-truck traffic along the way. Watch for falling chunks of coal as the trucks pass, and as usual watch for potholes, especially on the descents.

As mentioned previously, dogs will probably be a problem, but they are easily dealt with if you carry a pepper-based spray and use common sense. How much pepper spray will you need? Dick Davis, my fellow cyclist for one week of the ride, wrote me later, "I tell everyone that I spent $27 on Mace just to spray dogs in the state of Kentucky." I spent about $12.

Summertime weather is usually hot and sticky due to high temperatures and equally high humidity. To make the journey more bearable, wear lightweight clothing, cycle early in the day, and stop to take in the sights along the way.

If you decide to go off route, note that the interstates are closed to bicyclists. For more bicycling information, contact State Bicycle Coordinator, Transportation Cabinet, 501 High St., Frankfort, KY 40622; (502) 564-4890; website: www.kytc.state.ky.us.

Breaks Interstate Park to Pippa Passes AYH (69.4 miles)

You'll exit the lengthy state of Virginia today and enter the second of ten states that embrace the TransAmerica Trail. Entering a new state is always a joyous occasion, and this segment is no different. Welcome to Kentucky!

Although the day is a long one, the first half should zoom by if you skip the alternate route. (Some find it too steep, although I heard more than one bicyclist say, "It wasn't that bad!") The paved alternate shaves 11 miles off the total (making it 58 miles instead of 69), and it's also nearly traffic-free, unlike the main route. Regardless of which route you choose, remember to save some energy for a couple of long, steep climbs near the end of the segment.

The scenery remains pleasant as you roll through rural Kentucky, where homes vary from tiny shacks to wealthy estates. As in Virginia, the vegetation is green and lush, the hills numerous, the grades steep at times.

View into Kentucky from Stateline Overlook, Breaks Interstate Park, Virginia.

Most of the roads through Appalachia are narrow and shoulderless, so you'll want to use extra caution when the traffic is heavy.

MILEAGE LOG

0.0 Entrance to Breaks Interstate Park; head left on Hwy. 80 West for a speedy downhill.

2.0 Market on the right. Terrain is easy to moderate rollers for miles and miles as you continue.

3.0 Cross into Kentucky!

3.7 "Unknown Soldier" gravesite on the left. An interpretive sign tells the story: "Here rests the body of a soldier of the Confederacy struck down by an unknown assassin in May of 1865. Apparently on the way to home in the south. He was buried in a coffin made of boards rived from a great oak by four men in the community. After the turn of the century a rose bush marked this final resting place of a soldier who is 'known but to God.'"

4.3 Scenic overlook on the left.

4.7 Steep downhill to Russell Fork River and Breaks Interstate Park.

5.0 Exit Breaks Interstate Park.

6.1 Elkhorn City, an all-service town with a Laundromat.

6.4 Cross over Russell Fork River and railroad tracks via a bridge.

6.9 Make a left on Hwy. 197 (also known as the Trail of the Lonesome Pine) and head through downtown Elkhorn City, where there is another restaurant and a variety of shops.

8.0 Market on the left. Look for one more in the next 3 miles. As you continue, the roadway hugs Elkhorn Creek now and again.

13.9 Junction Hwy. 195 in downtown Ashcamp, where there's a post office and a market. **ALTERNATE ROUTE:** If you'd like to cut 11 miles out of your day, make a right on Hwy. 195; when you reach Lookout (it's about halfway), where there's a market and post office, go left on Hwy. 611. It's steeper than the main route, but shorter. The main route is easy, a cycler's dream, but it can be plagued with traffic. The alternate is virtually traffic-free.

17.0 Mini-market on the right.

23.2 Shelby Gap Post Office on the left.

23.7 Junction; stay north on US 23/US 119/Hwy. 610. Market on the right.

28.9 Hwy. 610 leaves the route in Dorton; continue right on US 119/US 23 and pass a post office.

29.2 Market/deli on the right. The roadway is four lanes now and sports a shoulder, a nice change. Begin a long uphill climb.

31.1 Top of hill.

33.0 Hwy. 611 (the alternate route) joins US 119/US 23 here. Look for a mini-market at the junction.

36.7 Restaurant on the right.

36.8 Make a left on CR 1469, a narrow, shoulderless country road. Now the hills begin.

40.0 Turn right on Hwy. 610.

40.2 Grocery store on the left.

40.9 Turn left on Hwy. 122 West.

44.1 Begin a steep climb and ascend about 700 feet.

46.2 Top of hill.

49.3 Junction Hwy. 466 in Melvin. Continue on Hwy. 122.

50.7 Junction Hwy. 306 in Bypro. There's a restaurant, market, and post office nearby.

52.0 Junction CR 1498 on the left. This is Bevinsville; restaurant, mini-markets, post office close by. Stay on Hwy. 122.

52.7 Turn left on CR 1091. Begin another climb and ascend several hundred feet.

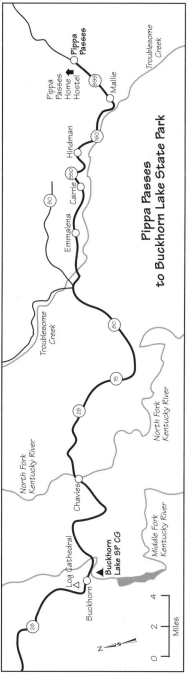

Pippa Passes
to Buckhorn Lake State Park

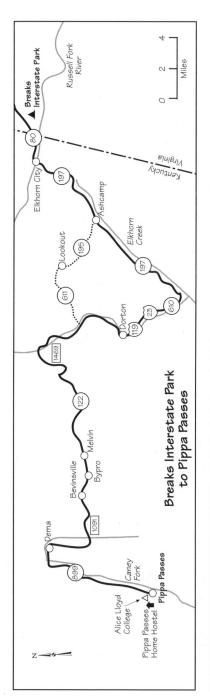

Breaks Interstate Park
to Pippa Passes

53.6 Top of hill.

55.8 Store on the right; just past the store, turn right on Hwy. 7. Easy to moderate rollers begin and remain until day's end.

59.1 Dema Post Office on the left.

60.4 Bear left on Hwy. 899.

61.1 Raven Post Office on the right.

68.1 Mini-market on the left.

68.6 Pizza establishment on the left.

68.8 Alice Lloyd College on the right. To avoid the upcoming hill, turn right here and pedal through the school via Purpose Rd.

69.4 Stop sign. Turn right and pedal up a steep hill to the third house on the right. Pippa Passes Home Hostel is owned and managed by Charlotte and Ed Madden, who started the hostel in 1976 when the first group of bicyclists rode through. Reserve a spot at the Maddens by calling (606) 368-2753; they offer eight beds and warm hospitality.

Pippa Passes AYH to Buckhorn Lake State Park Campground (54.9 miles)

Although it's a hilly day in most respects, you'll hit some nice rolling areas as well, although you can expect to climb more than 3,000 feet in elevation en route to day's end at Buckhorn Lake State Park Campground.

While pedaling this segment, I had one stray dog after another bearing down on my legs, bike, and panniers. I tried screaming at them, outracing them, and aiming my bike for the dogs in the hopes of intimidating them, usually to no avail. Using a pepper-based spray on them worked best for me.

The roads through eastern Kentucky remain mostly shoulder-less, although certain highways, such as Hwy. 80, do bear shoulders. Upon reaching Hwy. 15, you'll have to contend with heavy truck traffic—coal trucks in particular—and narrow roads.

Rain may dampen your spirits and deliver you to the campground coal-covered and messy. That's how I arrived, but a hot shower and a pineapple milkshake made the effort worthwhile.

MILEAGE LOG

0.0 Pippa Passes AYH. Head back to the main road.

0.1 Junction Hwy. 899. Continue pedaling southwest through rolling hills and along fairly busy roads where shoulders are either nonexistent or minimal.

0.4 Pippa Passes Post Office on the left.

0.5 Market on the left.

2.0 Top of a steep (but short) hill.

3.3 Junction CR 1393 on the left. Mallie Post Office at the junction. Keep right on Hwy. 899.

5.5 Grocery store and restaurants on the left. Hwy. 899 merges onto Hwy. 160.

8.2 Turn left on Hwy. 550 in downtown Hindman. The post office and a restaurant are at the junction, and to the right is a Laundromat. You'll also find the Quiltmaker Inn, a quaint place I heard nothing but good things about. The inn offers reasonably priced lodging in quilt-decorated rooms.

10.5 Market on the left. The hills continue to roll as you parallel Troublesome Creek for the next few miles. If you're lucky, the traffic may let up some.

12.4 Grocery and feed store on the left.

12.7 Carrie Post Office on the left.

13.8 Country store on the left.

15.9 Junction CR 1102; remain on Hwy. 550.

16.7 Emmalena Post Office on the right.

19.0 Junction Hwy. 721 and Fisty Post Office on the left. Keep straight on Hwy. 550 West.

Bicycle after day of riding in the rain along coal-coated highways in Kentucky

21.3 Stop sign; make a right on Hwy. 476. (If you head left about 100 yards from the junction, you'll find a post office and a market.)

22.4 Cross under Hwy. 80.

22.7 Make a left onto the Hwy. 80 onramp and merge right onto a four-lane highway with a wide shoulder. Expect a lot of truck traffic, especially coal trucks. Begin climbing a long hill.

24.4 Top of hill. Drop down, then climb again. You'll do the same thing—climb up and drop down—about four times in the next 5 miles.

29.9 Take the Hwy. 15 exit, where a sign points the way to Jackson. If you need a motel or restaurant, stay straight on Hwy. 80 for less than a mile.

30.1 Offramp leads to T-junction; make a left on Hwy. 15 toward Buckhorn Lake State Park. There's a narrow shoulder as you descend. Expect heavy traffic.

30.3 Mini-market on the right. Begin climbing.

31.0 The highway sports four lanes now; there's a narrow shoulder most of the time.

31.4 Bonnyman Post Office on the left.

31.6 Top of hill. Highway shrinks to two lanes; narrow shoulder continues.

32.4 Restaurant on the right.

33.2 Top of hill.

34.8 Restaurant on the right.

35.8 Turn left on Hwy. 28 West, a two-lane shoulderless road with light traffic.

36.1 Market/deli on the left. Look for another market/deli about 3 miles ahead.

41.6 Cross bridge over North Fork Kentucky River and enter Chavies; post office, country store.

42.0 Junction Hwy. 451 to Trace Branch Recreation Area on the left.

42.5 Start climbing. The grade is gradual at first; then it increases. Beware of false summits.

46.4 Junction CR 1833 on the left.

47.4 Top of hill. You'll descend and then gain before finally dropping.

47.6 Gays Creek Post Office on the left.

48.6 Restaurant on the right.

49.9 Junction CR 1110 North on the right. Keep straight on Hwy. 28. Climb again, then drop, then climb, and so on.

52.6 Cross Middle Fork Kentucky River, then climb and descend.

54.0 Restaurant on the left.

54.6 Junction CR 2022; head left, following signs to Buckhorn Dam. There's a post office and grocery store in Buckhorn.

You'll also see the Log Cathedral, a Presbyterian church that is home to hundreds, if not thousands, of bats. The bell of the Log Cathedral has been heard throughout the valley each evening for more than sixty years. Even today, softball games are brought to a halt while everyone bows their heads in silent prayer until the last echo dies away.

54.9 Turnoff to Buckhorn Lake State Park Campground on the left. The campground offers all services and nice shady sites.

Buckhorn Lake State Park Campground to Irvine (60.2 miles)

Today's ride is much like the others—quite a few miles and a more than 3,000-foot gain in elevation. Stray dogs are just as rampant, so be alert!

Traffic is basically light, especially on CR 1209, where you'll feel as if you're bicycling through the jungles of Africa. Vines intertwine in this lush haven of green trees, green plants, green grass, green leaves, and green moss. Occasional wildflowers, farms, and scattered homes dot this part of rural Kentucky.

The day ends in civilization, however, with fast-food restaurants, wonderful buffets, and a motel for those who are ready for a bed.

SPECIAL NOTE: If you're not interested in staying in Irvine, or cycling through the city for that matter, you can take the following shortcut, which cuts 11 to 12 miles off the main route. You'll end up pedaling about 88 miles with a nearly 4,000-foot gain in elevation. All of the bicyclists I spoke with took advantage of it, and I don't blame them. I rode the original route because, although I did go off route on occasion, I tried to stick to the TransAmerica Trail

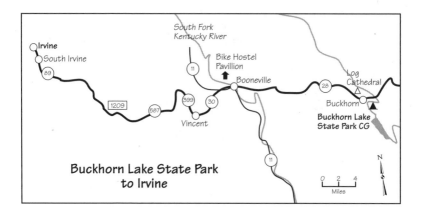

whenever possible. **SHORTCUT:** Upon reaching Hwy. 89 at the 52.1-mile mark, go left instead of right. After about 0.5 mile, cross a bridge over Station Camp Creek and turn right onto a paved, one-lane road. It connects with Hwy. 594 in about 3 miles. The connecting point on the Irvine to Berea segment would be at about the 6.5-mile mark.

MILEAGE LOG

0.0 Buckhorn Lake State Park Campground entrance.

0.3 Back to the junction of Hwy. 28/CR 2022. Climb up Hwy. 28, a moderate to steep grade.

1.7 Top of hill.

3.9 Junction Hwy. 315; keep left on Hwy. 28.

4.7 Mini-market on the left.

6.0 Begin uphill; it's a moderate, sometimes steep grade.

7.7 Top of hill. Descend and continue rollers with an occasional steep pitch through rural Kentucky. The roads are shoulderless, but fairly quiet.

15.4 Junction CR 2024 on the right; just ahead is junction CR 2024 on the left.

16.5 Begin climbing.

17.1 Top of steep hill.

18.2 Market on the right.

18.3 Cross the South Fork Kentucky River.

18.6 Road curves at this point and becomes Hwy. 30 West/Hwy. 11 North. This is downtown Booneville, where there are all services, including a church hostel. Booneville Methodist Church (Bike Hostel Pavilion) is about 4 blocks from downtown. Ask locals for directions.

Road curves right, then left, then right. In other words, you'll end up heading straight from where you first entered town. Now the highway is four lanes with a narrow shoulder, and traffic increases. Begin climbing.

20.4 Turnoff on right for Old Kentucky Rt. 11.

20.6 Summit.

21.0 Turn left on Hwy. 30, a two-lane, shoulderless road; Hwy. 11 continues straight. Hwy. 30 is mostly rolling, with an occasional short, steep hill.

25.5 Junction Hwy. 399; make a right. Just to the left is the Vincent Post Office and market.

29.3 T-junction; head left on Hwy. 587. There's a market on the corner. Begin uphill climb at a mostly moderate to steep grade. Prepare to descend a short distance on occasion, then climb again and again, sometimes at a very steep grade.

38.7 Stay straight on CR 1209 and begin a fun descent along an uncrowded backcountry road where vines choke just about everything.

39.1 Small grocery store on the right.

44.0 The road levels off somewhat and continues to be rolling as you pedal past farms, fields, and rural homes.

52.1 T-junction; turn right on Hwy. 89. Terrain is now rolling, but mostly uphill. If you're interested in the shortcut, this is where you'll make a left turn.

57.8 Short, steep climb into South Irvine.

58.6 Junction Hwy. 851; keep left on Hwy. 89. Market on corner.

59.1 Cross bridge over a small creek.

59.4 Junction Hwy. 52; make a left. The busy highway sports a narrow shoulder at times. (To the right of the junction in downtown Irvine, you'll find a Laundromat and other services.)

60.1 Turn left on Hwy. 499 to continue on route.

60.2 Motel on the left. There are also several restaurants and a market.

Irvine to Berea (30.6 miles)

After cranking out a lot of miles the past few days, you should find this segment pure pleasure as you enter central Kentucky's bluegrass region. En route there will be plenty of time for petting box turtles, gazing at the many ranches, enjoying the ease of rolling hills (with a couple of short, steep climbs), and exploring the lovely town of Berea.

You'll enter Berea, known as "the Folk Arts and Crafts Capital of Kentucky," near the Boone Tavern Hotel and Dining Room, "Where Southern Hospitality Begins." Featuring fine regional

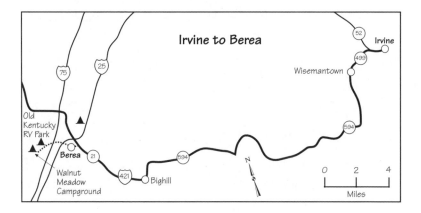

foods and attractive guest rooms, the Boone Tavern Hotel is part of College Square, a potpourri of shops and restaurants. Highlights include the Log House Craft Gallery, which features goods made by Berea College students as well as a full line of handcrafted traditional furniture.

To learn more about the region, which is rich in both history and cultural heritage, visit the Appalachian Museum. You may also tour Berea College, a unique institution in the world of higher learning. Founded in 1855, the college provides a high-quality liberal arts education at minimal cost. Students, 80 percent of whom are selected from the southern Appalachian area and Kentucky, pay no tuition. Room, board, and health and incidental fees for each student total $3,600 a year, met all or in part by students' earnings in the work program. They work 10 to 15 hours a week while carrying a full academic course load.

With forty-six arts and craft shops, studios, and galleries in town, it's not surprising that Berea is the site of many craft fairs and festivals. Outdoor galas are held in May, July, and October. A few annual events include the Kentucky Guild of Artists and Craftsmen Spring Fair in May, the Berea Craft Festival in July, and the Celebration of Traditional Music in October.

Berea College Crafts, Log House Sales Room, Berea, Kentucky

Cemetery along Hwy 594 east of Berea, Kentucky

The day ends at a campground, but it could just as easily end at the fanciest of hotels, a quaint bed-and-breakfast inn, or a budget motel. No matter where you stay, be sure to sample the inexpensive but delicious all-you-can-eat pizza buffet at Mario's Pizza, a favorite of bicyclists.

MILEAGE LOG

0.0 Motel entrance. Continue west on Hwy. 52.

0.1 Make a left on Hwy. 499; no shoulder, very little traffic.

2.1 Junction Hwy. 594; head left on Hwy. 594. There's a market at the junction. This highway is a bicyclist's dream: a smidgen of traffic, farm scenes, and rolling terrain. Expect a few steep pitches, but nothing too difficult.

19.5 Market on the left.

22.4 T-junction at US 421; head left along the busy two-lane highway.

23.5 Bighill Post Office on the right.

23.6 Turn right on Hwy. 21, a busy two-lane road, and climb to Berea. There's a market on the corner.

27.6 Market on the right.

28.6 Old downtown Berea and Hwy. 595 junction. To continue on the 76 Route, make a right on Hwy. 595 (Main St.) and ride north. **SIDE TRIP:** To reach the campground, which is off route, continue straight. There's a wonderful hotel on the right near the junction.

28.7 T-junction at stoplight. Make a left, now traveling Chestnut St., also called Hwy. 21 North/US 25 South (I know this doesn't really make sense, but Hwy. 21 curves to the west before heading north). Pass Berea College and a variety of amenities as you ride through this all-service town. Greyhound bus service is also available.

29.3 Exit Broadway St. **SIDE TRIP:** Turn right on Broadway to reach the visitor center, which is on the left in 0.3 mile.

29.6 Mario's Pizza and Pasta Bar on the right.

30.1 Junction I-75. Plenty of motels or restaurants in this area.

30.6 Old Kentucky RV Park, on the right, offers special rates for touring bicyclists. In addition to the usual services, there's a Laundromat, market, and swimming pool. Or try Walnut Meadow Campground just beyond (but note that the sites are a bit more expensive and the terrain a bit hilly).

Nearby is the reasonably priced Waffle Pantry, where I had some of the biggest pancakes of the entire route. According to one waitress, their pancakes are so outrageously big that some folks even photograph the hotcakes before eating them!

Berea to Chimney Rock Campground (41.3 miles)

Another short day leaves plenty of time for exploring Berea before continuing on your westward journey through the bluegrass region. Today, Kentucky starts to look more like the images of the state we've all seen: a maze of tobacco and hay fields, with enormous ranches, some surrounded by rock fences.

The only disappointment is seeing cows instead of horses. When I first thought of bicycling through Kentucky, I dreamed of seeing

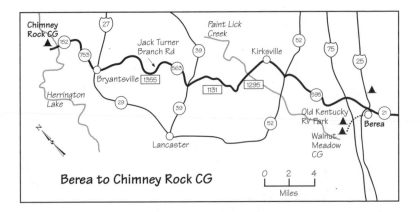

Berea to Chimney Rock CG

jumbo horse ranches framed by freshly painted white fences. As I later found out, I would never see Kentucky's famous ranches on the TransAmerica Trail. Most of the ranches are found to the north, in and around Lexington.

Still, the vistas are wide and pleasant as you continue through the hills in roller coaster fashion. Although there are a few short, steep grades, most of the pavement follows ridges where the pedaling is fun and you can enjoy one magnificent view after another.

Traffic is usually light, although you should expect heavier traffic in some areas, particularly as you exit Berea.

MILEAGE LOG

0.0 Old Kentucky RV Park entrance. Return to town and the 76 Route.

2.0 Back to the corner of Hwy. 595 (Main St.) and Hwy. 21 in downtown Berea. Head northwest on Hwy. 595.

4.5 Cross under I-75; stay straight. At the crossing are a restaurant, motel, and mini-market. Traffic decreases as you proceed.

10.5 Turn left on Hwy. 595, which merges onto Hwy. 52. Market/deli at the junction.

Bicyclist pedaling Jack Turner Branch Road, north of Lancaster, Kentucky.

Herrington Lake, Kentucky

11.3 Exit Hwy. 52 and turn right on Hwy. 595.

13.4 Make a left on CR 1295; Hwy. 595 stays straight. There's a market about a mile east in Kirksville.

14.9 Cross Paint Lick Creek.

17.4 Turn right on CR 1131.

18.0 CR 1131 takes off to the left; CR 1666 is straight ahead. Stay on CR 1131 as the moderate rollers (with an occasional steep one) continue.

22.1 Turn left (south) on Hwy. 39; market at junction.

22.7 Top of hill.

23.1 Turn right on Hwy. 563.

25.4 Junction Jess Ray Rd. on the left.

26.2 Go left on Jack Turner Branch Rd., a one-lane, paved road through the trees.

27.8 T-junction; turn right on unsigned CR 1355.

28.9 Road levels off somewhat after a steep ascent, then continues to roll with an occasional steep climb.

34.6 Turn right on US 27, a very busy road; market on corner in Bryantsville.

35.2 Turn left on Hwy. 753.

38.0 Go left on Hwy. 152.

39.0 Marina/restaurant sign on the right.

40.1 Grocery store on the left.

40.3 Cross bridge over Herrington Lake.

41.1 Hwy. 152 curves to the left; go right and follow signs to the Chimney Rock Campground and Marina.

41.3 Campground office; all services are available, including a Laundromat, a swimming pool, and special rates for bicyclists.

Chimney Rock Campground to Bardstown (59.6 miles)

I don't know whether it was the mostly rural scenery through bluegrass country, the superb weather, the moderate rollers that occasionally challenged me, or the nearly traffic-free roads, but this was one of the best rides to date. And the thought wasn't just mine. I rode with three other bicyclists that day, and as the sun bid another good-bye we all unanimously agreed it had been one heck of a great day!

Rolling hills, alfalfa fields, lovely rural homes, and box turtles in need of rescue escort you to day's end at Bardstown. Along the way history is prevalent, with recommended stops at both Old Fort Harrod and Lincoln Homestead state parks.

Old Fort Harrod features a replica of the historic 1774 fort. Here, costumed workers engage in old-time crafts such as broom making, quilting, basket making, and woodworking. The park also includes an animal corral, a cabin believed to be the site where Abraham Lincoln's parents were married, a pioneer cemetery, and the 1830 Mansion Museum, which displays native American and Civil War artifacts.

If you spend the night in Harrodsburg sometime from June through August, you may want to attend "The Legend of Daniel Boone," an outdoor drama performed at the amphitheater behind the state park. You'll enjoy comedy, romance, adventure, and

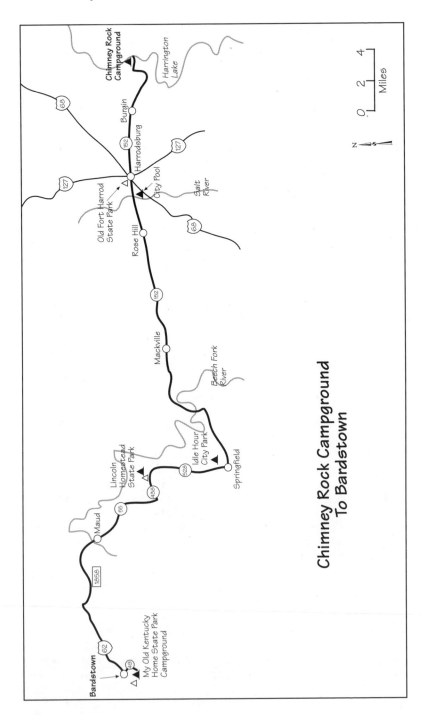

Chimney Rock Campground
To Bardstown

danger as you observe a skillful mix of historic happenings and tales of the brave pioneers who settled the wilderness.

Lincoln Homestead State Park is next on the agenda. The park includes a reproduction of the cabin built on the site of the original log house in which the president's grandmother raised her five children. Lincoln's father, Thomas Lincoln, lived here until he was twenty-five years old. In addition, the park offers the actual house in which Nancy Hanks, the president's mother, lived during her courtship with Thomas.

If you haven't had enough by day's end, you can enjoy a musical featuring the tunes of Stephen Foster at My Old Kentucky Home State Park in Bardstown. Beforehand, you may want to walk the grounds or tour the mansion known as Federal Hill, the home of Foster's cousin, Judge John Rowan. The famous composer wrote "My Old Kentucky Home," Kentucky's state song, while a guest here.

"The Stephen Foster Story" is a professional musical tribute performed outside under the stars. (The Saturday afternoon show and any nighttime shows threatened by the chance of rain are held in an air-conditioned indoor theater.) Enjoyed by millions since it opened in 1959, the drama recounts the composer's life and includes more than fifty of his songs.

Bardstown is known for more than just Stephen Foster, however. Situated in the state's famed bluegrass region, Bardstown is

Cows and rock fence off Hwy. 152 east of Berea, Kentucky

Kentucky's second oldest city. Also recognized as the "Bourbon Capital of the World," Bardstown was home to twenty-two distilleries at one time. Today, four remain open, three of which—Jim Beam, Maker's Mark, and Heaven Hill—offer tours or films of the distilling operation.

Another place to explore is the Oscar Getz Museum of Whiskey History in downtown Bardstown. Look for it in Spalding Hall along with the Bardstown Historical Museum, the Jim Cantrell Pottery and Painting Gallery, and La Taberna restaurant.

Other area highlights include the Old Talbott Tavern, built in the latter part of the 1700s. Mid-America's oldest stagecoach stop, this historic building is the oldest inn in continuous operation west of the Allegheny Mountains.

MILEAGE LOG

0.0 Chimney Rock Campground and Marina entrance. Enjoy rolling countryside and open farmland as you proceed.

3.9 Burgin; junction Hwy. 33. There's an excellent café on the corner, run by friendly folks who serve up tasty, delicious meals. You'll pass a post office and market as you continue on Hwy. 152.

7.5 Enter Harrodsburg, the first permanent English settlement west of the Allegheny Mountains. You're now pedaling through a residential area.

8.5 Downtown Harrodsburg. Post office is to the right; café across the street.

8.6 T-junction at US 127/Hwy. 152/US 68; Old Fort Harrod State Park across the street. Make a left onto the busy four-lane road.

8.9 Junction; head right on Hwy. 152 and US 68. (Harrodsburg is an all-service town with a Laundromat. The majority of services are found less than a mile south on US 127.)

9.1 US 68 exits the route as Hwy. 152 takes off to the right; keep right on Hwy. 152 and descend.

10.4 Cross a bridge over the Salt River. There's a pool and bathrooms on the east side, a picnic area on the west. Bicyclists can spend the night if they contact the police (734-3311) first. However, there are no facilities (including rest rooms) at the picnic area, which provides only picnic tables and trash cans.

13.2 Country market on the right.

20.5 Junction Hwy. 442 on the left.

22.5 Enter Mackville; at this point Hwy. 152 curves to the left. There are a couple of markets nearby and a post office as you continue.

29.3 Cross Beech Fork River.

33.5 US 150 joins Hwy. 152. There's a motel just past the junction; look for a grocery store and post office as you head straight into downtown Springfield, where there are all amenities.

33.9 Turn right onto Hwy. 528 East. (If you were to continue straight on US 150 for less than a mile you'd find a restaurant and shops.)

34.9 Cross Hwy. 555; there's a pizza place here as well as an all-you-can-eat buffet. If you need a place to camp, you'll find Idle-Hour City Park (it's free) about 0.3 mile east on Hwy. 555. Check in with police (336-3933) before camping.

39.8 Head left on Hwy. 438 West. This will take you directly through Lincoln Homestead State Park. (If you want to camp for free, there's a shelter, picnic tables, and rest rooms near

Old farm off Hwy. 55 near Maud, Kentucky

the junction of Hwys. 528 and 438.) A self-guided tour gives visitors the chance to explore the homes of Lincoln's parents. The site is a nice place for a break; you'll find rest rooms, a pop machine, and a gift shop.

42.0 Turn right on Hwy. 55.

45.1 Junction Hwy. 458 in Mooresville (no services).

47.5 Enter Maud (no services).

48.4 Cross a bridge over Beech Fork River.

49.1 Make a left on CR 1858 West; Hwy. 55 stays straight.

52.9 Cross over the Blue Grass Pkwy.

53.4 T-junction; make a left on US 62, a shoulderless road. Expect heavy traffic.

56.0 Enter Bardstown, an all-service town with a bicycle shop and Laundromats.

57.6 Junction Hwy. 245; remain on US 62.

58.1 Cross railroad tracks.

58.3 Turn left on Guthrie Rd. and ride through a residential area, where traffic is light.

58.8 T-junction; turn left on E. Stephen Foster Ave. There are restaurants, a motel, and a Laundromat at the junction. **SIDE TRIP:** Turn right on E. Stephen Foster Ave. to go into downtown for more accommodations, restaurants, Laundromats, and a bike shop. Also, you'll see the magnificent architecture of St. Joseph Proto-Cathedral. Began in 1816 but not fully completed until 1823 this national landmark is a parish church, hence the title "proto-cathedral."

58.9 Turn right on Hwy. 49.

59.6 Go right and enter My Old Kentucky Home State Park Campground. In addition to the usual services, there's a golf course and a shuttle (although it's an easy walk), to the Stephen Foster Musical and the Federal Hill mansion.

Bardstown to Hodgenville (38.7 miles)

Rural countryside reigns again as you climb just over 1,500 feet in elevation. Although there are a few steep grades, it's nothing compared to the knee-pounding eastern half of the state.

Traffic remains light, although Hwy. 49 may be a bit busy at times. Hwy. 31E into Hodgenville sports a lot of traffic as well.

A highlight for some will be a visit to one of several distilleries. (The distilleries are located out of town; check at the Bardstown Visitor Center for directions and more information.) Others may want to make a short side trip to the Abbey of Our Lady of Gethsemane, a Trappist monastery. The monks support their monastery by making cheese and fruitcake. The fruitcake, flavored with

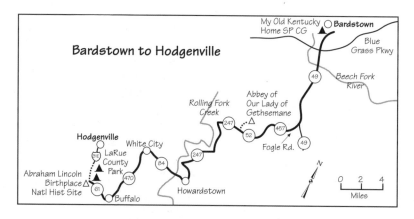

premium Kentucky bourbon, rated first among mail-order fruit-cakes in a *Newsday* taste test.

The monks lead a simple life. They wake up at 3:00 A.M. and pray for several hours before baking fruitcake, making cheese, filling orders, and so on. At lunch they pray, and early afternoons are spent resting and reading. There's more prayer in midafternoon, more at dinner, and then an early bedtime at 7:30 P.M.

This segment ends near Abraham Lincoln Birthplace National Historic Site, which is just outside Hodgenville. A memorial building protects the crude cabin from further deterioration. It is known locally as Sinking Spring Farm, after a large limestone spring that surfaced near the cabin. You can see the spring, hike a trail, see a film (*Lincoln: The Kentucky Years*), and enjoy a picnic, all near the spot where Lincoln was born in 1809.

The Lincoln Museum is located downtown. The people of Hodgenville built the museum with donated money, nightly volunteer labor, and a lot of determination. It features wax figures in displays that are as historically accurate as possible. For instance, for the recreation of Ford's Theater on April 14, 1865, the theater supplied measurements and detailed drawings of the entire scene the night Lincoln was assassinated. The scene is painstakingly precise. There's also a gallery of Lincoln art, and much more.

MILEAGE LOG

0.0 Campground entrance. Continue south on Hwy. 49. You'll pedal rolling hills once again.

1.8 Cross over the Blue Grass Pkwy.

3.0 Cross Beech Fork River.

5.9 Country market on the left.

6.9 Junction Hwy. 46 on the right.

8.7 Hwy. 49 bears to the left; turn right on Fogle Rd.

9.7 Stop sign; turn right on unsigned Hwy. 457. You'll see Holy Cross Rd. written on local mailboxes.

13.6 Stop sign; turn right on Hwy. 52.

15.4 Hwy. 247 joins the route; keep left. **SIDE TRIP:** It's 0.7 mile via Hwy. 247 (to the right) to Abbey of Our Lady of Gethsemane. I stopped for a visit and was sent back on the road with prayers and hugs for a safe journey ahead. According to one of the monks, this region is known as "Kentucky's Holy Land," for it's the first place Catholics settled after crossing the Allegheny Mountains.

17.7 Hwy. 52 leaves the route; head left on Hwy. 247 South.

25.4 Howardstown and junction Hwy. 84; make a right on Hwy. 84. There's a market/deli and a post office at the corner.

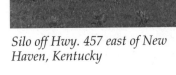

Silo off Hwy. 457 east of New Haven, Kentucky

26.2 Cross Rolling Fork Creek. Begin the longest and steepest climb of the day, about 400 feet.

29.9 Junction US 31E/Hwy. 84 in White City (no services); head left on Hwy. 84.

30.1 Turn left on Hwy. 470 West.

33.4 Junction Hwy. 916 on the left; 0.4 mile ahead Hwy. 916 takes off to the right.

34.7 Junction Hwy. 210; keep straight on Hwy. 470 toward Buffalo.

36.4 Buffalo; junction Hwy. 61; make a right on Hwy. 61. Look for a mini-market near the junction; a post office and market are to the left in 0.1 mile.

38.7 Junction US 31E. To continue on the 76 Route, go south (left) on US 31E. To reach a campground or motel, turn right. **SIDE TRIP:** To reach the Abraham Lincoln Birthplace National Historic Site, turn right on US 31E North. Go 0.1 mile to reach the entrance on the left. Continue another 0.1 mile via US 31E and you'll see a picnic area on the right; rest rooms here. After an additional 0.1 mile, you'll find a motel/campground (all services) on the right and another motel on the left. For free camping, continue about 1.5 miles via US 31E to LaRue County Park, located behind the high school in Hodgenville. Showers, water, and rest rooms are available with prior arrangements through the LaRue Chamber of Commerce at 358-3411. There are several restaurants nearby.

Hodgenville to Rough River Dam State Park (55.6 miles)

If I had to choose one word to describe today's segment, it would be "wonderful."

Everything about the ride makes it so. The elevation gain is just about 1,000 feet and most of the climbs are easy, although there are a couple of steep ones. Traffic is light as you travel two-lane roads through quiet countryside. (You can expect an increase in volume upon reaching Hwy. 259 near Rough River Dam State Park, however.)

Best of all, you'll roll through rural Kentucky, where the friendly folks are emblematic of small-town America. You may see the Amish at work on some of the farms, using horse-drawn plows to till their fields.

The day ends at Rough River Dam State Park, located at Rough River Reservoir, a man-made lake designed and built by the Louisville District of the U.S. Army Corps of Engineers in 1955. In addition to camping, lodging, and dining facilities, you can look forward to fishing, golfing, swimming, nature trails, and boating here. In addition, there are many special events, including Bass and Crappie Tournaments, the Kentucky Old Time Fiddlin' Contest, and a great Fourth of July celebration.

MILEAGE LOG

0.0 Junction Hwy. 61 and US 31E. Go south on US 31E.

0.2 Turn right on McDowell Rd. and enjoy some great country where rolling hills are a true delight.

2.8 Turn left on unsigned Hwy. 84.

3.3 Fork in road; junction Hwy. 357 takes off to the left; keep right on Hwy. 84.

9.9 Stop sign and junction US 31W. Keep straight on Hwy. 84. There's a mini-market and restaurant in the area.

10.2 Cross over I-65. Just past the junction is a restaurant.

10.6 Sonora Post Office on the left. Hwy. 84 heads over railroad tracks, then curves right through downtown, where there's a market/café.

16.4 Junction CR 1375.

21.2 Cross over the Western Kentucky Pkwy.

21.7 Cross US 62 and begin pedaling some steeper hills. There's a store at the crossing.

23.2 Enter Eastview. If you need a post office, go right for 400 feet on Eastview Rd.; the road is prior to the railroad tracks.

31.3 Hwy. 920 merges onto the route.

31.9 Hwy. 920 leaves the route; stay right on Hwy. 84. Look for a grocery store/deli at the corner.

35.1 Begin dropping in elevation.

35.8 Cross Rough River and begin climbing a steep hill. Just beyond, enter the Central Time Zone and move your watch back 1 hour.

36.1 Top of the steepest hills of the day! Now they are moderate to steep, but rolling; nothing long or abrupt.

39.6 Turn left on Hwy. 401. To the right is the Hudson Post Office and a market.

Bicyclists reading their mail in Sonora, Kentucky

43.8 Turn right on Hwy. 259.

46.4 Junction Hwy. 737 on the left leads to Peter Cave.

48.8 Enter McDaniels; market/deli on the right.

49.9 Junction Hwy. 110 on left. Laurel Branch Campground, one of several U.S. Army Corps of Engineers campgrounds, is down the road about a mile.

50.3 Turn left on Hwy. 79. **SIDE TRIP:** If you head straight on Hwys. 79 and 259 for about 0.8 mile, you'll reach North Fork Recreation Area, where there is camping. A restaurant is another 0.3 mile away.

50.4 McDaniels Post Office on the left.

50.9 Axtel Campground on the left. Sites vary; some are lakeside. Freestanding tents may be a problem, as tents must be staked on gravel pads.

53.7 Junction Hwy. 79 and Hwy. 105; keep left on Hwy. 79. Country store at junction.

55.3 Cross over Rough River Reservoir.

55.6 Tailwater Recreation Area on the right. This all-service campground offers both shady and sunny sites. (If you need a market, restaurant, or motel, continue on route for another mile or so via Hwy. 79.)

Rough River Dam State Park to Sebree Springs Park (74.5 miles)

Unless you've combined days or segments, this is the twenty-second day of your ride and the news is more of the same—you'll roll along quiet two-lane roads through the hills of Kentucky, passing fields of corn and other crops en route to Sebree. The people are friendly, often stopping to wave or smile. Traffic is relatively light, although you should expect more of it between Fordsville and Whitesville and then again heading into Sebree. And the grades are moderate with a steeper incline on occasion. (You can look forward to relatively flat terrain at the end of the day.) In other words, it's bicycling at its best.

As you ride from Rough River Dam State Park to Sebree, you'll pass through Falls of Rough, tucked away in the hills of northern Grayson County. A "small town with big assets," according to Cheryl Junker, vice president of tourism for the Falls of Rough Area, historic Falls of Rough was once a flourishing community of 250 people. Today little remains of the various town businesses, which once included a gristmill, a bank, and a sawmill. Listed on the National Register of Historic Places, Green Farms General Store has been in operation since the early 1820s. Today it houses a museum containing much of the Green family memorabilia.

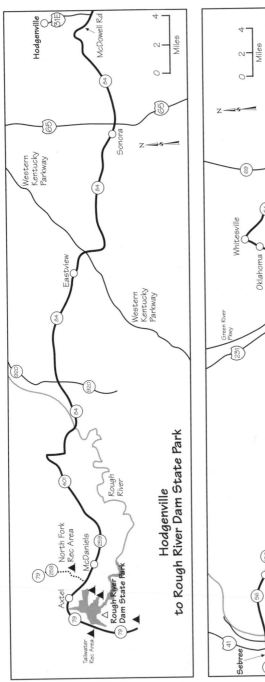

**Hodgenville
to Rough River Dam State Park**

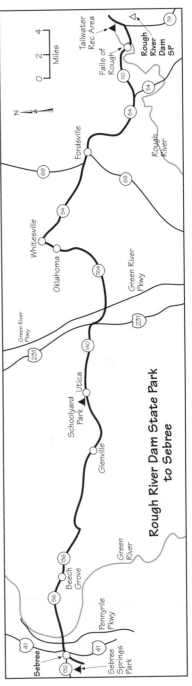

**Rough River Dam State Park
to Sebree**

The segment ends at a city park where the people are friendly and there's a pool and showers for cooling off after the day's climb of about 2,500 feet in elevation.

MILEAGE LOG

0.0 Tailwater Recreation Area entrance. Continue south on Hwy. 79.

0.9 Market and restaurant on the right. Rough River Dam State Park lodge to the left.

1.1 Motel on the right.

1.3 Motel, restaurant, post office on the right.

1.7 Turn right on Hwy. 110 West.

3.6 Cross the Rough River via a new bridge.

10.1 T-junction; turn right on Hwy. 54 West. Market on corner.

12.6 Junction Hwy. 919; keep straight on Hwy. 54.

16.5 Junction Hwy. 261; market and restaurant on the left at the junction, which is to the right.

17.7 Hwy. 69 joins the route in downtown Fordsville, where there's a post office, shops, a restaurant, and a market.

19.3 Hwy. 69 takes off to the north and leaves the route. Traffic increases as you head from Fordsville to Whitesville.

27.6 Enter downtown Whitesville, population 900, and turn left on Hwy. 764. Pass the post office and a restaurant as you head out of town. (If you continue straight on Hwy. 54 for a short distance you'll reach Peg's Diner, where good food and reasonable prices abound. There's a drugstore and market too.)

29.1 Enter Oklahoma; market on the right.

36.0 Junction Hwy. 762 on the right; keep straight on Hwy. 764 West.

38.1 Cross under the Green River Pkwy.

39.4 T-junction at stop sign; continue right on Hwy. 764 West; grocery/general store at junction.

40.2 Stop sign; make a right on US 231. Traffic may be heavy—use caution.

40.6 Turn left on Hwy. 140 West. Look for a mini-market at the junction.

47.2 Junction US 431 in Utica; keep straight on Hwy. 140 West.

47.5 Schoolyard Park on the right. There are picnic tables, rest rooms, and a water hose for taking cold outdoor showers.

47.7 Mini-market and post office on the left.

52.8 Stop sign; Hwy. 140 curves to the right at this point.

53.1 Another stop sign and junction Hwy. 81 in Glenville. Keep straight on Hwy. 140. Signs proclaim that Glenville sports a population of three.

56.8 Junction Hwy. 815; keep straight on Hwy. 140.

61.2 T-junction; turn right on Hwy. 136 West; Hwy. 140 joins the route, but leaves it in 0.2 mile.

Rough River Dam State Park, Kentucky

61.4 Hwy. 140 leaves the route; keep straight on Hwy. 136.

65.5 Downtown Beech Grove. Nearby is a café as well as a market where you can get fresh sandwiches.

65.6 Junction Hwy. 256 on the left; keep straight on Hwy. 56 and Hwy. 136, which head straight, then curve to the right. There's a post office at the junction.

68.4 Hwy. 136 takes off to the right; stay on Hwy. 56.

71.0 Cross the Green River. Coal-truck traffic increases as you continue.

71.6 Cross the Pennyrile Pkwy.

73.4 Hwy. 56 merges onto US 41 at this point. Make a left and pedal 3 blocks, then stay on Hwy. 56 as it takes off to the right. (US 41 continues south.) Look for a mini-market and pizza shop near the junction. There's a café, drugstore, and Laundromat in town too.

73.8 Turn left on Hwy. 132.

74.1 Turn left off the main route via Sebree–Roger Powell Rd. to go off route to the park. Hwy. 132 curves to the right.

Scene along Hwy. 140 between Utica and Sebree, Kentucky

74.5 Sebree Springs Park on the left; rest rooms and picnic facilities. (If you need a hot shower or a swim, continue another
0.2 mile to the pool.)

Ohio River ferry crossing at Cave-in-Rock State Park, Kentucky

ILLINOIS

Pedaling through Illinois is certainly slight on the miles, but not on things to see and do. The journey begins as you ferry across the Ohio River, a wide, wet border separating Kentucky and Illinois. It ends as you bicycle across another river border, the unstoppable Mississippi River.

Originating in northwest Minnesota, the Mississippi River flows 2,340 miles and drains 1,247,300 square miles of land before empty-ing into the Gulf of Mexico. The second-longest river in the United States (only the Missouri is longer at 2,540 miles), "Old Man River" drains almost all of the plains between the Rocky Mountains and the Appalachians.

The Mississippi is the nation's chief inland river, carrying about 60 percent of the freight transported on the nation's inland water-ways. With a depth of 9 to 100 feet, the Mississippi spans 3.5 miles at its widest point just north of Clinton, Iowa; it certainly deserves its name, which means "big river" in several local Indian lan-guages.

The big river, a traveling route for Spanish and French explorers during the 1500s and 1600s, is known not only for its size but also for its muddy character. Clear until the Missouri River (known as the "Big Muddy") joins it near St. Louis, the Mississippi takes on a muddy look from there to the Gulf.

The Ohio River is the second most heavily used commercial river in the United States, with coal making up almost half of the total freight shipped on the waterway. Flowing 981 miles through some of the nation's busiest industrial regions and richest farmlands, the Ohio begins life in Pittsburgh, Pennsylvania, where the Allegheny and Monongahela rivers collide, and ends at Cairo, Illinois, where it empties into the Mississippi River.

You'll encounter two state parks on your ride through Illinois: Cave-in-Rock State Park, which hugs the Ohio River and provides modern-day visitors with a place to relax and enjoy their surround-ings, and Ferne Clyffe State Park, a botanical wonderland.

Plains cover about 90 percent of Illinois, the most populous Mid-west state, giving it one of its nicknames, the Prairie State. Other nicknames include the Land of Lincoln because Abraham Lincoln spent most of his life in Illinois and was buried in Springfield.

Farmland covers about three-fourths of the state. Part of the Midwestern Corn Belt, Illinois ranks among the leading states in agriculture. However, you won't see much evidence of that during

Scene off Hwy. 91, Kentucky

your stay. Instead, you'll ride through the Shawnee Hills, also called the Illinois Ozarks and known for their numerous valleys, woods, river bluffs, and forested hills.

While most of the state is prairie-flat, you'll spend just over two days riding 132.4 miles through the southern tip of the state, which is full of hills. I did, however, find one flat area that is worth going off route, thanks to the Carbondale bike shop employees and bicyclists who recommended that I skip the TransAmerica Trail to Chester and pedal through the flatter region south of Chester instead. See the Ferne Clyffe State Park to Chester segment for more information.

You can expect road conditions similar to those of the past two states: narrow, shoulderless roads and light traffic. Note that traffic does increase near the following areas: Cave-in-Rock State Park, Ferne Clyffe State Park, Carbondale, Murphysboro, and Chester.

The weather is similar too, with high humidity and hot temperatures common in the summer. Thunderstorms are prevalent as well.

If you decide to go off route during your stay in Illinois, do not ride the interstates. They are off-limits to bicyclists. For more information on bicycling in Illinois, contact State Bicycle Program Manager, Illinois Department of Transportation, 2300 S. Dirksen

Parkway, Room 110, Springfield, IL 62764; (217) 782-3194; website: www.dot.state.il.us/bikemap/bikehome.htm.

Sebree Springs Park to Cave-in-Rock State Park (55.2 miles)

Today's segment ends in a new state—Illinois! Rural scenes continue to feature occasional homes along with abundant fields of corn and soybeans. The terrain is mostly flat with a few rollers for the first half of the ride; the second half consists of a lot of rollers; some are steep, although most are short climbs. Total elevation gain for the entire day is about 2,000 feet.

En route you'll pass through the delightful, super-friendly town of Marion. If you'd like to learn more about the area, be sure to visit the Bob Wheeler Museum, which houses native American artifacts, a quilt made in 1810, a variety of military uniforms dating back to the Spanish-American War, a collection of old clothes, and many antique pieces of farm equipment.

The day ends at Cave-in-Rock State Park, a pleasant spot along the banks of the Ohio River. The 25-foot-high, 55-foot-wide cave, carved from limestone rock by water thousands of years ago, was named Caverne Dans Le Roc by the French explorer deLery in 1729. It is frequently mentioned in the journals and diaries of later travelers. One of Illinois' most popular trails leads modern-day visitors a short distance to the cave, where there is a full view of the Ohio River. Unfortunately, extensive graffiti mars the rock.

After the Revolutionary War, the cave provided a hiding place for pirates, bandits, and outlaws who preyed on folks traveling the broad Ohio River. In 1797, Samuel Mason, who was once an officer in George Washington's revolutionary army, converted the cavern into a tavern. It was named Cave-in-Rock.

But this was not a tavern for socializing; rather, Mason would send comrades upriver to offer "assistance" to needy travelers. Upon reaching the cave, these outlaws would either disable the boats or send the victims into the gaping cavern. Either way the travelers lost, for they were robbed or worse. Unfortunately, it was usually worse: few people lived to tell their story.

MILEAGE LOG

0.0 Sebree Springs Park entrance. Head back to Hwy. 132.

0.4 Turn left and continue on Hwy. 132 West. There may be heavy coal-truck traffic on Hwy. 132; use caution.

7.6 Junction Hwy. 283 on the right.

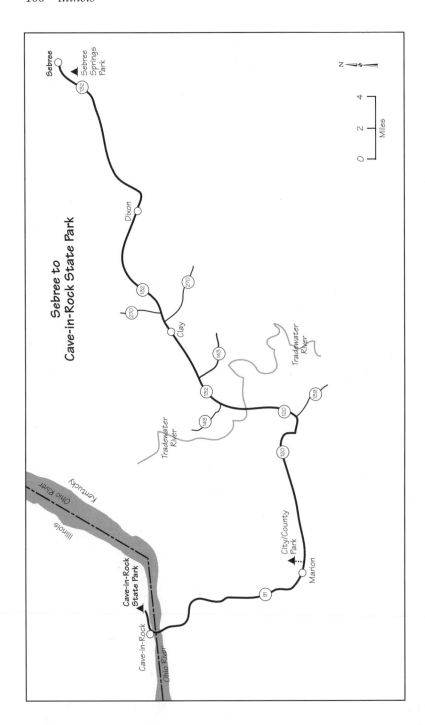

9.9 Junction Hwy. 138 on the left.

11.5 Junction Hwy. 630 on the left.

12.1 Junction US 41A and downtown Dixon. There's a café to the left via US 41A in about 0.5 mile and a market in about a mile. You'll pass the post office en route.

18.5 Junction CR 1340 on the left.

19.7 Junction Hwy. 270 East merges onto the route.

20.4 Hwy. 270 leaves the route.

21.0 Junction Hwy. 109 on the right. Enter downtown Clay and stay on Hwy. 132. There's a post office, café, drugstore, market, and Laundromat in town.

24.9 Hwy. 143 North merges onto the route.

27.0 Hwy. 143 makes an exit to the right.

28.8 Cross over the Trade-water River.

30.7 T-junction; turn right on Hwy. 120 West.

32.2 Junction Hwy. 139; keep right on Hwy. 120 toward Marion.

37.9 Junction Hwy. 654 on the right.

40.4 Junction CR 1905 on the right.

42.1 Enter the town of Marion.

42.6 Junction Old Shady Grove Rd. **SIDE TRIP:** If you'd like a free place to camp, turn right on Old Shady Grove Rd. A sign, "Park and Fairgrounds," leads the way. After 0.6 mile make a left on Club Dr.; reach the park in another 0.2 mile. The park offers shade, water, and chemical toilets; check in with police at 965-3500.

43.1 Junction US 60 and Hwy. 91 in downtown Marion, where there are all services, including a Laundromat. Continue northwest on Hwy. 91. (If you want a fast-food restaurant or another motel to choose from, go right on US 60 for about a mile.) **SIDE TRIP:** The Bob Wheeler Museum is to the left at the junction via US 60, then left on W. Carlisle St. Look for it in 0.1 mile, just past the library.

51.6 Junction Hwy. 387 on the right.

53.1 Junction Hwy. 135 on the left.

54.5 Reach the Ohio River and the Ohio River ferry. The ferry runs seven days a week, from 6:00 A.M. through 5:40 P.M. There's a small fee for the crossing.

54.8 Exit ferry and enter downtown Cave-in-Rock. There's a café, a variety store with very limited groceries, and a post office. Signs point the way to the state park. (If you'd rather spend the night at a motel, continue north of town for 1 mile via Hwy. 1.)

55.1 Enter Cave-in-Rock State Park.

55.2 Road on the left leads to the campground, where there are picnic facilities, pit toilets, and water. The cave, a restaurant, and Cave-in-Rock Lodge are located nearby.

Cave-in-Rock State Park to Ferne Clyffe State Park (62.5 miles)

Although most of Illinois is flat, southern Illinois is not; you'll find hills and valleys and some steep climbs to negotiate. You can also expect some heavy truck traffic, although relatively uncrowded roads make most of the ride through rural Illinois a pleasant one.

You should mentally prepare for hot, sticky weather as you proceed through the Ohio River Valley, where heat and humidity are typical. Showers are available at Ferne Clyffe State Park.

There's enough to do for a layover day or two in Ferne Clyffe State Park, which lies in the majestic Shawnee Hills and covers more than 1,100 acres. An outstanding natural scenic spot, Ferne Clyffe is prized for its botanical treasures, which include more than 700 species of ferns. In addition, wooded trails lead visitors to fascinating rock formations and awe-inspiring vistas.

George Rogers Clark and party passed through the region en route to Fort Kaskaskia in 1778. Some historians believe that the Cherokee used the area for hunting while on their Trail of Tears march. In 1899, two Cairo brothers purchased Hawks Cave/Rocky Hollow and named it Ferne Clyffe because of the abundance of ferns growing in the area. It was eventually sold to Emma Rebman, who later sold the park to the state of Illinois. The year was 1929.

A rainbow of colors provides two options: Visit in late April and early May for an explosion of springtime wildflowers; visit in October for the best in fall foliage.

MILEAGE LOG

0.0 Campground entrance. Head back into town.

0.4 Cave-in-Rock and junction Hwy. 1; go north.

1.5 Motel on the left; no air conditioning.

2.4 Turn left on Hwy. 146 West. Just past the junction is a market.

9.2 Turnoff to Tower Rock Recreation Area on the left. Tower Rock is 4 miles away.

9.8 Cross Hosick Creek.

10.7 Enter Elizabethtown, a quaint village nestled along the banks of the Ohio River.

11.2 Laundromat on the left.

11.4 Downtown Elizabethtown; market, restaurant, post office, and other stores.

12.2 Cross Big Creek.

14.0 Hwy. 34 merges onto Hwy. 146.

16.8 Turnoff to Horsebend Campground via Hwy. 115 on the left. It's about 2 miles away.

17.5 Hwy. 34 leaves the route and leads to a number of different Shawnee National Forest recreational areas.

19.0 Cross Grand Pierre Creek.

19.9 Top of a long, steep hill. Prior to this point there have been rollers, most of them mild.

21.9 Country store/deli on the left. The store owner welcomes many cyclists each summer and seems pleased to visit with everyone.

24.7 Turn right on unsigned Eddyville Rd. (A sign points the way to Eddyville.) Unfortunately, the rollers increase in pitch as you continue. **SIDE TRIP:** If you continue south on Hwy. 146 you'll reach Golconda (all services) in about 2.5 miles. If you want to camp at Steamboat Hill in the Ohio River Recreation

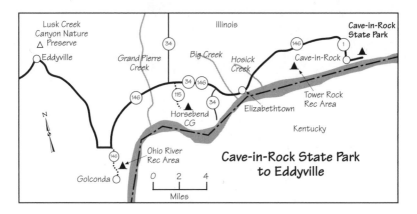

Cave-in-Rock State Park to Eddyville

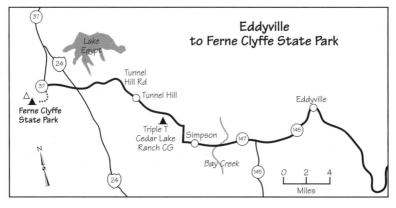

Eddyville to Ferne Clyffe State Park

Cave-in-Rock State Park, Illinois

Area, the turnoff is 1 mile prior to reaching town, then about 0.7 mile southeast via a gravel road.

34.0 Road on the right leads 2 miles to Lusk Creek Canyon Nature Preserve and Indian Kitchen. A 1.5-mile trail penetrates the Lusk Creek Wilderness, leading to a 70-foot precipice called Indian Kitchen.

34.4 Junction Hwy. 145 in Eddyville; market on the right. Make a left on Hwy. 145.

39.8 Turn right on Hwy. 147.

40.1 A sign points the way to Big Creek Ranch Campground, about 1 mile away.

42.5 Cross Bay Creek.

44.9 Enter Simpson; the post office in this virtual ghost town is to the right in 0.2 mile via the "Business District."

46.3 Turn right on Simpson Rd. The road is unsigned, but there is a "Bike Route" sign to make life easier.

49.6 Triple T Cedar Lake Ranch Campground on the left; all services, including some grocery items and a café (limited hours). There's also a lake for swimming (for a fee), and a barn dance is held on Friday and Saturday nights. The campground is used mostly by horse people, so be prepared for noisy nights and lots of dust, especially on the weekends and holidays.

51.7 Stop sign. Cross US 45; stay straight on Simpson Rd. toward Lake Egypt. The road remains nearly traffic-free and is fairly flat with some rollers.

52.9 Enter the no-services town of Tunnel Hill. Simpson Rd. changes to Tunnel Hill Rd. along the way.

53.0 Turnoff to Lake Egypt on the right.

58.3 Mini-market on the left.

58.5 Cross over I-24.

61.1 Junction Hwy. 37; the route continues to the north (right) via Hwy. 37. **SIDE TRIP:** Head to the left (off route) to Ferne Clyffe State Park via Hwy. 37.

61.7 Entrance to Ferne Clyffe State Park; go right.

62.5 Campground registration. This all-service campground offers the usual amenities plus hiking trails.

Ferne Clyffe State Park to Chester (66.4 miles)

The ride from Ferne Clyffe to Chester is one of pure pleasure, with rollers (sometimes short and steep) for the first half or so and mostly flatlands during the latter half. Traffic is basically light, the people friendly, and the scenery mostly rural.

As you cycle through portions of the Shawnee National Forest, look for an assortment of animal life. The forest is home to white-tailed deer, fox, gray squirrels, wild turkeys, Canada geese, quail, and a variety of ducks, including America's most beautiful, the wood duck, as well as mallards, widgeons, and bluebills.

Carbondale offers more amenities than most of the towns on the TransAmerica Bike Route in recent days. It's a college town with three bike shops (including the home of the famous "Bike Surgeon," who'll not only fix your bike but let you stay at his place for free), movie theaters, and even a mall. There is also Amtrak and Greyhound bus service.

The TransAmerica Trail touches only the outskirts of Carbondale, adding about 20 miles to the ride in its aim to guide bicyclists to the town of Chester. All of the cyclists I spoke with decided to go off route with a trip through Carbondale and then a wonderful journey through the hills and west to the Mississippi River. I opted to do the same. Check your Adventure Cycling maps if you'd rather stay on the route. (It's marked as the alternate route on my map.)

After a pleasant ride along the Mississippi, the day ends along the river at Chester, home of Popeye. Popeye's creator, Elzie C.

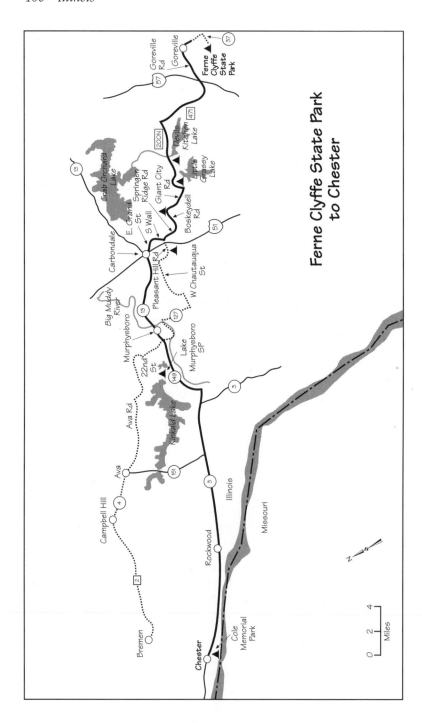

Ferne Clyffe State Park
to Chester

Segar, was born here in 1894 and is honored here with a 6-foot-tall bronze sculpture of Popeye the Sailor. If you're in town the weekend after Labor Day, you may want to attend the annual Popeye Picnic.

Located in Randolph County, where the motto is "Where Illinois Began," the all-service town of Chester also harbors a wonderful little park with a terrific fifty-year-old pool and hot showers, all for free.

MILEAGE LOG

0.0 Ferne Clyffe State Park entrance. Turn left to head back on route.

0.6 Back to the TransAm Trail at the junction of Tunnel Hill Rd. and Hwy. 37. Keep straight on Hwy. 37, then make a quick left onto unsigned S. Fly Ave. The road is signed by name, however, after climbing a short steep hill.

1.4 Turn left on S. Broadway St. and head through downtown Goreville. There's a mini-market, a pizza shop, and several other shops plus a post office and café.

2.0 Turn left on W. Main St. (Just beyond, via Hwy. 37, is a Laundromat.) As you head out of town, W. Main St. becomes Goreville Rd.

5.4 Cross over I-57. Now the route consists of bumpy, lightly traveled back roads. Steeper rollers begin.

6.4 T-junction; turn right on unsigned CR 471. A "Bike Route" sign points the way.

11.6 Turn left on CR 200N; now the rollers are easy to moderate.

12.3 Crab Orchard National Wildlife Refuge sign points the way to "Information" in 3 miles.

12.8 Devil's Kitchen Lake area begins. Numerous side roads lead to the lake. The highway finally smooths out somewhat as you proceed.

15.2 Cross bridge spanning the inlet between Crab Orchard Lake and Devil's Kitchen Lake.

15.9 **SIDE TRIP:** Road leads to Devil's Kitchen Lake Campground and Marina in 0.2 mile. Swimming is not allowed here because an underground forest exists in this man-made lake. You can rent motorboats and canoes, however, and there's an all-service campground with a snack bar at the marina. The fishing is reportedly good, with seven-pound bass and five-pound rainbow trout inhabiting the waters.

16.0 T-junction; turn left on unsigned road toward Little Grassy Lake.

17.8 Little Grassy Lake on the left.

19.1 **SIDE TRIP:** Turnoff on left leads a short distance to Little Grassy Lake Recreation Area. The campground offers all

Marina at Devil's Kitchen Lake, Illinois

services, including a beach area. Swimming is allowed in the 1,200-acre lake, built in 1940.

19.6 T-junction at junction Giant City Rd.; make a right. Giant City State Park is about 4 miles away to the south and east.

21.9 Turn left on Boskeydell Rd., where there's a motel, campground, market, and Laundromat at the corner. Rollers begin again. Fortunately, most are not too steep!

24.1 Turn right on Springer Ridge Rd.

26.0 T-junction at Pleasant Hill Rd.; from this point the 76 Route continues left on Pleasant Hill Rd. If you'd like a free place to camp, try Evergreen Park about 0.6 mile from the route and US 51.

As mentioned previously, I decided to take the Carbondale to Chester shortcut. If you'd like to do the same, continue into Carbondale by pedaling to the right on Pleasant Hill Rd.

26.1 Turn left on S. Wall.

27.3 Make a left on E. Grand St.

27.8 T-junction; turn right on S. Illinois Ave. (US 51). Watch for traffic on this busy, shoulderless, four-lane roadway.

28.3 Junction Hwy. 13 (Walnut) and US 51. Those in need of repairs or supplies will find three bike shops in the area. If you want a motel, restaurant, mall, or movie theater, you'll find plenty to choose from within the first 2 miles if you head east on Hwy. 13.

28.4 Turn left on Hwy. 13 West (Main St.). There's a Laundromat and other services as you ride out of town via a six-lane highway with no shoulder.

29.2 The highway narrows to four lanes, but a shoulder begins shortly afterwards, making the ride to Murphysboro one of pure joy. And to top it off, the terrain is flat to gently rolling.

35.1 Cross the Big Muddy River.

35.3 Junction Hwy. 127 South and Hwy. 149 West in downtown Murphysboro; keep straight on Hwy. 149. The shoulder disappears as you head through this all-service town, which includes a Laundromat.

36.5 Murphysboro Ranger Station, Shawnee National Forest, on the left.

39.2 Road on the right leads to Lake Murphysboro State Park and Kinkaid Lake on the right.

40.3 Sign for Kinkaid Lake and camping on the right. Hwy. 149 is now two lanes, no shoulders. Traffic is basically light through this part of rural Illinois, although you should expect some truck traffic. Also, the ride is once again roller-coaster-like, with some steep climbs on occasion.

42.5 You'll reach the top of the last hill on this stretch of roadway. On a clear day you'll see into Missouri.

44.0 T-junction at Hwy. 3, also known as the Great River National Route. There's a mini-market on the corner. Head right on Hwy. 3, a wonderfully flat road for miles and miles.

48.4 Junction Hwy. 151. This road also leads to Kinkaid Lake and the town of Ava.

57.6 Enter Rockwood, a small town with no services.

62.0 About this time you'll begin seeing the Mississippi River.

64.0 Cross another bridge and some railroad tracks. A truck route takes off to the left; stay on Hwy. 3 and climb a steep hill; then it's a gentle up-and-down to Chester, located on a bluff overlooking the Mississippi River.

66.4 You'll enter the south end of Chester prior to this point at Cole Memorial Park. Make a left and enjoy this wonderful park, where the camping is free. In addition to the usual services, there's also a pool; check in with police at 826-5454.

"Across Missouri" bicyclists take a dip at Johnson's Shut-Ins State Park, Missouri

MISSOURI

Missouri was a lot more scenic than I had expected, with such compelling natural highlights as Elephant Rocks State Park, Johnson's Shut-Ins State Park, and the Ozark National Scenic Riverways.

The state was named for the Missouri River, Missouri being an Indian word meaning "town of the large canoes." The longest river in the United States (it stretches from Montana to the Mississippi River), the Missouri spans the state from west to east.

Nicknamed the "Show Me State," Missouri is sometimes called the "Mother of the West," with good reason. Once it lay at the frontiers of the country, a virtual starting point for those who were headed west. Westbound pioneers began their overland odysseys at such locations as St. Louis, St. Charles, Independence, St. Joseph, and Westport Landing (now Kansas City).

The state's residents seem to be a potpourri of sorts. Although I had encountered mostly kind folks on my journey thus far, and I found friendly folks in Missouri as well, I also encountered some of the craziest drivers of the entire trip.

Earl Norman, another coast-to-coaster, said he came across more hostile drivers in Missouri than anywhere else. Other bicyclists I met as I passed through the state said the same. On the other hand, when I had bike trouble in Missouri, not only did a kind family fix the problem for me, but they insisted that I join them for a generous piece of cake and iced tea. Fortunately, as in most places, the kind folks definitely outnumbered the unkind.

Cycling through southern Missouri is a 355.5-mile, six-day journey through varied terrain. In the east there are the Ozarks, Missouri's largest land region, with many steep grades, but nothing too long in duration. Not surprisingly, the only flat areas found in the Ozarks rest in the river valleys. Yes, riding the Ozarks is like riding a continuous roller-coaster, only you have to pedal hard to get to the top of each hill. Look for rolling terrain in western Missouri, with some hilly sections.

Although traffic is basically light, there are some sections, especially around Eminence and Alley Spring, where it may be quite heavy. And in the Ozarks, road visibility is very limited, so use extra caution. (The Ozarks are one of the major recreation areas of the Midwest, so watch for heavy traffic in some areas.) Bear in mind that the roads are shoulderless.

As in the other states traveled to date, bicycling on the interstate is prohibited. If you decide to go off route and would like additional

Mississippi River crossing near Chester, Illinois

information, contact State Bicycle/Pedestrian Coordinator, Missouri Department of Transportation, P.O. Box 270, Jefferson City, MO 65102; (888) ASK-MODOT; email: comments@mail.modot.state.mo.us.

Bicycle suitability maps are available from the Missouri Department of Natural Resources. Cost for the series of maps is $1.50 prepaid. For more information, contact the Missouri Department of Natural Resources, Division of State Parks, P.O. Box 176, Jefferson City, MO 65102; (888) 334-6946; email: moparks@mail.dnr.state.mo.us.

Chester to Farmington (47.9 miles)

Today's ride is special and just cause for celebration on two accounts. First, you will now be pedaling west of the Mississippi! Second, you will reach Missouri, the fourth of ten states! Best of all, you're probably having more fun then you ever thought imaginable.

Be sure to remember how much fun you're having as you continue west, where roller-coaster-like hills make the day more challenging. Although some grades are steep, they aren't nearly as tough as those in Virginia. As if to help ease some of the pain, the Missouri countryside welcomes cyclists with an abundance of farms and quiet roads. Best of all, the people are generous.

The day ends at Farmington, an all-service town with all-you-can-eat buffets, free camping at two city parks, a variety of motels to choose from, and Greyhound bus service.

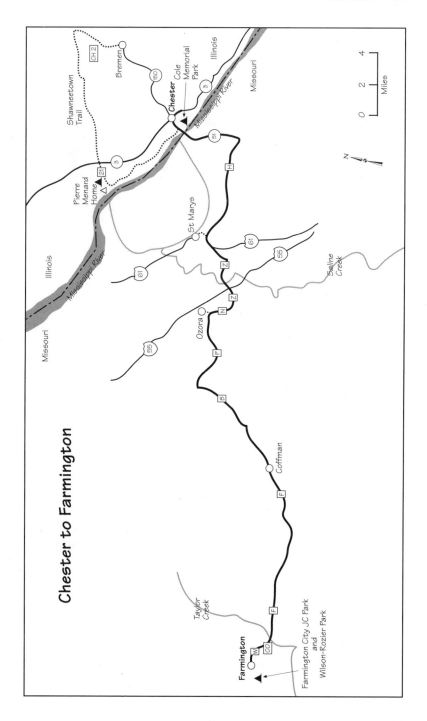

Chester to Farmington

Miles

Shawneetown Trail

CH 2

Bremen

150

Chester

Cole Memorial Park

3

Illinois

Missouri

Mississippi River

51

Pierre Menard Home

21

3

H

St Marys

61

61

55

Z

Z

Saline Creek

N

Ozora

P

55

B

Coffman

F

Taylor Creek

F

Illinois

Missouri

Mississippi River

Missouri

Illinois

Farmington

W

CO

Farmington City JC Park and Wilson-Rozier Park

If you have time before heading out of Chester, you may want to consider a side trip up the Mississippi River to the Pierre Menard Home, a model of southern French Colonial architecture often referred to as the "Mount Vernon of the Midwest." One of the most exquisite examples of upper-class French-American life during the late 1700s and early 1800s, the home is in the process of being restored by the Department of Conservation. Named as a National Historic Landmark and listed on the National Register of Historic Places, the home remains intact and contains many original furnishings. You can tour the home free of charge, although donations are accepted and appreciated.

You may also want to visit the nearby Fort Kaskaskia Historic Site. But don't expect to see some sort of old structure or link to the past, as I did. Instead of seeing the actual fort, you'll see the site where the fort once stood. Still, you might find it worth exploring, especially if you combine it with a visit to the Menard Home.

MILEAGE LOG

0.0 Cole Memorial Park entrance. Continue northwest on Hwy. 3 (Opdyke St.)

0.6 Junction Hwy. 150 in downtown Chester. There's a Laundromat at the junction. (To the right via Hwys. 150 and 3 you'll find a variety of motels and restaurants.) Turn left on Spur Hwy. 150.

1.4 Reach the county courthouse, where Hwy. 150 curves to the right. En route you'll pass a bakery, restaurant, and other miscellaneous shops.

1.8 T-junction at Hwy. 150 West (Truck Route—River Bridge Route); make a left.

2.0 Junction Branch Rd. Keep straight on Hwy. 150, passing a tiny park and a Popeye statue on the left. At this point the TransAm Trail hooks up with my off-route odyssey. **SIDE TRIP:** If you followed my route and would like to head up river to see Fort Kaskaskia and the Pierre Menard Home, follow Branch Rd. (on the left) to Kaskaskia Rd. in 0.2 mile. Here you'll make a right and continue past the Menard Correctional Center in 1.1 miles. Reach the junction to the Pierre Menard Home and Fort Kaskaskia Historic Site about 5 miles northwest of Chester. The Pierre Menard Home is straight ahead in 0.2 mile; head right for 0.3 mile to the Fort Kaskaskia turnoff, then travel another 0.5 mile to the park information office. You'll pass a picnic area and overlook en route. There are shaded campsites, chemical toilets, and water.

2.1 Cross Chester Bridge over the Mississippi River and enter Missouri. You are now traveling Hwy. 51, a flat but very busy road. Watch for traffic—use caution.

Pierre Menard Home, northwest of Chester, Illinois

2.9 Mini-market on the left.

5.9 Make a right on CR H. (If you need supplies before turning, there's a mini-market about 0.5 mile ahead on Hwy. 51.) CR H is also fairly busy, so watch for trucks and other traffic. The roadway is fairly level for a while; hills, some of them steep, are common later.

12.8 T-junction at US 61; make a left. US 61 is two lanes, no shoulder, and the traffic is moderate. **SIDE TRIP:** St. Marys, a virtual ghost town, is 1 mile to the right via US 61. There's a post office and a store (limited groceries) that serves hot prepared foods.

13.8 Make a right on CR Z, a two-lane road with light traffic.

16.6 Cross Saline Creek.

17.0 Cross over I-55.

18.2 T-junction; go right on CR N.

20.3 Junction CR P; make a left. **SIDE TRIP:** To reach Ozora, where there's a motel, restaurant, mini-market, and Laundromat, continue 1 mile on CR N.

25.8 T-junction; turn left on CR B.

30.3 Junction CR CC on the right.

33.7 Reach a fork in Coffman, a town without services; CR WW on the left, CR F on the right; go right on CR F.

36.2 Junction CR MM on the left.

38.6 Junction CR AA on the right.

44.9 Cross Taylor Creek.

45.7 T-junction; make a right on CR OO, a busy road with a narrow shoulder. There's a motel soon after turning.

46.5 Enter Farmington.

46.7 Junction CR W and Hwy. 32. Stay left on CR W, which is St. Genevieve Ave. There's a motel, restaurant, and mini-market in the area.

47.4 Long Park on the left. Although you can't camp here, there are showers and a pool available for your use.

47.6 CR W curves to the right on Main St., then makes an immediate left on Liberty St. A bike shop is on the left as you continue.

47.9 Junction Washington St. The day ends here, giving each cyclist a couple of options: you can stay in a motel or camp at one of two city parks for free. Both parks—Farmington City JC (no facilities) and Wilson-Rozier (toilets, water)—are located off Perrine Rd. Check in with police at 756-6686 before camping.

   If you need a Laundromat, from the junction go right on Washington St. for 0.1 mile. If you're interested in restaurants, motels, and other services, continue on Washington St. for about a mile to Hwy. 32. You'll have plenty of options to choose from along Hwy. 32.

Farmington to Johnson's Shut-Ins State Park (35.2 miles)

By this time you've probably heard about the dreaded Ozarks. I know I had; nearly everyone spoke of grades that cars could barely climb; of walking their bikes over one hill after another; of the terribly high humidity that nearly zapped them of all their strength.

Well, the humidity did wear me down at times, but the grades did not (although I must admit I was very happy to reach the

Elephant Rocks State Park, Missouri

"flatlands" of Kansas). And the same thing happened to other cyclists I spoke with—or at least, to most of those who were headed west. Whereas some westbounders found the Ozarks tough, it was mostly the eastbounders who considered them extremely difficult. I found the Ozarks similar to slopes in Virginia, Kentucky, and Illinois, but the climbs were shorter. Some westbounders and I came to the conclusion that since the eastbounders had just crossed Kansas, they likely just weren't as used to the hills as we were.

Although the Ozarks never materialized in the sense I was expecting, there are some steep grades. You'll climb about 1,300 feet during this segment, which is only 30-plus miles. It's short primarily because there is so much to see and do. On route you'll pass Fort Davidson State Historic Site, and just off the route is the must-see Elephant Rocks State Park.

Fort Davidson was attacked by Major General Sterling Price and his Confederate troops, which numbered 10,000 to 12,000 men, on September 27, 1864. The attack occurred during the famous invasion known as Price's Raid, an expedition that ultimately covered 1,434 miles and involved forty-three battles and skirmishes. The tiny earthen fort that once stood here was defended by a Union force of about 1,400 men, including fifty members of a local black militia. Although Price eventually occupied the fort, it was not without heavy casualties.

A visitor center at the fort offers exhibits, but if you visit at the proper time you'll see more than just displays. Every three years, the Missouri Department of Natural Resources co-sponsors a Civil War reenactment at the site.

A Missouri Natural Area, Elephant Rocks is composed of perhaps the most curious geological formations in all of Missouri. Is there any other place where "billion-year-old giant granite rocks stand end-to-end like a train of circus elephants," thus giving the site its name?

A 1-mile trail leads around and through the rocks, the largest of which stands 27 feet tall, 35 feet long, and 17 feet wide and weighs an amazing 680 tons. Designed especially for the visually and physically handicapped, the path is paved and wheelchair accessible; Braille signs describe the origin of the rocks. As mentioned previously, camping is not permitted, but there are picnic sites near the boulders.

This segment ends at 2,490-acre Johnson's Shut-Ins State Park, formed by ancient rocks nearly 1.5 billion years old. Volcanic in origin, the rocks were molded when fierce eruptions spewed clouds of ash, debris, and turbulent gases. Shallow inland seas then covered the volcanic mountains until major uplifts forced the seas to retreat. Streams eventually formed river valleys, carving the chutes and potholes seen today.

Within the park the East Fork Black River slices through a gorge located in the St. Francois Mountains. Trails enable visitors to see the rhyolitic rocks, play in the various nooks and crannies of the river, and explore the glades—Missouri's equivalent of deserts. Located between forests, these barren areas provide homes for such species as prickly pear cactus, pineweed, and fame flower as well as scorpions and the rare eastern collared lizard, Also known as the mountain boomer, this lizard rises up on its haunches and runs on its hind legs when disturbed.

Trails lead through the park, which contains more than 900 species of plants, including Missouri's largest assemblage of Virginia witch hazel. In addition to hiking and observing the flora and fauna native to the area, swimming and fishing are also popular activities here.

Two-lane roads provide access to day's end. Some of the roads are busy (CR W is particularly troublesome as you head out of Farmington), while others are slow and mostly traffic-free.

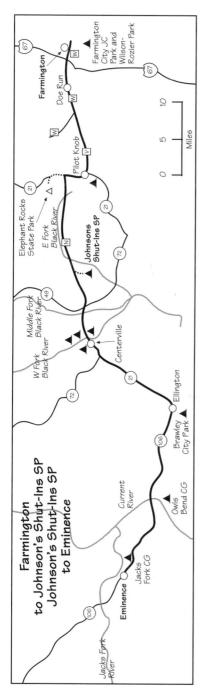

Farmington
to Johnson's Shut-Ins SP
Johnson's Shut-Ins SP
to Eminence

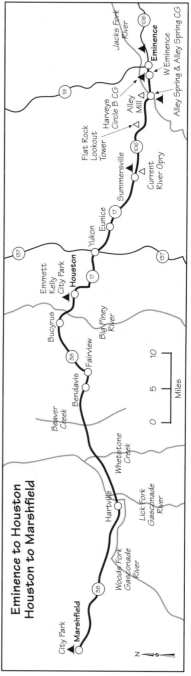

Eminence to Houston
Houston to Marshfield

MILEAGE LOG

0.0 Junction Washington St. and Liberty. Head out of town via Liberty St. (CR W).

1.3 Junction US 67; make a left, now riding US 67, which sports a shoulder. Two motels and several restaurants are in the area.

1.6 Exit US 67 at the CR W offramp and make a right. (At this point cyclists headed east should stay straight on W. Columbia St., riding directly into downtown.) Beware of heavy traffic, including trucks, on CR W.

4.9 Doe Run; there's a mini-market, a restaurant, and a post office as you head through town.

8.8 Junction; CR W continues straight ahead; make a left on CR V. You'll find a mini-market at the corner. Traffic is light now.

17.1 Enter Pilot Knob city limits. Pilot Knob is an all-service town with restaurants and a motel (camping available), and it's also the home of Fort Davidson State Historic Site.

17.5 Stop sign; keep straight on CR V, passing a post office and market en route.

18.1 T-junction; go right on Hwy. 21; there's a wide shoulder on this busy road.

20.4 Junction CR W. Make a left and proceed on Hwy. 21.

20.9 Junction CR N on the left; mini-market. Turn left on CR N and remain there until reaching Johnson's Shut-Ins State Park. Traffic is light once again. **SIDE TRIP:** Stay straight on Hwy. 21 to reach Elephant Rocks State Park. Pedal 0.5 mile to CR RA and make a left; go another 0.6 mile to the park entrance, which is on the right.

28.1 Cross the Black River.

29.6 Bar and grill on the right.

33.9 Cross East Fork Black River.

34.2 Entrance to Johnson's Shut-Ins State Park; make a left.

35.2 Here you'll find a small market, a changing room, an information center, and a trail leading to the river. There's a campground with all facilities and a Laundromat prior to this point.

Johnson's Shut-Ins State Park to Eminence (54.0 miles)

It's another wonderful ride through the Ozarks as you pedal quiet lanes, including a section of the Ozark National Scenic Riverways area, which encompasses more than 80,000 acres and 134 miles of the Current and Jacks Fork rivers. Both rivers are crystal clear, spring-fed waterways, with the Jacks Fork River a tributary of the

Current River. Together they create the nation's first and longest free-flowing protected riverway. The choice scenery makes this segment extra special.

Canoeing, tubing, and fishing are popular pastimes. In fact, according to *Life* magazine, the Jacks Fork River is one of the world's seven most scenic float fishing streams. Anglers will find ninety-five types of fish, including smallmouth bass, trout, and goggle-eye.

The Current River, one of Missouri's most beautiful rivers, begins life at Montauk Spring in the Ozarks. Here, about 40 million gallons of water spill out each day. Springs are common in the Ozark Plateau, where about 10,000 bubble from the ground at any given moment.

Although this segment involves a lot of elevation gain and loss, with some short, very steep climbs, the grade still doesn't seem as tough as in Virginia. Best of all, traffic is relatively light.

SPECIAL NOTE: Today's text is based on estimates because my microcassette recorder was on pause all day and I missed getting the precise mileages. I did, however, use Adventure Cycling's maps, which have proved to be quite accurate.

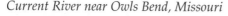

Current River near Owls Bend, Missouri

MILEAGE LOG

0.0 Campground entrance. Head west on CR N, a two-lane road with little traffic and some steep, rolling grades.

7.0 T-junction; turn right on Hwy. 72/21/49; then in a short distance make a left on Hwy. 21/72. Hwy. 49 forks off to the right. Cross the Middle Fork Black River soon after turning.

13.0 Centerville. Prior to town (about a mile east) is Pines 21 Campground, which offers all facilities. In addition, two other campgrounds (West Fork and Jackson's) are nearby, and camping is allowed at the city park. Check with town hall about camping in the park; Centerville Market can help with campground directions.

The town offers two cafés, a market, and a post office. Cross the West Fork Black River as you exit town, then climb a long, moderate to steep hill.

15.0 Hwy. 72 leaves the route; continue on Hwy. 21. Long hills and rolling terrain are a delight.

28.0 Reach Ellington. This town offers all services and free camping at Brawley City Park, 1.2 miles south on Main St. After about a mile you'll reach a stop sign. Make a right on Hwy. 106, a two-lane road with more traffic than encountered earlier in the day. Rural countryside and rolling hills continue (some of the grades are quite steep) as you pedal the next 15 miles.

43.0 Turnoff to Owls Bend Campground. Located along the Current River, the campground offers water, toilets, and hiking trails.

As you proceed, the road is still roller-coaster-like with some very steep climbs. Perhaps visions of Virginia and Kentucky will come to mind as you continue on to Eminence.

54.0 After a long stretch of up-and-downs, reach Eminence and junction Hwy. 19. Deemed the "Canoe Capital of the World," Eminence offers all services, including canoe and inner-tube rentals. In addition, year-round floating is available on the scenic, spring-fed rivers of the Ozarks, and the fishing is reportedly superb, with smallmouth bass, walleye, and drum virtually yours for the asking. Eminence is also the site of the nation's largest trail ride, which is offered several times a year.

You'll have to decide where to spend the night. There's a bed-and-breakfast inn near the junction. To the right via Hwy. 19 are motels, a Laundromat, and a mini-market. To the left via Hwy. 19 are a motel, market, and restaurants. If you'd rather camp, you'll pass Jacks Fork Campground just prior to entering town. Located along the Jacks Fork River, the campground provides all services, cabins, a limited selection of groceries, and canoe and tube rentals.

Another campground, Harvey's Circle B, is straight ahead from the junction via Hwy. 106 and then 0.5 mile east. See the Eminence to Houston segment for more details.

Eminence to Houston (42.8 miles)

Today's segment is more of the same—a ride through rural Missouri, where ranches and homes are spread wide and far. You'll continue through the Ozark National Scenic Riverways area, where you can stop and canoe, hike, or just plain relax.

I found the two-lane, shoulderless roadways literally traffic-free, even on a warm summer weekend. However, park ranger Bill O'Donnell of the Alley Spring Ranger Station warns of heavy traffic along some roads, especially Hwy. 106, which is plagued with logging trucks all year long. RVs are also increasing in numbers as the "Branson phenomenon" brings more people to the area. (Branson boasts a mix of celebrity-owned theaters and supper-clubs where country music is king.) O'Donnell also reminds riders to ride single file.

Sign in Eminence, Missouri

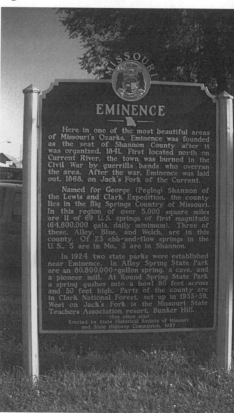

Fortunately, the worst of the steep grades are over, although you will encounter some heavy-duty rollers for the first 7 miles. After that you'll pedal along a ridge where there are some moderate rollers. At about the 20-mile mark, the terrain becomes more rolling, although you should expect an occasional short, steep climb.

The day is a relatively short one since camping areas are far apart and you may want to spend some extra time lingering around Alley Spring. Canoeing, fishing, and visiting the mill are popular activities.

The day ends in downtown Houston. I was with a friend, and we opted to share the cost of an inexpensive motel room. It proved to be the right decision because of the huge thunderstorm that pounded the area that night, with tornado-like winds ripping through the area and creating quite a stir. We were thankful to be inside the safe confines of our room.

MILEAGE LOG

0.0   Junction Hwy. 19 and Hwy. 106. Head west on Hwy. 106.

0.2   Harvey's Circle B Campground turnoff on the right; there's a market too. A 0.5-mile partially paved road leads to the campground, which offers the usual amenities plus groceries, a recreation hall, and river swimming in the clear waters of the Jacks Fork River. Harvey's offers special rates for bicyclists.

1.0   Enter West Eminence; no services.

1.3   Cross Mahans Creek; beware of slippery grid bridge.

3.6   Mini-market on the left.

3.7   Junction CR E on the left.

5.0   Enter Ozark National Scenic Riverways, a wonderful place to fish or float on the river.

5.2   Canoe rentals/store on the right.

5.3   Entrance to Alley Spring Campground on the left. The campground is 0.4 mile away, set along the banks of the Jacks Fork River. You'll find all the usual amenities plus snack items.

5.6   Cross Jacks Fork River.

5.8   Alley Spring Picnic Area on the right. The largest of the Jacks Fork springs, Alley Spring is the seventh-largest spring in the state, emitting 81 million gallons daily.

Nearby is Alley Mill, located a mere 20 yards from Hwy. 106. Blocked by leaf-laden trees during the summer, the mill is easily seen from the roadway in the winter. The old red mill building was completed in 1895 and is open during the summer; admission is free. There is also a one-room schoolhouse on the site.

7.4   Enter Alley Spring Conservation Area.

7.7   Leave Ozark National Scenic Riverways area.

12.7   Junction CR D on the right leads to Flat Rock Lookout Tower, visible from the road as you approach the area. You are welcome to climb the fire tower, owned and operated by the Missouri Department of Conservation, although the observation room at the top is not open to the public.

17.3   Cross Spring Valley Creek.

18.2   Junction CR Z on the right.

18.5   Current River Opry on the left. Performances are held Saturdays at 8:00 P.M. and include blues, gospel, bluegrass, and country music.

19.4   Downtown Summersville. A number of shops, including a post office, market, and other businesses, surround the city park, where camping is free. Note, however, that the park is sans rest rooms or water. If you decide to camp, check in with city hall at 932-4299.

19.5 Café on the left.

19.7 Hwy. 106 ends and Hwy. 17 begins; head to the right at the fork and proceed on Hwy. 17 North.

20.5 Junction CR K on the right.

24.1 Dragon Lady's house on the right. Peter and Phyllis Lowe welcome bicyclists here; all they ask is that you call in advance (932-5368). And Phyllis asks to be called the Lemonade Lady, as the name Dragon Lady tends to scare people off. (Peter and Phyllis began hosting cyclists in 1985. In the beginning, Phyllis was known as the Lemonade Lady. Three months later the couple planted a 6-foot by 6-foot wooden dragon in the front yard, and she was quickly crowned the Dragon Lady.)

24.4 Junction CR W on the left.

26.3 Junction CR TT on the right.

28.3 Eunice; post office, small store with limited groceries.

33.2 Hwy. 137 joins the route. Make a right on Hwy. 137 North and Hwy. 17 North. There's a market at the junction.

34.0 Hwy. 137 leaves the route; there's a post office at the junction. Stay left on Hwy. 17.

37.1 Junction CR DD on the left.

42.6 T-junction at US 63 in Houston, where you'll find all services, including a Laundromat. Pizza Express, near the junction, is especially good, and their buffet is inexpensive. Make a right on US 63/Hwy. 17.

42.8 Junction and end of today's segment. US 63 continues straight, make a left on Hwy. 17. Camping is allowed at Emmett Kelly City Park, but was not recommended when I passed through due to kids harassing bicyclists. Check with the sheriff (967-4165) before camping and for information regarding possible problems. The park is located 0.3 mile north on US 63; there are restaurants nearby.

KINDNESSES ALONG THE WAY

Without a doubt, one of the best things about touring across the country is talking with the local folks and realizing that although we live in a world sometimes filled with violence and hatred, there are still many kind people who will go out of their way to make life easier for us. Woven into the text of this book are descriptions of just a few of those special people: June Curry, the Cookie Lady, of Afton, Virginia; Peter and Phyllis Lowe, who live 5 miles west of Summersville, Missouri; the Dusty Gilmore family of Ashgrove, Missouri; Kathryn "Yodeling Katy" Lopeman of Chanute, Kansas; and Bonnie Edmondson of Fairplay, Colorado.

I also found families who were more than willing to offer me a plot of land where I could pitch my tent, and a warm shower for my sweat-dried skin. Some even offered me a room for the night. In addition to those who offer a part of their homes or yards for cyclists to sleep in, a number of generous folks manage various hostels across the land and provide kindnesses too numerous to mention.

Acts of kindness were common along the route as well. A Missouri farmer fixed my gearshift cable when it broke in the middle of nowhere. (Fortunately, I always carry a spare, but I had no idea how to use it.) And in Tribune, Colorado, when Carol and I stopped at a grain co-op to use the rest room, the co-op people alerted us about a severe thunderstorm warning that was in effect for the area ahead. Pedaling our fastest, we made it to a motel minutes before the storm hit.

In Kentucky, I stopped at a monastery and was invited to stay for lunch. Best of all, after my simple meal the monks sent me off with their heartfelt prayers. In addition, neighboring campers often stopped by; some offered popcorn, watermelon, and toasted marshmallows, but most important of all, they offered their company, which was worth more than all those things, especially when I was riding alone.

Other bicyclists spoke of similar kindnesses. When Dick Davis had a desperate desire for a beer, one kind soul drove 44 miles round-trip to buy him a six-pack. She shared the beers with him and made him and his companion dinner as well.

Yes, if there's one "best" thing about bicycling across the country, it most certainly has to be meeting new folks. That's what bicycle touring is all about.

Houston to Marshfield (65.3 miles)

Today's ride is one of open spaces, making it possible to find solitude (or something close to it) on the road. You'll pass through just one bona fide town—Hartville—en route to the day's destination in Marshfield.

During the 60-plus-mile day you'll gain about 2,800 feet, most of it moderate, although there is an occasional steep grade, especially toward the end of the day. Climbs are usually of short duration, though, and tend to be longer than those earlier in the journey. Fortunately, they are usually not as steep. Roads are two lanes and traffic-free until you near Marshfield.

The day ends at another nice, free city park where there are all amenities, including a pool.

MILEAGE LOG

0.0 Corner of Hwy. 17 and US 63 in Houston. Head west on Hwy. 17.
2.7 Big Piney River crossing.
2.9 Dog's Bluff public fishing access on the right; outhouses, picnic tables, grills.
4.5 Enter Bucyrus, where there is a post office.
5.6 Junction CR ZZ on the left.
7.7 Turn left on Hwy. 38 West as Hwy. 17 takes off to the right.
11.3 Junction CR FF on the right.
15.3 CR M merges onto the route as Hwy. 38 curves to the right.
17.2 CR M exits the route to the right.
17.7 Junction CR MM on the left; town of Bendavis. No services.
22.6 Graff Post Office on the right.

Cows near Houston, Missouri

Expansive scene off Hwy. 38 east of Marshfield, Missouri

23.9 Cross Beaver Creek, a great place for swimming.
24.8 Cross Hwy. 95.
29.7 Cross Whetstone Creek; just past is junction CR E on the right.
31.9 Junction CR E on the left.
36.3 Junction CR Y on the left.
36.8 Cross the Lick Fork Gasconade River.
37.5 Cross the Woods Fork Gasconade River.
37.7 Enter Hartville; there's a supermarket, two restaurants, a post office, and miscellaneous shops. Camping is allowed at the city park—no water or rest rooms—south of town on the other side of Woods Fork Gasconade River.
37.9 Cross Hwy. 5 and continue west on Hwy. 38. There's a long hill as you continue.
44.8 Odin Woods Fishing Area on the left; outhouse.
45.6 Enter Odin; no services.
49.0 Junction CR F; country store.
50.2 Enter Duncan; no services.
53.8 Junction CR C on the left.
57.9 Cross Osage Fork Gasconade River.
59.9 Junction CR P on the left.
63.6 Enter Marshfield, a town with all services.
64.2 Mini-market on the left.

64.5 Junction CR A is straight ahead; Hwy. 38 curves to the right. Follow Hwy. 38.

64.8 Hwy. 38 curves to the left. To continue to the city park you'll have to go off route. **SIDE TRIP:** Keep straight on S. Crittenden, following it around to the left, then make a right on N. Marshall and follow the signs to the city park.

65.5 City Park on the right. Shady or open sites; all amenities, including a pool. Check in with city hall (468-2310) before camping.

Marshfield to Ash Grove (48.1 miles)

Missouri continues to be a wonderful state for biking with another day of roller-coaster ups and downs, and pleasant riding along almost traffic-free roads.

The trip from Marshfield to Fairgrove is a breeze, with gentle rolling hills and some fun rollers where you can zoom up to the top of one hill without pedaling, then zoom down the other side. The story is different from Fairgrove to Ash Grove, however, as there are quite a few short, steep hills. Total elevation gain for the day is 2,000 feet.

The journey lingers through rural Missouri, past many small streams and through small towns where friendly folks stop to chat and wonder. In Ash Grove, Dusty Gilmore and family provide a wonderful hot meal as well as comfortable lodging in the VFW building. (If you'd rather stay in the city park, you can.)

I first met Dusty after I had just shared a large pizza with a fellow bicyclist, Don, whom I had met only hours before. Both of us were bicycling alone at the time and hoping to hook up with

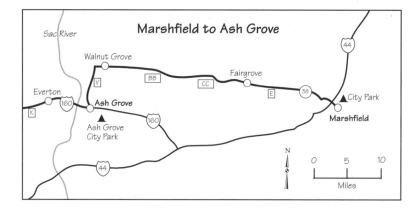

Marshfield to Ash Grove

someone else. After stuffing ourselves, we emerged from the restaurant only to find Dusty, who asked, "Where have you been?" I wondered who he was, wondered if he was some sort of strange fellow or something. Then he said his name and all was fine, for I had heard legends of his grand hospitality. He invited us to a Mexican dinner at his home, and wouldn't take no for an answer. Before we knew it, we were off to share enchiladas, beans, and watermelon with the Gilmores.

Dusty and his wife, Jane, and children Jacque, Jimmy, and Tyesha started opening the VFW in 1991 when a storm came through the area, causing havoc for a group of bicyclists. In late 1992, the family started feeding cyclists who passed through town. Although the Gilmores are not bicyclists themselves, they enjoy feeding those who are, listening to their stories, and hearing from them once they are back on the road. If you'd like to stop and see the Gilmores, you can contact them at 109 S. Webster, Ash Grove, MO 65604; (417) 751-2981.

MILEAGE LOG

0.0 Junction Hwy. 38 and S. Crittenden. Continue west on Hwy. 38; there's a shoulder.

0.8 Market and Laundromat on the left.

1.2 Wal-Mart, restaurants, and other shops as you head out of town.

1.4 Cross over I-44; stay on Hwy. 38.

7.9 Hwy. 38 heads to the right; keep straight, now riding Hwy. E, a two-lane shoulderless road. Traffic is minimal. (Most of the following roads are similar—shoulderless with light traffic.)

15.1 T-junction at stop sign; go right on Hwy. 125.

16.1 Fairgrove; post office, café, and market.

16.4 Cross US 65 and continue onto Hwy. CC.

26.2 Cross over Hwy. 13 North and pedal what is now Hwy. BB; mini-market at junction.

26.4 Cross over Hwy. 13 South.

32.3 T-junction; Hwy. Z merges onto Hwy. BB. Go right.

33.3 Hwy. Z stays straight; turn left, now riding Hwy. BB. Mini-market at junction.

40.0 Downtown Walnut Grove and junction Hwy. 123; post office nearby. To the left are a café, market/deli, and several other shops. As you proceed on across the junction, the road changes to Hwy. V.

41.4 Hwy. V curves to the left; Hwy. U is straight ahead. Stay on Hwy. V.

48.1 Downtown Ash Grove and junction US 160. Although the route heads right onto US 160, you'll end the day at Ash Grove

City Park or the VFW center. There are restaurants, a Laundromat, and other shops in town. Check in at city hall to camp for free at the city park, where there is a pool in addition to the usual amenities. If you'd rather spend the night indoors, Dusty Gilmore will open the VFW Hall for you. To reach the VFW and city hall, head straight on Hwy. F for 0.1 mile.

Fort Larned National Historic Site, Kansas

KANSAS

"Kansas is flat and ugly." It's a remark I heard again and again as I prepared for my cross-country journey, the minute I told people I'd be cycling through the flatlands of Kansas. And I always responded, "Well, I've heard the same, but I've also heard that the friendliest people live in Kansas, so perhaps it won't be all that bad!"

Indeed it wasn't. Kansas was indeed flatter than any other state to date, and I enjoyed every moment. I'm hoping to replace the Kansas image of flatlands and boring scenery with one of the friendliest folks in the country as well as some downright pretty farm scenes. I've never bicycled through any state where roughly 99 percent of the motorists, including truck drivers, waved a friendly greeting. It was truly remarkable, and the generous waves did a lot to keep me going through the more monotonous regions such as the dry, desolate western half.

Rather than dwell on the drab points in the state, I'd like to recommend enjoying the solitude of a ride where you get almost the same feeling as if you were out on a wilderness trail. At times you may feel as though you are one of only a handful of people left on planet Earth.

From just east of Pittsburg to the Colorado border, the Kansas portion of the journey leads almost due west, except for a couple of short northward or southward stints and a longer northward ride out of Larned.

In the eastern part of the state you'll find corn and cattle-grazing operations; in the central part, cornfields and masses of sunflowers that bloom in summer. You'll also pass through the Flint Hills, where lush bluestem grasses are more common than cornfields and oil rigs (nearly 200 kinds of grasses grow in the state). West of there you'll pedal through the Great Bend Prairie, a land of broad river valleys and rolling hills.

In the western portion of the state is the Great Plains area, a vast, dry grassland stretching from the eastern edge of the Rocky Mountains to points roughly 400 miles east. Remarkably, the Great Plains extend 2,500 miles from northern Canada to New Mexico and Texas. Drier than the eastern half of the state, the Great Plains appear tortilla-flat, but in fact they slope from about 1,500 feet to about 4,000 feet at the Colorado border.

An important agricultural and mining region, the Great Plains is one of the world's chief wheat-growing areas. Other major crops

Scene along US 54 near Rosalia, Kansas

include alfalfa, barley, oats, and rye. The plains also produce more oil than any other area in North America.

Kansas is probably best known as the Sunflower State after the state flower, which originated in North America and was introduced into Europe during the 1500s. More than sixty species exist, with the largest sunflower heads measuring more than a foot in diameter and producing up to 1,000 seeds. Rich in protein, sunflower oil is the world's third most important vegetable oil. Only soybean and palm oil are used more.

Kansas boasts several nicknames. Also known as the Wheat State and the Breadbasket of America, Kansas leads all states in wheat production. For a real treat, ride through Kansas in early summer and witness golden seas of grain swaying in the breeze. Don't arrive too late, or busy mills will have already ground the wheat into flour for the world's bakers.

Although many early Kansas farmers cultivated corn and wheat, insects and drought often destroyed their crops. Things changed in the 1870s, when a religious group—the Mennonites—arrived in Kansas from Russia, bringing a variety of winter wheat with them. Instead of being planted in the spring, Turkey Red was planted in the fall and harvested in early summer, thereby eluding the summer heat and hordes of insects. In 1894, wheat became the state's leading crop.

Kansas was named for the Kansa, or Kaw, Indians who once lived in the region (the name means "people of the south wind"). The reference to wind should be of no surprise to those traveling through the state. If there's one thing you can predict in the plains, it is that the weather will be unpredictable, especially the tornadoes, which occur more often on the plains than in any other region. Although the prevailing winds are generally from the south or southwest, you can expect a tailwind one minute, a headwind the next. I was fortunate enough to enjoy a brisk tailwind throughout the entire state.

I did experience a perfect example of wind change late one afternoon in Kansas, though. As fellow cyclist Carol Kaufman and I were aiming toward Tribune for the night, an enormous, scary storm developed right before our eyes. As we blew toward town, a tailwind shoving us along, Carol kept insisting that we had to hurry because the wind could change within seconds. Sure enough, once we were safe inside our motel room, the wind rotated 180 degrees and blew ten times as hard.

If you dream of cycling lightly traveled roads, then you'll love the ride through Kansas. Plan on spending nine days and 505.6 miles in Kansas, the third-most miles of any of the ten Trans-America states. You'll ride along an assortment of county roads, most of which are average in width and shoulderless. However, upon reaching some of the more heavily traveled roads, such as US 54 and Hwy. 96, you'll encounter wide shoulders. And if you're thinking of going off route, avoid the interstates, where bicycles are prohibited.

SPECIAL NOTE: Towns in Kansas are far apart. Be sure to stock up on food and water, since you will ride up to 39 lonely miles without any services.

For more information on bicycling through Kansas, contact State Bicycle and Pedestrian Coordinator, Kansas Department of Transportation, 2nd Floor, Thacher Building, 217 S.E. 4th, Topeka, KS 66603; (913) 296-7448; website: www.ink.org/public/kdot/burrail/3bike.htm; email: bikeped@ksdot.org.

Ash Grove to Pittsburg (70.2 miles)

In your cross-country quest there are ten states to traverse. Today you'll reach Kansas, the fifth and flattest state in your endeavor.

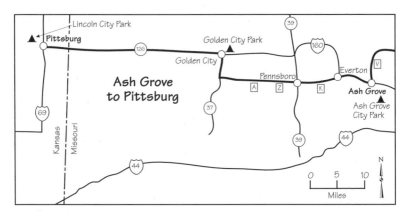

Today also marks the last day of steep pitches until Colorado (and even most of Colorado's grades are mild in comparison to those in the East; they're just longer).

Expect rolling hills with some steeper grades from Ash Grove to about 3 to 4 miles west of Pennsboro. From there the terrain flattens out to gentle rolling hills as you make your way to Pittsburg, where the segment ends.

Traffic remains light (except on US 160) as you travel quiet roads past farms, ranches, and rural homes. Most of the farms produce wheat, soybeans, and other crops; some even raise pigs (and lots of them). Highways are two lanes except in downtown Pittsburg, where Broadway boasts four lanes.

Pittsburg is a university town with an active nightlife. And if you have the urge for Chinese, Mexican, or some other type of cuisine, this is the place to look. The town also has Greyhound bus service—and a Wal-Mart.

To learn more about the area, visit the Crawford County Historical Museum, where you'll see displays of vintage clothing, coal-mining and farming artifacts, horse-drawn vehicles, and photographs. Outdoor exhibits include an authentic neighborhood grocery store and a one-room schoolhouse.

Annual events are many. A small sampling includes the Old-Fashioned Picnic in the Park, held during the Fourth of July holiday, and the Crawford County Fair, held the first full week in August.

Labor Day weekend offers up Little Balkans Days. More than 40,000 people come from all around to celebrate the coal-mining history and heritage of the Pittsburg area. The multitude of activities includes golf, bocci, softball, tennis, and volleyball tournaments, and horseshoe pitching. There are also an assortment of bands, hot-air balloons, vintage cars, a gigantic sidewalk sale by downtown merchants, a Coal Car 500 race, and a Doo-Dah Parade.

In addition, festivalgoers can enjoy more than 100 arts and crafts booths and a potpourri of ethnic foods.

MILEAGE LOG

0.0 Junction Hwy. V and US 160. Head west on US 160. Be careful; there will be some truck traffic.

2.1 Cross the Sac River.

4.3 Junction Hwy. FF on the right and Hwy. MM on the left.

6.8 Junction; keep straight, now pedaling Hwy. M. US 160 takes off to the right. If you need groceries or snacks, stay on US 160 for a short distance. If not, head through Everton, where there's a bed-and-breakfast inn and a post office.

8.0 After climbing a short, steep pitch, turn right on Hwy. K.

10.3 Cross Sinking Jordan Creek.

12.4 Cross Turnback Creek.

15.5 T-junction; head left on Hwy. 39 in Pennsboro.

15.8 Turn right on Hwy. Z. Mini-market at junction.

23.2 Cross Hwy. 97 and continue straight on what is now Hwy. A.

27.2 Junction Hwy. N.

27.6 Cross Muddy Creek.

31.3 Junction Hwy. 37; make a right on Hwy. 37, which sports a shoulder.

35.4 Reach junction Hwy. 126 and make a left. **SIDE TRIP:** For a real treat, explore Golden City, about 0.2 mile to the right (east). If you're like most cyclists, you'll definitely want to log in at Cooky's Café and try a piece of their famous pie. In addition, you'll find a post office, a market, several other shops, and a couple of restaurants.

If you'd like to spend the night in the city park, head east of town for another 0.1 mile on Hwy. 126 and turn left on Wyatt Ave. Make a right in another 0.1 mile at the park entrance. There are the usual facilities, but unlike some city parks, this one has no pool. Call 537-4412 for more information.

Golden City fans can join in the annual Golden Harvest Days if they're in the neighborhood the third weekend in July. There are crafts, thrashing displays, tractor pulls, and music Friday and Saturday nights. It's a typical small-town celebration; unfortunately, it's also usually very, very hot.

40.9 Cemetery on the right with shade and an outhouse.

46.5 Junction; cross US 71.

47.1 Cross North Fork Spring River.

56.7 Junction; cross Hwy. 43.

57.3 Cross Little North Fork Creek.

59.4 Cross another creek.

64.1 Mini-market on the right.

64.3   Enter Kansas; continue on Hwy. 126.

68.2   As you first enter Pittsburg, look for Farris' Café—it's highly recommended by locals who like its good, home-cooked food and great prices.

68.5   Schlanger City Park on the right. Wading pool, rest rooms, water, picnic facilities. Camping is not allowed.

69.1   Turn right on US 69 Business (Broadway). (If you've been craving scrumptious Mexican food, from the junction go straight on Hwy. 126 for 0.8 mile to Antonio's Mexico Restaurant. There's also a motel.)

69.2   Junction 6th St. There's a bike shop to the right in 0.1 mile.

69.5   Junction W. 10th St. If you want to camp at Lincoln City Park, turn left on W. 10th St. and ride about 0.5 mile to the park. There's a pool and other amenities, including an eighteen-hole public golf course, miniature golf, batting cages, fitness trail, and more. Notify the Parks Department (231-8310) or the police (231-1700) before camping.

70.2   Turn left on W. 20th St. (To reach Wal-Mart and a number of restaurants, markets, and motels, continue on Broadway for about a mile.)

The segment ends here, allowing you to choose between a motel or camping at 116-acre Lincoln City Park.

Pittsburg to Chanute (57.5 miles)

The Kansas "flatlands" are a welcome treat for those who are tired of climbing steep grades. (Don't think the hills have totally disappeared, though—there are still a few short, steep ones to negotiate.)

If you're one of the lucky ones, you'll whiz through the state with a brisk tailwind to push you along. Note, though, that the wind doesn't always blow east to west. Much of the time it blows from the west. My fellow cyclists Dick and Earl, who were a few weeks ahead of me, told of braving tough headwinds across the entire state. To ease the pain, they woke up before dawn and cycled as fast as they could until noon, when the wind really kicked in.

From Pittsburg to Chanute the terrain is flat to rolling, and there's little traffic until Hwy. 7, where you'll encounter some trucks. Expect an elevation gain of roughly 1,000 feet.

You'll pedal through Girard en route to Chanute. Surrounded by farms and ranches, the town boasts several other industries. In fact, it claims to be the "Printing Capital of the Nation." If you'd like to get a feel for the area, be sure to visit the Museum of Crawford County, Inc. It's housed in the former St. John's Episcopal Church,

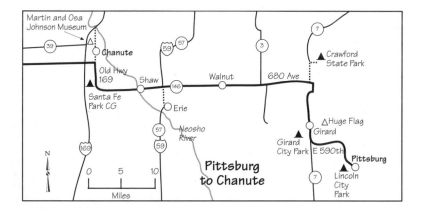

which was built in 1886 and is listed on the National Register of Historic Places.

If you arrive in downtown Chanute early enough in the day, you can enjoy the pool at the city park (free for cyclists). Chanute also boasts a bike shop and the Martin and Osa Johnson Museum, the most popular Kansas museum. The Johnsons were world-famous wildlife photographers who traveled the world between 1917 and 1936, taking safaris through the South Seas and Africa. For directions to the museum, see the Chanute to Eureka segment.

Chanute offers several options for the long-distance cyclist. You can stay at a campground, motel it, or camp out at "Yodeling Katy" Lopeman's. A visit with Yodeling Katy is the most entertaining option, of course. The sixty-nine-year-old opened her home to bicyclists in 1981 after she was in a doughnut shop and met a bicyclist who was grateful for her offer of a shower. Katy offers a place to camp in her yard as well as a shower, and she often serves delicious home-baked goods too. In addition, she'll be sure to amuse you with her yodeling and ukelele as she sings you a greeting song, a bedtime song, and a good-bye song.

Katy, the mother of three sons and seven grandchildren, asks little in return. She does ask that you sign her guest book and allow her to take your photo. She also requests that all bicyclists refrain from using bad language.

MILEAGE LOG

0.0 Junction W. 20th St. and Broadway in downtown Pittsburg. Go west on W. 20th St.

0.7 Cross unsigned US 69/Hwy. 57 and proceed on.

2.1 Turn right on unsigned road. (At the next junction a sign claims this road is S. 200th St.) There's a power pole at the corner that reads "P7-F901."

Kathryn "Yodeling Katy" Lopeman at home in Chanute, Kansas

5.1 Stop sign; turn left on E. 590th.

6.1 Mini-market on the right.

10.3 E. 590th ends; merge onto Hwy. 7. In 0.3 mile the road curves to the north.

13.1 Junction Orange St. **SIDE TRIP:** Girard City Park is to the left in 0.2 mile. There's a pool in addition to the usual facilities; check in with police at 724-6217.

13.7 Junction Hwy. 57 and Hwy. 7 in downtown Girard; continue straight on Hwy. 7. At the junction there are restaurants, a post office, a Laundromat, and other shops. To the left on Hwy. 57 are restaurants and a market, all within 0.5 mile. **SIDE TRIP:** If you'd like to see one of the largest flags in America, go right for a mile via Hwy. 57. Standing 130 feet high, the actual flag is 30 feet by 60 feet and can be seen for miles around. It flies 24 hours a day above a memorial honoring all war veterans.

13.9 Bed-and-breakfast inn on the left. Bicyclists are welcome without a reservation as long as there is room at the inn.

18.6 Hwy. 7 curves to the right.

19.1 Hwy. 7 curves to the left.

20.1 Junction; turn left on signed 680 Ave. **SIDE TRIP:** Those interested in exploring Crawford State Park should stay straight on Hwy. 7 for about 3 miles, then head east for another mile or so. This scenic 500-acre park boasts a 141-acre lake with a swimming beach, two bathhouses, several campgrounds, a marina, and a restaurant.

27.3 Stop sign; junction Hwy. 3 and end of 680 Ave; turn right on Hwy. 3.

27.7 Keep straight on Hwy. 146 when Hwy. 3 heads north.

33.6 Downtown Walnut. There's a combination restaurant/minimarket and a post office.

43.4 Hwy. 146 ends at the US 59/Hwy. 57 junction, which runs north and south. Continue straight onto unsigned road. There's a rest area at the junction. Although camping is permitted, I wouldn't recommend it. Facilities include dilapidated toilets, shade, and running water. **SIDE TRIP:** If you need supplies, the all-service town of Erie is located about 2.5 miles south via US 59/Hwy. 57.

47.0 Enter Shaw—no services.

47.2 Cross Neosho River.

54.4 Stop sign at junction of unsigned Old Hwy. 169; make a right. Traffic increases along this narrow two-lane road.

57.3 Enter outskirts of Chanute.

57.5 This segment ends at the Chanute 35 Pkwy. junction, where you'll see Santa Fe Park Campground on the left. At the campground, a sign states that tents must go on the gravel. According to park employees, the sign is wrong; instead, tents must go on the grass near the rest room. You'll find all amenities at this free (for up to 48 hours) campground. If you'd rather motel it, there's a motel and restaurant at the junction, and more as you head into town. (See the Chanute to Eureka segment for more information.) If Yodeling Katy is your choice, she lives 0.4 mile north of the junction off Santa Fe St. (US 169). You can call her at 431-4038 to let her know you're in town.

Chanute to Eureka (64.3 miles)

Four bikers said it best when they exclaimed, "We like Kansas—it's easy!" And if, like them, you have a tailwind, today's ride is just that. But don't expect it to be perfectly flat. Kansans seem to be proud of their "mountains," with most of the locals anxious to warn you of the climbs up ahead. There are some actual hills in the Flint Hills, but nothing like those you've already experienced.

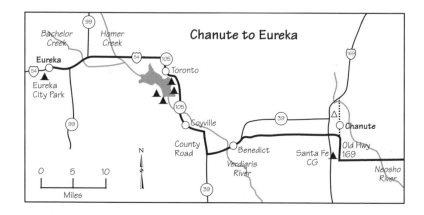

Like most of the trip to date, today's ride roams through rural America, embracing quiet roads and typical Midwest scenes.

Eureka is the destination for the night. It is also the place where an early pioneer shouted "Eureka!" in August 1857, after discovering a spring of cool, clear water near what is today Fall River. The pioneers had several top priorities in deciding where to settle; abundant drinking water was one of them, and so the town of Eureka was born.

A horse-racing mecca, Eureka is a small, agriculture-based town (oil is also an important resource) of just over 3,000 people. If you're into horses, you'll find the finest in quarterhorse racing at the pari-mutuel track, Eureka Downs. Horses from throughout North America have raced here from May through July since 1872.

MILEAGE LOG

0.0 Junction Chanute 35 Pkwy. and Santa Fe St. The road is busy, with two lanes and no shoulder. Continue north on Santa Fe St.

0.4 Yodeling Katy Lopeman's place is on the left. As you continue, you'll pass a Wal-Mart and other assorted shops and restaurants.

1.5 Junction; make a left on W. 14th St. **SIDE TRIP:** From this junction, the Martin and Osa Johnson Museum is 1.5 miles north on Old Hwy. 169 in downtown Chanute.

2.5 Turn left on S. Plummer Ave., a quiet two-lane road.

3.0 Turn right on W. 21st St., another quiet two-lane county road.

3.6 Cross over New US 169; now the road is flat to rolling, uncrowded, and extremely rough at times.

13.0 Cross US 75; gas station.

16.1 The road turns to hard-packed gravel that is actually smoother than the paved road.

17.3 Gravel ends and asphalt returns.

17.5 Turn left on Hwy. 39 West, a somewhat busy (some truck traffic) two-lane highway. The terrain is flat to gently rolling, with an occasional short, steep section.

19.5 A county road on left leads a very short distance to Benedict, where there is a post office.

20.1 Cross the Verdigris River.

21.3 Cross Snake Creek.

24.7 Junction; Hwy. 39, Hwy. 96, and a county road, which leads to Coyville and Toronto State Park. Make a right on the county road.

28.2 Road curves to the left; a gravel road leads straight to the Verdigris River in 100 yards or so.

32.3 Stop sign in downtown Coyville; turn right and continue on to the lake.

32.4 Coyville Post Office; pop machine out front.

35.9 Gravel road on left leads to Toronto Lake, East Spillway. There's a short, steep climb from here.

Cornfield near Buhler, Kansas

36.2 Road becomes Hwy. 105 North and improves dramatically. On the left is a road leading to the Hilltop Café and Holiday Hill Campground in 1.5 miles. You'll find groceries there in addition to all services. Woodson Cove Campground is down the same road in 0.2 mile. Sites are free and shaded. Facilities are limited to toilet and picnic tables.

38.5 Mann's Cove Campground on the left. Fee area. Shaded sites, toilets, picnic facilities, and water.

41.6 Road on left leads to Toronto State Park in about 1.5 miles. The park has all amenities, including lake swimming, fishing, and limited groceries.

42.0 Downtown Toronto. There's a market, two restaurants, several other shops, and a post office.

42.1 Hwy. 105 curves to the right and gently rolls onward.

44.8 Stop sign and end of Hwy. 105. Turn left on US 54, a smooth two-lane highway with a shoulder and moderate rolling terrain. You'll find a market/deli on the corner.

46.9 Rest area on the left; water, pit toilets, shade.

51.9 Turnoff on left to Neal, which is about 0.1 mile away; post office.

53.3 Cross Homer Creek.

57.5 Hwy. 99 merges onto the route; stay on US 54/Hwy. 99.

58.1 Cross Bachelor Creek.

61.0 Hwy. 99 leaves the route.

62.9 Enter the all-service town of Eureka. There's also a Laundromat near downtown.

64.3 Junction Main St. To camp at the Eureka City Park, go left on Main St. for 0.2 mile. You'll find everything you need, including a pool. Bicyclists must register with police (583-5526).

Eureka to Newton (75.4 miles)

If a tailwind prevails, today's ride will be a breeze—yes, even considering the mileage. You'll climb about 1,100 feet, quite a bit considering that most folks expect all of Kansas to be flat.

Towns are few and far between and so are ranches, with some boasting more than 20,000 acres. Folks are friendly and the scenery pleasant as you pass through the lower reaches of the Flint Hills.

The day ends in Newton, where you can enjoy the annual Chisholm Trail Festival if you roll into town during the Fourth of July holiday. Whenever you visit, you may enjoy the Kauffman Museum, which documents the strong Mennonite heritage of the area. It also displays the cultural and natural history of the Central Plains, along with the birds and mammals of the North American prairies. An award-winning living prairie representing more than 100 species surrounds the museum.

MILEAGE LOG

0.0 Corner of River St. (US 54) and Main in downtown Eureka. Continue west via US 54. There's a shoulder; the highway may be busy.

0.3 Cross the Fall River as you exit town. There's a motel/café just prior to the crossing. After crossing, you'll climb one long grade after another. None are very steep, but you will end up at over 1,600 feet in elevation.

18.1 Make a right toward Rosalia on S.E. Rosalia Rd.

18.6 Rosalia; post office, restaurant/mini-market on the right. The terrain is open as you continue to gently roll along the un-crowded, rural county road.

35.0 Hwy. 177 joins the route. Continue straight into Cassoday, the "Prairie Chicken Capital of the World." There's a post of-fice, café, and a couple of shops.

35.5 Turn left on Sunbarger St. There's a city park at the corner where bicyclists can camp for free. There are outhouses and picnic tables. If you need grocery items, continue straight on Hwy. 177 for a block or so to a mini-market. There are no ser-vices for many miles, so stock up.

35.9 Cross over I-35. This county road is rolling to flat and it's a pure pleasure, especially with a tailwind. Traffic remains light until approximately 10 miles east of Newton.

47.7 Stop sign and junction US 77. Cross US 77 and continue.

49.6 Turnoff to Burns on the right. **SIDE TRIP:** It's approximately 4 miles to the Burns Post Office, café, and mini-market.

54.9 Cross Whitewater River.

62.3 Turnoff to Elbing (post office, groceries) on the right. **SIDE TRIP:** You'll reach the post office and mini-market in about 0.5 mile.

63.9 Road is now called Harvey County Road 570.

66.9 Turnoff on the right leads to Harvey County East Park via CR 835. **SIDE TRIP:** A gravel road leads to the park office in 0.4 mile. You'll find all the necessary amenities, including a bait shop that offers limited groceries.

68.9 Les Walton's Camping Area on the left; rest rooms, water, and pond swimming.

73.0 Enter Newton, an all-service town. You'll also find a Laun-dromat. CR 570 is now called E. 1st St. and it is shoulderless with four lanes of traffic, which may be heavy.

73.3 Cross over US 50 West, I-135, and US 81.

74.5 Turn right on Main St.; grocery store, restaurants, and other shops are visible as you continue.

74.8 Junction Main St. and 5th. Turn left on 5th and ride 0.6 mile to City Athletic Park, where you can camp for free. The park of-fers all facilities, including a pool.

Newton to Buhler (30.4 miles)

This segment continues the pattern of grand country riding on mostly flat, traffic-free roads. As you continue through Kansas farm country, you'll pedal through the Central Lowlands, or Great Bend Prairie. The lowlands were formed by debris carried eastward after the Rocky Mountains were born. Today most of the area is drained by the Arkansas River (called the AR-kansas, not the Arkan-SAW, by native Kansans).

Today is a short-mileage day, although it certainly doesn't have to be. For this guidebook I made it a short one because whenever possible I try to end the day at a city park or some other place where the camping is free. As I pedaled across the country I found that most of the bicyclists I met were like me—short on funds. And even if they weren't, most folks still enjoyed doing the trip as inexpensively as possible.

The only problem with this philosophy is that in this part of the country, towns are spread far apart, so the parks are too. The quaint little town of Buhler offers a beautiful little park, free for the asking, that's definitely an enjoyable place to pitch a tent for the night. The next free on-route campground is another 56 miles west in the town of Hudson. Ride a total of 96 miles to Hudson City Park for the night and you'll find rest rooms and water. Follow my planned route and you'll enjoy a shower as well.

But if you'd rather ride more miles you can continue west, going off route about 6 miles to Hutchinson, where there is a hostel at the Zion Lutheran Church, a couple of bike shops, and anything else you might need in a town of 40,000. See the next day's route, Buhler to Larned, for more information.

MILEAGE LOG

0.0 Main St. and 5th. Continue north on Main St.

0.7 Turn left on W. 12th St. The roadway is two lanes and no shoulder, but it widens to four lanes for a short distance. Look for a market and a restaurant at the junction.

2.2 Junction CR 568 and CR 817; continue on CR 568.

5.2 Turn right on CR 811 toward Hesston.

10.2 Enter Hesston, where the road turns into four lanes.

10.7 Junction Old 81 South; make a left. There's a restaurant at the junction.

11.0 Downtown Hesston; post office, market, several other shops. Hesston is also home to the Wheat Bin, an authentic Kansas wheat-milling operation and farmstead. Here you can watch the process of milling Kansas hard winter wheat into whole wheat flour while you snack on a variety of goodies, including freshly baked whole wheat buns.

11.3 Road narrows to two lanes.

11.6 At the blinking light turn left on Lincoln Blvd. (CR 556), a two-lane road. **SIDE TRIP:** Restaurant, motel, and campground to the right in less than a mile near the I-135 junction. Cottonwood Grove Campground offers the usual facilities, including a Laundromat.

20.1 Junction CR 793.

24.2 Junction CR 785.

30.0 Junction Main St. at flashing light. Turn left to head into downtown Buhler.

30.3 Turn left on Curtis Ave. and reach the Wheatland Park entrance in 0.1 mile. There's a wonderful picnic area with a pond, pool, and all the usual amenities. (Downtown Buhler is another 0.3 mile south. You'll find a post office, market, Laundromat, and café.)

Buhler to Larned (85.7 miles)

Nearly flat riding makes the day a real treat, especially if you have a tailwind. And the day ends at a nice park with a pool in a place where the Santa Fe Trail intersects with the TransAmerica Bicycle Trail: the rustic town of Larned, "Heart of the Santa Fe Trail," located midway along the historic trail.

The Santa Fe Trail stretched nearly 1,000 miles from Missouri to New Mexico. The exact mileage isn't known, since there are numerous ways to figure the mileage of the trail. According to park ranger George Elmore of the Fort Larned National Historic Site, the most common measurements are 865 miles for the Cimarron Route and 909 miles for the Mountain Route. Amazingly, numerous wagon ruts are still visible in the Larned area. For detailed information about the trail, contact the local chamber of commerce, or visit the Santa Fe Trail Center or the Fort Larned National Historic Site. Directions to both are listed in the next segment, Larned to Ness City.

Between towns, you'll pedal through a patchwork of farm fields—some corn, some sunflower, others maize and silage. The roads are mostly uncrowded, and shade is hard to come by.

En route you'll pass the 21,820-acre Quivira National Wildlife Refuge, a preserve that embraces both the lush vegetation of the eastern prairie and the arid grasslands of the western prairie. The refuge was named for the Indian tribe that lived in the region when the Spanish explorer Coronado visited in 1541.

Sod House, Santa Fe Trail Center, Larned, Kansas

In earlier times, the refuge grounds provided an abundant food source for native Americans and early settlers, who hunted waterfowl in these marshes many years ago. Although regulated hunting is permitted today, the refuge continues to serve as home to more than 250 species of birds, most of them migratory. (More than 300,000 ducks, geese, pelicans, and other migrants may flock to the refuge in spring.) In addition, a number of endangered species—the bald eagle, peregrine falcon, whooping crane, and least tern—share the grounds with deer, pheasants, and a whole slew of other species.

The best times to visit the refuge are in spring and fall, when animal life, especially waterfowl, is more abundant and more easily seen. Hikers will find much of the refuge open to foot travel. Photographers will find two blinds available on a first-come, first-served basis. Overnight camping is not permitted on the refuge; your best bet would be to pitch your tent in Hudson and make it a two-day trip to Larned.

MILEAGE LOG

0.0 Junction Main St. and CR 556 near Buhler. Continue west via CR 556.

4.2 Cross the railroad tracks and turn left on Hwy. 61, then make an immediate right on an unsigned paved road. Medora Antiques is at the junction.

4.4 T-junction; make a right on unsigned N. Medora St.

5.1 Turn left on unsigned road toward Nickerson. A sign at the next junction claims this is E. 95th Ave.

9.1 T-junction; turn left on N. Plum St., a busy two-lane, shoulderless road.

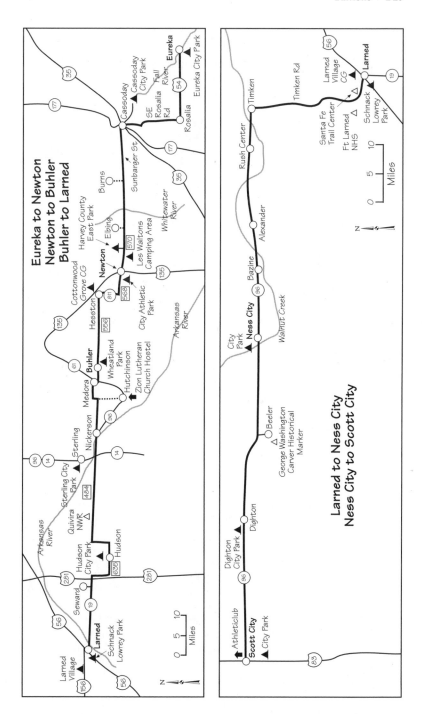

10.1 Turn right on E. 82nd Ave. toward Nickerson. E. 82nd Ave. offers a fine view into the Arkansas River Valley and is a favorite haunt of my favorite bicycling buddy, Carol Kaufman, who lives in Hutchinson and rides the trail as often as possible in the summer so she can stop and chat with all the cross-country bicyclists. **SIDE TRIP:** Hutchinson, an all-service town with two bicycle shops and a campground, is about 6 miles south from the junction. There's also a church hostel with showers at Zion Lutheran Church, at the corner of 11th and Washington. Call 663-3513 or ask at Harley's Cycle Supply (663-4321) for more information.

    In addition, Hutchinson is the home of the Kansas Cosmosphere and Space Center, where you'll find the world's largest collection of space suits, hands-on computerized exhibits, an Omnimax movie theater, and a planetarium.

14.7 Cross Cow Creek.

18.8 T-junction; turn left on N. Nickerson St. in downtown Nickerson. Two-lane Hwy. 96 joins the route as you continue west. The town of Nickerson has brick roads, a market, a café with good food and prices, friendly folks, and a post office.

19.1 Hwy. 96 curves to the right; expect some truck traffic.

20.5 Cross the Arkansas River.

24.2 Hwy. 14 North joins the route.

27.0 Turn left on W. 101st Ave., which eventually becomes CR 484. This road, like all the others for the day, is two lanes with limited amounts of traffic. A sign points the way to Quivira National Wildlife Refuge. **SIDE TRIP:** Hwy. 96/14 leads about 3 miles north to Sterling, a small town with all facilities, including a free place to camp at the city park. Check in with police (278-2100) before camping.

42.0 Turnoff to Quivira National Wildlife Refuge on the right. A gravel road guides you through the northern part of the refuge.

43.0 Turnoff to refuge on the left; a gravel road leads 8 miles to headquarters via the southern portion of the refuge. There's an information board with brochures at the junction.

46.0 Artesian Well on the left.

49.1 Make a left onto unsigned road at the four-way stop; look for a power substation at the junction.

53.2 Turn right onto unsigned road CR 635. A previous sign points the way to Hudson.

56.4 **SIDE TRIP:** Turn right at Hudson Market and continue 0.3 mile to a city park, where there is camping. Rest rooms and water are the only park conveniences. A café, a post office, and a craft shop are nearby.

61.2 Stop sign; turn right on US 281.

65.2 Turn left on Hwy. 19 West.

67.6 **SIDE TRIP:** Junction CR 219 leads north about a mile to Seward; post office and café. If you'd like to camp there, check with the owners at J & J Café.

73.2 Turnoff on right leads to Radium in a mile—no services.

84.2 T-junction; turn right on Spur Hwy. 19 to Larned.

84.6 Cross bridge over Arkansas River.

85.2 Junction US 56 and Hwy. 19. To reach Schnack Lowrey Park and home for the night, make a left and go off route via US 56. After 0.3 mile go right on W. 1st St. Continue another 0.2 mile to Carroll Ave. and the park entrance. Schnack Lowrey Park offers a pool in addition to the standard facilities. Be sure to check in with police at 285-3188 before camping.

From the junction, downtown Larned is straight ahead via Hwy. 19. The town itself offers all services, including a Laundromat. You'll find the majority of businesses at the junction of US 156, a mile to the north. There's also a private campground, Larned Village, located on US 156, just west of the Broadway (Spur 19)/US 156 junction.

Larned to Ness City (65.4 miles)

This segment includes two noteworthy side trips—Fort Larned and the Santa Fe Trail Center—but it is reward enough if all you do is cycle Timken Rd. a two-lane "bumpity-bump," as Kansas cyclists like to call such roads. There's another benefit to pedaling Timken Rd.; you'll get the opportunity to view fence posts made of rock, or rock posts, as they are often called.

A gaze at the surrounding countryside clearly reveals that trees are at a premium in Kansas. Sometimes you can ride miles upon miles without seeing a single one. Thus, when farmers and ranchers began fencing their parcels of land, they built fences made of limestone posts. Limestone was plentiful; in fact, it was the most widely used building material on the plains.

The average post rock was extremely heavy, often weighing between 250 and 450 pounds. Consequently, horse-drawn teams managed to haul only four to eight posts per load. The fee for such a service? A mere twenty-five cents per post.

As you continue up Timken Rd. and beyond, the scenes are very Kansas-like: wide open country and uncrowded vistas all around. Traffic is usually light, and when it isn't, such as on Hwy. 96, the truckers are friendly and courteous, often waving a hearty hello. The segment ends at Ness City, where the folks continue to smile and the old town buildings beg you to take a look.

The Santa Fe Trail Center is the closest side trip, 2 miles west of Larned on Hwy. 156 and a mere 0.5 mile off route. A nonprofit regional museum designed and built as a research facility, the center reveals the story of the Santa Fe Trail, a transportation route that linked native American, Spanish, and American cultures.

Displays begin with the prehistoric days of the trail, when millions of bison blanketed the plains. The story picks up speed in 1821, when new trade opportunities became available to both Mexicans and Americans when Mexico attained independence from Spain. The Santa Fe Trail began in Independence, Missouri, climbed through the valley of the Arkansas River, stretched across the Cimarron Desert to Bent's Fort, and then went south through Raton Pass to Santa Fe, New Mexico. From 1822 until 1880, when trade was shattered after the railroad arrived near Santa Fe, the amount of merchandise taken from Santa Fe increased continuously; its value in 1855 was estimated at $5 million. In 1860, 3,033 wagons, 9,084 men, 6,147 mules, and 27,920 oxen were used in the commercial-freight wagon trains that traversed the plains. The story concludes with a look at life on the plains just after World War I.

In addition, there's an Outdoor Museum in the center's 25-acre

Bicyclist riding along Hwy. 96 in Kansas

complex that includes a one-room schoolhouse, a sod house, a dug-out house, a Santa Fe Railroad depot, and a limestone cooling house. And if you're interested in doing some research, there's a research library and archives.

Fort Larned National Historic Site is another must-see. Located 6 miles west of Larned and 2.7 miles off the main route, it is well worth the bit of energy needed to get there.

The fort, "Guardian of the Santa Fe Trail," was the northern mainstay of the string of forts—stretching south from Fort Larned, through Fort Cobb in present-day Oklahoma, to Forts Griffin, Concho, McKavett, Clark, and Duncan in Texas—that defined the southwestern military frontier. During the late 1860s, Fort Larned was also a fundamental post in the Indian wars.

Although the original fort was made of adobe in 1860, the buildings were poorly constructed and inadequate, according to many high-ranking officers, who feared a large-scale Indian war. New construction began in 1866 and was completed two years later. Today stone and timber buildings surround the quadrangular parade ground. You can tour the various buildings, which include both an old and a new commissary, barracks, post hospital, storehouse, and officer's quarters.

SIDE TRIP: If you'd like to see some trail ruts, from the Fort Larned entrance go west on Hwy. 156 for 0.3 mile. Turn left on the paved county road and ride about 4 miles south. Make a right, ride a mile, then make a left on a gravel farm road for 0.8 mile to a well-marked parking area. In addition to the ruts, there are old buffalo wallows where the behemoths used to roll in the dust, begging for relief from the biting flies.

MILEAGE LOG

0.0 Larned City Park entrance; head back the way you came.

0.5 Junction Spur Hwy. 19 and US 56. Continue to the left on Broadway (US 56/Spur 19).

0.9 Make a left on 8th St., an uncrowded two-lane (only one-lane for a while) brick street.

4.0 Stop sign; turn right onto Hwy. 264 North. To the left is the state hospital.

4.6 T-junction; make a left on Hwy. 156, a busy two-lane road with truck traffic. **SIDE TRIP:** Go right for 0.5 mile to the Santa Fe Trail Center.

5.7 Turn right on paved, unsigned Timken Rd. (CR 584), a wonderfully beautiful, uncrowded country road with some "bumpity-bumps." (More than one Kansan said that what I would call "ups and downs" or "roller-coaster-like hills," they call bumpity-bumps.) **SIDE TRIP:** Instead of turning onto Timken Rd., head straight on Hwy. 156 to Fort Larned, which is 2.7 miles to the west.

25.4 Turn left on Hwy. 96 West, a two-lane road with some truck traffic. **SIDE TRIP:** Timken, a post office–only town with a city park for camping (no water) is 0.5 mile straight ahead via CR 584.

28.6 Cross Walnut Creek.

32.4 Junction US 183 and Hwy. 96 in downtown Rush Center. There's a café, mini-markets, and a post office. You can camp at the Walnut City 4-H Park; there's water but no rest rooms, and the markets close early.

45.8 Enter Alexander, which consists of a café/market (minimal groceries). Just beyond is a rest area with toilets, water, and picnic facilities.

50.8 Cross Walnut Creek.

53.4 Enter Bazine, which has a couple of restaurants, a mini-market, and a post office.

65.1 Junction US 283 in downtown Ness City. The city offers all the usual services, plus a Laundromat and downtown shopping area. As you explore the streets of Ness City, you'll see some fine historic buildings such as the Ness County Bank Building, located at the corner of Main St. and Pennsylvania Ave. The four-story stone building was called, upon its completion in 1890, "the finest and most imposing structure west of Topeka."

65.4 Lake St. on the right leads to the city park, where there's a pool in addition to the standard facilities. Check in with the police at 798-3596.

Ness City to Scott City (56.5 miles)

The ride through the flatlands, with a slight rise in elevation, continues. Farms are even farther apart, the land more rural than ever before.

Kansas drivers, including truckers, continue to be some of the friendliest yet; nearly everyone waves.

The segment ends at Scott City, the largest city on the western Kansas route.

MILEAGE LOG

0.0 Lake St./Hwy. 96 junction near the city park. Continue west on Hwy. 96, a two-lane, shoulderless road until Dighton.

0.4 Cross North Fork Walnut Creek.

Old building in downtown Ness City, Kansas

15.3 CR 523, a gravel road on the left, leads to Beeler, where there is a post office.

15.6 Cemetery on the left; water and shade here.

15.9 George Washington Carver historical marker on the left. Born in Missouri in 1864 to parents who were slaves, Carver moved to Kansas as a boy. He became a scientist and was instrumental in using peanuts and sweet potatoes to make paint, milk, cosmetics, medicine, and more than 500 other products. He has been called the foremost genius of the African-American people; the "Homestead of a Genius" is about 1.5 miles south of here.

29.1 Rest area on the right. Camping is permitted; however, the facility lacks rest rooms. Amenities include a shelter, water, and picnic tables. The Dighton sheriff (397-2452) asks that you check in before camping.

31.2 Junction Hwy. 23 in downtown Dighton, where there are all services, including a Laundromat.

31.4 **SIDE TRIP:** To reach the city park, where camping is allowed, make a right on N. 2nd St. You'll reach the park in 0.1 mile. There's a pool in addition to the usual facilities. Check in with the sheriff at 397-2452.

40.0 Continue on Hwy. 96; now the road is two lanes with a shoulder. Reach Amy—no services—at this point.

46.2 Enter Grigston—no services.

56.4 SIDE TRIP: To reach Athleticlub, where there is a pool and jacuzzi in addition to a hostel, turn right on Washington St. Follow it 0.2 mile to the club, which is on the right. Athleticlub (872-3807) is open May 1 to September 1.

56.5 Junction US 83 and Hwy. 96 in downtown Scott City. Scott City has a Laundromat and all services. **SIDE TRIP:** If you'd prefer camping at the city park (corner of 12th and Main) where there are rest rooms and picnic facilities but no pool or showers, head left on US 83 for about 0.6 mile. Check in with police (872-2133) prior to camping. There are plenty of restaurants in the area.

Scott City to Tribune (47.9 miles)

As you continue across the High Plains, cows, a slight rise in elevation, and more of the same friendly Kansans make this another pleasant day. Truck traffic may be prolific, but the truckers are usually great.

MILEAGE LOG

0.0 Junction US 83 and Hwy. 96 in downtown Scott City. Continue west on Hwy. 96, a two-lane road; shoulders are now narrow to nonexistent. Pass an occasional stockyard as you proceed west.

10.3 Modoc—no services—to the right.

17.4 Junction CR 167 on the right leads to Marienthal—no services.

18.9 Rest area on the right; you'll find a shelter and rest rooms.

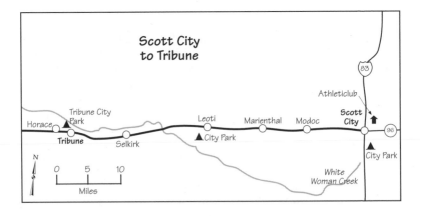

25.4 Junction Hwy. 25 in downtown Leoti, where you can explore the Museum of the Great Plains. Camping is available at the New City Park, which is near the hospital. Go 0.4 mile to the south (left) on Hwy. 25 to check in at the sheriff station (375-2723). There's a pool and showers at the park, but no rest rooms; at night you can use the bathroom at the hospital. In town are the usual services plus a Laundromat.

32.5 Cross White Woman Creek.

35.5 Selkirk turnoff on the right—no services.

36.9 Cross into the Mountain Time Zone.

42.9 Enter Whitelaw—no services.

47.2 Junction Hwy. 27 in downtown Tribune. All services, including a Laundromat, are available in this town of 900-plus.

Tribune City Park is located at the northwest edge of town. From the junction of Hwys. 27 and 96, go north on Hwy. 27 for 0.6 mile. Turn left on Zenaide St. and reach Tribune City Park in 0.1 mile. There's a pool in addition to the usual facilities. Before camping, check in at the police station (376-4543), next door to the Horace Greeley Museum.

Sheldon Jackson Memorial Chapel, Fairplay, Colorado

COLORADO

Colorado. Say its name and most people immediately conjure up images of tall peaks, great skiing come winter, and an abundance of other outdoor activities come spring, summer, and fall.

But Colorado is much more than that. It is home to an assortment of animal life, including moose, elk, deer, and bear. It boasts small towns, beautiful lakes, lush mountain streams, grand vistas, and, for a change of pace, great pizza at Fatty's in Breckenridge.

Colorado also boasts Hoosier Pass, the highest point on the entire TransAmerica Trail. (In addition, Colorado claims the highest average elevation—6,800 feet—of any state in the nation.) The climb is steep but certainly doable, and the beauty of the Rocky Mountains eases any climbing hardships.

The Rocky Mountains truly are spectacular. In the wintertime they become a mecca for the millions of visitors who come to carve turns at Colorado's ski resorts. In the summer, the Colorado Rockies draw a large number of hikers and backpackers who want to reach for the stars. Often called the "Roof of North America," Colorado's Rockies comprise more than fifty peaks extending 14,000 feet or more into the heavens. In fact, the peaks are the tallest in the Rocky Mountain Range, which stretches from Alaska to New Mexico.

There are five main mountain ranges in the Rockies: Front Range, Park Range, Sawatch Range, the San Juan Mountains, and the Sangre de Cristo Mountains. Fortunately, you won't have to ride up one range and down another. A number of nearly level, almost tree-less areas called "parks" are sandwiched between the various ranges and provide great terrain for the long-distance bicyclist.

The Great Plains, a vast, dry grassland that extends from Canada to Mexico, makes up the eastern two-fifths of Colorado. In this area, the most populated region of the state, tunnels bored through the mountains bring water to the plains, where most residents live and work. The plains are also a mecca for the wheat and corn farmers whose fields spread across the landscape. In addition, irrigated farms produce rich crops of sugar beets and potatoes.

You'll ride 440.9 miles and nine days through Colorado, which in Spanish means "colored red." The name was first given to the Colorado River because it flows through canyons of red stone. The state was later named for the river and nicknamed the Centennial State because it joined the Union in 1876, the 100th anniversary of the Declaration of Independence.

Stopping for a snack, Currant Creek Pass, Colorado

You'll enter the second largest (in square miles) of the Trans-America states east of Eads, then gradually climb west to Pueblo. From there, you'll curve northwest toward Wyoming, exiting the state in the middle of nowhere, about 27 miles south of the nearest town of Riverside, Wyoming.

Expect wind and dust when pedaling across eastern Colorado. If a thick dust storm materializes, it's best to get off the road if possible. The same is true of the thunderstorms and hailstorms that are common during warm summer afternoons. Look for some type of shelter if possible, although it'll be difficult to find in some parts of the state.

Eastern Colorado is semiarid with warm or hot summer days, although low humidity makes the temperatures more bearable than in the East. In the central and northern portions of the state you'll ride in the Rocky Mountains and the high basin areas known as South Park and North Park. Here you can expect weather typical of the mountains: warm days and cool nights. Note that daytime temperatures can be cool, even cold, atop Hoosier Pass and other high-elevation places.

Bicyclist fishing, Straight Branch Creek, Virginia

Bicyclists on CR 618 near Bumpass, Virginia

Resting at a cemetery west of Golden City, Missouri

Prairie scene near Newton, Kansas

Relaxing atop Hoosier Pass, Colorado

LEFT: *Farm along Highway 9, south of Hartsel, Colorado*
RIGHT: *Grand Teton National Park, Wyoming*

Red rock area near Dubois, Wyoming

LEFT: *Farm scene near Philipsburg, Montana*
RIGHT: *McKenzie Pass (Mount Washington in the background), Oregon*

ABOVE: *Tide pools north of Pacific City, Oregon*
OPPOSITE PAGE: *Georgetown Lake, Montana*

The West Coast, at last!

As you travel in the high-altitude regions of the western countryside, you may experience some problems acclimating to the elevation. Symptoms may include headaches, shortness of breath, and insomnia. If you have any problems, rest at a comfortable elevation before you continue climbing.

The route to Pueblo is lightly traveled, although you will see more traffic than you've seen in days upon reaching Pueblo. A shoulder-blessed interstate leads you into town. Although eastern Colorado is full of quiet roads, those of central Colorado are anything but, especially near the popular towns of Breckenridge, Frisco, and Dillon. As you head away from the aforementioned towns, traffic decreases and the ride is usually quite pleasant.

If you decide to go off the main route, note that riding the interstates is prohibited except where no alternate route exists. For more information on bicycling in Colorado, contact State Bicycle Program Manager, Colorado Department of Transportation, 4201 East Arkansas, Room 225, Denver, CO 80222; (303) 757-9982; email: info@dot.state.co.us; website: www.dot.state.co.us/index.htm.

Tribune to Eads (57.9 miles)

One Tribune resident told me that things got bleaker after Tribune. I thought it impossible, since towns were already set far apart, but lo and behold, she was right. As I slowly climbed up a vast plateau, better known as the Great Plains, even the farmhouses were set far back from the main road, and I had fewer people to wave to. It really didn't matter, though, as I was immersed in the kind of "see-forever" scenes one sometimes dreams of.

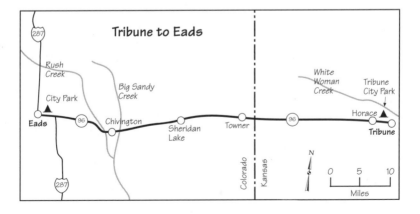

Grain mill at sunset in Eads, Colorado

Of course, I also had a friend with me, and we talked about books and bicycling and food and husbands and boyfriends and ex-husbands and ex-boyfriends for miles upon miles. The time literally zoomed by. I think things might have been different, probably a lot more difficult, had I been alone. I talked to some cyclists who were emphatic about wanting to get through the "boring part" of Kansas as quickly as possible!

Even if you do find eastern Kansas boring, today should be quite a historic day for you because this segment reaches into Colorado. I don't know about you, but I, and everyone else I talked to, was anxiously awaiting Colorado. Personally, I had many reasons. First, I love mountains, especially the high, granite types with jagged peaks, and Colorado has plenty. Second, I was looking forward to drier weather—not necessarily less rain, because I really couldn't complain about the rain I had experienced in previous weeks, but less humidity (which Colorado delivered). My third reason had nothing to do with grand scenery; rather, I was anxious to enter state number six in my ten-state quest.

The day ends at Eads, a small Colorado town of less than 900 folks. The all-service town rests on the Great Plains, far from the mountain scenes you'll enjoy during the next few days. Visit the city during Eads Appreciation Days, an annual event held in mid-July, and you'll be welcome to attend the barbecue and free dance. A note of caution: We stayed over during the event and encountered noisy, sometimes rowdy people who slapped our tents, threw bottles, and yelled until the wee hours of the morning. Other bicyclists, however, had nothing but wonderful things to say about the people of Eads.

MILEAGE LOG

0.0 From the park, head back to the main route.

0.7 Junction Hwys. 96 and 27; the shoulder is narrow and the traffic is light as you continue west on Hwy. 96, a two-lane highway.

2.6 Turnoff on the right for Horace, named for Horace Greeley, a prominent newspaper publisher who founded and edited the *New York Tribune*. A leader in the antislavery movement, Greeley's writings and remarks were widely quoted. Perhaps the most popular, "Go West, young man," was first used by an Indiana newspaperman, John Soule, in 1851. However, Greeley popularized the phrase when he used it in his newspaper as advice to the unemployed of New York City.

16.6 Enter Colorado. As you do so, the traffic only gets lighter and the landscape, if possible, only more desolate.

18.3 Enter Towner, a town without services, although there is a post office.

30.2 Junction US 385 in Sheridan Lake. The lake wasn't much more than a mud hole when I cycled through town. There's a post office in town, and the Wheatland Café, visible to the north via US 385, offers good food and a limited supply of groceries. From town, continue west on Hwy. 96.

31.0 US 385 heads south to Granada; stay on Hwy. 96.

38.3 Enter Brandon—no services, although there is a post office.

42.2 Cross Big Sandy Creek.

43.6 Enter Chivington—again, no services except for a post office.

44.6 Cross Rush Creek.

55.2 Junction US 287 South to the left; US 287 North joins the route at this point and traffic increases a bit. A shoulder makes the ride more enjoyable.

57.6 Enter Eads, an all-service town with a Laundromat. Proceed west through town.

57.9 If you're choosing to camp instead of staying in a motel, make a right on Maine St. Cross the railroad tracks and turn right on the first street. Camping is allowed across from the courthouse. There are no rest rooms at the present time, but they are in the works for the future. Amenities include water and picnic tables.

If you want to use the public pool and showers, stay on Maine St. for 0.6 mile, then turn left at the baseball diamond and continue 0.1 mile. You'll pass a grocery store, post office, and other businesses en route.

Eads to Ordway (61.9 miles)

If you've ever wondered how lonely a highway can be, you should ride Hwy. 96 through eastern Colorado. We found the road so free of traffic that we almost craved the roar of a big rig. Now that's lonely!

Instead of motorists or truckers, we were entertained by the trains that often passed by. The conductors tooted their horns at us, waving briskly as we gradually climbed to Ordway, home for the night.

Between Eads and Ordway, service stops are few and far between. For instance, the once-bustling metropolis of Sugar City is now almost a ghost town.

Ordway is the county seat for Crowley County, established in 1911. With its roots in agriculture, principal crops include alfalfa, sugar beets, onions, and cantaloupes. In addition, each year turkeys are being produced in larger quantities.

Madeline Ferguson puts the finishing touches on the day from Hotel Ordway, which she manages with her husband, R. D. A stay at the historic hotel is a delight as you share a bathroom, television, and stories with fellow bicyclists and other boarders. Rooms are clean and simple; sheets and towels are not provided, so you'll have to supply your own.

MILEAGE LOG

0.0 Junction Hwy. 96 and Maine St. Head west on Hwy. 96. There's a narrow shoulder for the entire segment and very little traffic.

0.2 Junction US 287 takes off to the right; continue straight on Hwy. 96.

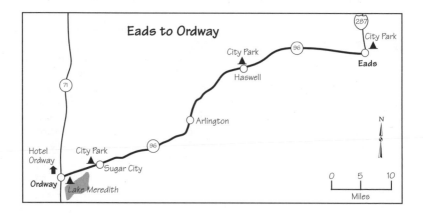

21.9 Enter Haswell, where there is a post office and camping at the city park, which is on the route. You'll find water, shaded shelters, and rest rooms.

35.9 Enter Arlington; post office only.

56.0 Enter downtown Sugar City. As you might have guessed, the city was named for the sugar beet, of which it saw plenty. Founded in the 1890s, Sugar City once boasted a population of about 2,800. The population declined, however, after the sugar factory closed down.

Besides friendly folks, and lots of fine fishing and boating at nearby Lake Meredith, the town offers little in the way of services. There's a bar where you can get cold sodas, pizza, nachos, and chips. Camping is allowed at the city park, which is on the route. Unfortunately, the park lacks rest rooms and water.

57.8 Road on left leads to Lake Meredith, where water sports and fishing abound. It's also a favorite place for waterfowl to stop over. As you continue on, you'll pass several stockyards en route to Ordway.

60.9 Hwy. 96 merges onto Hwy. 71 at this point. Turn left at the stop sign, now riding Hwys. 71 and 96.

61.1 Hwy. 96 curves to the right; Hwy. 71 continues south. Make a right on Hwy. 96. There's a restaurant (with public showers

Commemoration sign, Hotel Ordway, Ordway, Colorado

and a mini-market), a Laundromat, and a private campground here.

61.8 Turnoff to Ordway Business District on the right. Make a
right toward town.

61.9 Hotel Ordway is on the left. Native-born Madeline Ferguson
and her husband, R. D., have managed the hotel for nearly
thirty years. Home away from home for many, the hotel has
ten reasonably priced rooms for cyclists. Reservations are
needed for large groups. Call 267-3541 for more information.
In downtown Ordway (which is close by), you'll find a café, a
market, a post office, and other businesses.

Ordway to Pueblo (54.0 miles)

Today's ride is similar to yesterday's—you'll continue to climb
slowly—although the end will be much different. Instead of relaxing in a small town of 1,000, you'll enter the realms of Pueblo,
second-largest city on the
TransAmerica Trail. (Eugene,
Oregon, is the largest city, with
more than 113,000 inhabitants.)

*Prairie dog towns once covered
huge expanses of the Great Plains.
Now their numbers are dwindling,
but they still inhabit many short-
grass prairies.*

This city of more than
100,000 offers plentiful accommodations and other services
(including bicycle shops), located throughout town. If a
hostel or camping is more to
your liking, the city offers
those options too. In fact, the
day ends at Pueblo City Park.
If you need an airline or a
Greyhound bus, you'll find
those services here as well.

Pueblo offers many things to
see and do. The Pueblo Zoo
provides a home for more than
seventy species of animals and
is located in the city park. The
Colorado State Fair is held every year from the end of August through Labor Day and is
enjoyed by more than a million
visitors. In addition, there are
movie theaters, many fine local
performing groups including

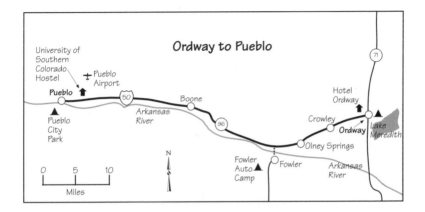

the Pueblo Symphony Orchestra, a number of museums, and an indoor ice arena. If you haven't had enough cycling, there are more than 20 miles of scenic biking and hiking trails along the Arkansas River at the Greenway and Nature Center.

Segment highlights include riding across the Great Plains, where traffic is nil (you won't encounter large amounts of traffic until you reach US 50 near Pueblo), seeing the Rocky Mountains far off in the distance, and watching prairie dogs play just off US 50. Best of all, there's a stopover at Dingo's Café in Olney Springs; you'll talk about the scrumptious free pie and friendly folks for days before and after your visit.

MILEAGE LOG

0.0 Hotel Ordway. Head back to Hwy. 96 and make a right. As you proceed west, the uncrowded highway is two lanes and sports a shoulder.

5.7 Junction Hwy. 207. As you continue on, you'll begin to see the Rocky Mountains in the distance. From the junction, if you head to the right for 0.1 mile you'll reach Crowley, the newest addition to Crowley County. The town was once a shipping point for many farm products (in 1924, about 1,000 railroad cars of produce were shipped) and was referred to as the "Biggest Little Town." Today, there's a post office, a café, and a store with limited items.

10.8 Olney Springs; market, post office, and Dingo's Café. Be sure to stop for a bite at Dingo's, where a slice of pie is not only free, it's also delicious.

15.3 Junction Hwy. 167 on the left. **SIDE TRIP:** The road leads 2 miles to the all-service town of Fowler, where there is camping at Fowler Auto Camp.

30.0   Enter Boone. There's a post office, and just past the park on the left look for a mini-market/deli/hardware store combination that serves sandwiches and such.

30.1   Junction Hwy. 209 on the left.

36.1   Hwy. 96 merges onto US 50 West, a four-lane road with a wide shoulder. Expect a huge increase in traffic.

41.3   Junction Hwy. 231 on the left.

43.1   Mini-market on the left.

43.4   Junction Hwy. 223.

43.8   Pueblo Memorial Airport turnoff on the right.

46.4   Shoulder narrows.

46.8   Exit US 50 via the Hwy. 47 and Hwy. 96 offramp.

47.0   Junction Hwy. 96 and Hwy. 47. Ignore the sign that promises "76 Bike Route" via Hwy. 47 unless you want to spend the night at the University of Southern Colorado hostel. The hostel, open May 15 through August 31, is less than 3 miles away via Hwy. 47. Reservations are a must; call 549-2601 for more information.

Head left on Hwy. 96 (4th St.) to continue on route. You'll find all services, including Laundromats, as you proceed.

50.0   Turn left on Santa Fe Ave.

50.1   Go right on 1st St., then pedal 1 block and make a left on Main St.

51.0   Cross the Arkansas River.

51.2   Main St. curves to the right and merges onto Abriendo Ave.

52.3   Make a left on Cleveland St. as you ride through a residential area.

52.7   Turn right on Dittmer Ave.

53.4   Merge onto Goodnight Ave. and continue to the right.

54.0   Junction Pueblo Blvd. You'll exit the park at this point. Tomorrow's segment crosses Pueblo Blvd. and proceeds westward. The swimming pool and bike camping are just prior to the intersection. (There's an automatic-sprinkler-free area near here—check in with the city parks and recreation department, 566-1745, weekdays before 5:00 P.M. to find the best place to pitch your tent.)

Pueblo to Royal Gorge (55.0 miles)

You'll probably greet today's ride with a lot of enthusiasm as you pedal ever closer to the heaven-piercing peaks of the Rocky Mountains, with thoughts of crossing Hoosier Pass in the not-so-distant future.

Upon leaving Pueblo, you'll climb most of the way to Wetmore, although you should expect a few downhills along the way. After

Bicyclists riding across Royal Gorge Bridge, Colorado

you reach Wetmore, it's downhill to Florence, nearly level to
Cañon (pronounced CAN-yon) City, and then uphill to Royal
Gorge. Total elevation gain for the day is quite an increase from
days past—about 3,000 feet.

From Florence to Cañon City, you'll pass through a couple of
small towns via Hwy. 115, which is narrow or shoulderless and
bears light to moderate traffic.

Cañon City, known as Colorado's climate capital and banana
belt, welcomes 330 days of sunshine each year and is a nice place to
stop and visit. Home of the Colorado Territorial Prison Museum
and Park, it offers several bike shops and all services, including
Laundromats.

The Territorial Prison, known as one of the hellholes of the Old
West, opened in 1871 and has been a museum since 1988. The institution has witnessed seventy-seven deaths, including that of
Alfred Packer, the first man in the United States ever to be con-
victed of cannibalism. Forty-five convicts were put to death by
hanging, thirty-two others by gas.

If you're interested in a whitewater rafting trip down the Arkansas River, you can make arrangements in town. There are half- and
full-day trips into Royal Gorge or Three Rock Canyon, and two-
day trips on the Upper Arkansas. If you have plenty of time and

money to spare, there are also four- or five-day trips on the Upper and Lower Arkansas.

Expect to climb at a mildly steep grade from Canon City to the Royal Gorge area. A side trip to Royal Gorge Bridge is a must if you can tolerate tourist traps and you have a lot of pennies to spare. It's exciting to peer down from a high suspension bridge to the Arkansas River more than 1,000 feet below.

In addition to walking or riding your bicycle across the bridge, you can ride the world's steepest incline railway to the bottom of the canyon. You can also soar above the chasm in an aerial tram and enjoy a variety of shows, including live entertainment. In addition, there are restaurants and gift shops.

All in all, I'm happy I made the side trip. Unlike the Grand Canyon, which is made up of layers of multicolored earth, the Royal Gorge has been cut through solid granite; it's a masterpiece of nature that has been more than 3 million years in the making. Even today, the thrust of sand and water continues to dig the chasm deeper at the rate of 2 inches every 1,000 years.

The nearly quarter-mile-long bridge itself is very impressive and is ranked as one of the world's outstanding suspension bridges. Built in 1929 for the sole purpose of tourism, it is the highest suspension bridge in the world, spanning the Royal Gorge at a height of 1,053 feet. From the bridge there are magnificent views down to the Arkansas River and across to the Sangre de Cristo and Greenhorn mountain ranges. For those who are wondering, the bridge can support more than 2 million pounds; two 300-ton cables, each containing 2,100 strands of wire, enable it do so.

Even if you don't pay to see the gorge, the side trip to the gorge area is nice in that you may see deer and other animal life en route. The view from the top is awesome as well; however, it's a bit of a steep climb to get there.

En route to the park you'll pass Buckskin Joe Park and Railway, a place that bills itself as the Old West's largest theme park. For a price (you can purchase a combination ticket that allows you to enjoy both Buckskin Joe and a train ride to the bridge), you'll get the chance to explore an antique and steam train museum, enjoy live entertainment, and pet the friendly animals at Buckskin Farm.

MILEAGE LOG

0.0 Junction Goodnight Ave. and Pueblo Blvd. Continue west on Goodnight Ave.

1.4 T-junction; turn right onto Hwy. 96. There's a nice shoulder and the road offers quiet riding with relatively little traffic. Begin climbing an easy to moderate grade to Wetmore.

4.2 Pueblo Reservoir State Recreation Area on the right.

10.9 Lake Pueblo State Park entrance on the right. Boasting 60 miles of shoreline and a magnificent backdrop of the Sangre de Cristo Mountains, Lake Pueblo is the state's most popular recreational site. Here you can go boating, windsurfing, water skiing, sailing, jet skiing, swimming, fishing, and camping.

14.2 Shoulder disappears, but the road is uncrowded.

23.6 Shoulder reappears; soon after, begin a steeper climb up Jackson Hill.

26.5 Enter Wetmore, where there's a restaurant, a mini-market that serves some hot foods, and a post office. At this point (the stop sign), turn right on Hwy. 67. The road is shoulderless, but the traffic isn't too bad until you get near Florence.

36.7 Shoulder begins; motel nearby.

37.7 Stop sign; make a left on Hwy. 115. There's a Laundromat in addition to the usual services, with facilities found both to the left and to the right of the junction. You'll head through downtown Florence, site of a refining center for oil and a gold ore reduction center in the late 1800s, by turning left.

38.0 Junction Hwy. 67. Continue straight on Hwy. 115, which is narrow or shoulderless. **SIDE TRIP:** If you want to stay at Pioneer Park, go right here (also called N. Pikes Peak Ave.) and travel 0.1 mile to the park. You'll find the standard amenities and a pool. Be sure to check in with police (784-3611) so they can shut off the automatic sprinklers. My companions and I didn't do so, and we, along with our belongings, got soaked.

42.7 Enter Brookside—no services.

43.9 Snack stand with vegetables, cold drinks, and candy. This is Lincoln Park.

44.3 Laundromat on the right.

45.5 Reach the outskirts of Cañon City; market, restaurant, and more services (including Laundromats) as you continue.

46.4 Cross the Arkansas River and enter downtown Canon City.

46.6 Junction US 50; make a left on US 50 (Royal Gorge Blvd.). US 50 is four lanes, no shoulder, as you travel through town. There are services to the right and left of this junction, and you'll find three bike shops in the area. For a place to camp, try the RV Station, which is off route, 2.5 miles east off US 50 at the Hwy. 115 junction.

47.9 Begin climbing out of town and pass the Territorial Prison as you leave town. US 50 sports a wide shoulder now.

53.9 Café on the left; campground with all services.

54.6 Fort Gorge Campground on the left; they offer the standard stuff as well as a washer/dryer and a store with limited groceries, and they allow bicyclists to share tent sites.

Pass River Outfitters, a rock shop, and horse stables as you continue.

55.0 Turnoff on left to Royal Gorge. There's also a motel, two restaurants, and a gift shop. This is the end of the segment, since there are several lodging options to choose from nearby. If you don't want to motel it, you can camp at one of the campgrounds you just passed, or you can try the Royal Gorge Eight-Eighty Campground, which is on the left after you turn toward the Royal Gorge. A Laundromat and store with limited groceries add to the usual services. And just ahead on the right is a KOA campground with a pool and Laundromat in addition to the standard amenities. **SIDE TRIP:** The Royal Gorge Bridge is located 4 miles from the US 50 turnoff. The first mile is level or downhill, then uphill to several picnic areas/rest rooms, which are available after you enter Royal Gorge Park.

Royal Gorge to Schechter Hostel (25.9 miles)

Except for a particularly steep grade once in a while, climbing the Rockies isn't as tough as you may think. Even if it were, the splendor of the scenes—mountains blanketed with grass, flowers dancing in the breeze, and turkey vultures soaring toward the heavens—make it a magical experience.

The segment is a short one and ends at the Schechter Hostel, where visitors include deer, porcupine, bear, and several family dogs, as well as Warren and Lynn Schechter, who are bound to make your stay a most interesting one.

As you may have guessed, the day is short for one particular reason. You're going to be climbing a lot during the upcoming days, and as you climb in elevation some of you may have problems adjusting to the high altitude, as one of my companions did. The shortness of this segment allows you to spend some time at the hostel acclimating to the elevation. I think you'll find it's time well spent: the scenery is lovely and quiet, and the Schechters are friendly.

Nevertheless, if you'd rather pedal more miles and you don't mind climbing 5,500 feet in a single day (you'll climb about 3,300 feet today), you can combine this day with the next, the Schechter Hostel to Fairplay segment, for a total of 67.2 miles.

MILEAGE LOG

0.0 Royal Gorge turnoff/US 50 junction; proceed west on US 50 West. There's a shoulder.

1.1 Head downhill to Yogi Bear Jellystone Camp Resort Park, which is on the right. Look for the standard amenities, as well as a pool, a store, and a Laundromat.

1.2 Turn right on Hwy. 9 toward Hartsel. There's a shoulder for the first 11 miles, then the shoulder is intermittently nonexistent until you reach the hostel. Traffic is limited, however, so it's not much of a problem. The road climbs and descends for a while, then climbs at a mostly moderate level, although there are one or two steep grades that will make your heart pound.

10.1 Hwy. 11 on the right. This leads to the Gold Belt Auto Tour.

19.7 Enter Park County and head downhill and uphill for some 150-foot, roller-coaster-like climbs and descents before climbing again.

21.6 Cross Thirty-One Mile Creek.

22.3 Hwy. 102 leads to the small community of Guffey, which is about 2 miles uphill. There's a restaurant, a market, a post office, and a bed-and-breakfast inn in this town of quaint, rustic buildings.

25.9 Turnoff to the Schechter Hostel on the left; it's located just north of Milepost 24 and is marked with a plaque bearing the

Currant Creek Hostel near Guffey, Colorado

name Schechter. Warren says of his nonprofit facility, "They call this the Lost Hostel of the Rockies. If you can find it you'll have a good time." Believe me, that's the truth! You can either sleep in cabins with cots or tent-camp. Excellent water, a cold-water bucket shower, and outhouses add to the amenities. A wonderful view makes the stay complete.

Schechter Hostel to Fairplay (42.1 miles)

The days continue to be short-mileage days, mostly because the scenes are too wonderful to pass quickly. Even by bicycle they seem to fly by, and you'll want to treasure them for as long as you can.

This segment was definitely the highlight of my Colorado trip to date. The jagged granite peaks of the Rockies loomed before me as I topped Currant Creek Pass. And as I zoomed down the west side of the pass to continue my quest, I couldn't help but feel that I was being pulled, as if by some magnetic force, to the sheer crowns of the Rockies.

The grades continue to be long, but they are gentle when compared to some you've experienced. In the East, for instance, I had poked up some of the hills on my 98-pound bike, averaging 2 to 3 miles per hour. Here, I managed 5 to 7 and sometimes even 9 mph. It seemed a breeze in comparison.

Broad, wide basins lead across a high plateau to the tiny town of Hartsel, set in what seems like the middle of nowhere.

Located at the 10,000-foot level, Fairplay sets the scene for day's end. A wonderful little town nestled in South Park and surrounded by the Mosquito and Park ranges, Fairplay offers craft shops, a gorgeous view, and delicious food. If you want to eat amid history, try the Fairplay Hotel, which features reasonably priced American food in a historic setting.

The South Park City Museum is definitely a town highlight for visitors, who come to the outdoor museum to see what life in a nineteenth-century Colorado mining town might have been like. (Gold was discovered in a stream bed in South Park in 1859.) Here, thirty-two authentic buildings from the 1870s through the 1900s are filled with up to 60,000 authentic artifacts.

If you are in Fairplay the last full weekend of July, be sure to attend the World's Championship Pack Burro Race, an annual festival that includes llama races, a parade, arts and crafts, and, of course, burro races.

A shoulder (part-time anyway) makes the day's ride smooth, giving you the chance to gaze at the sights. Expect more traffic on US 24 and US 285. Also, Hwy. 9 from Hartsel to Fairplay sports more traffic than the previous sections of Hwy. 9.

South Park area, Fairplay, Colorado

MILEAGE LOG

0.0 Hostel entrance and Hwy. 9. Continue climbing the steep grade; shoulder continues.

6.8 Currant Creek Pass. From this point you'll see the wide expanse of the Rocky Mountains before you. As you continue, the terrain is a series of ups and downs, with mostly downs to Hartsel.

22.9 T-junction; turn left on US 24. Hwy. 9 merges with US 24 at this point. The roadway is busy and shoulders are nonexistent—use caution. Downtown Hartsel is at the junction. You'll find a post office, a café, a mini-market, and a gift shop.

23.3 Shoulder begins.

24.0 US 24 continues straight. Stay right on Hwy. 9; a shoulder remains as you climb the easy to moderate grade through Badger Basin.

24.6 Shoulder disappears.

31.4 Cross the Middle Fork South Platte River.

36.4 Cross the Middle Fork South Platte River again.

40.3 T-junction; Hwy. 9 merges with US 285. Make a right and continue. There's a shoulder for most of the ride to Fairplay.

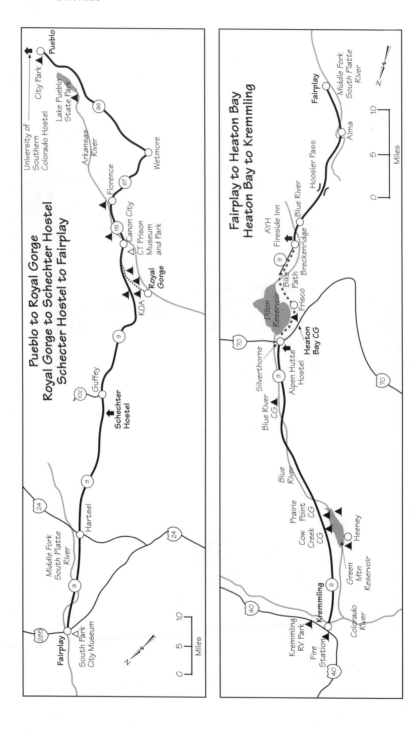

Pueblo to Royal Gorge
Royal Gorge to Schechter Hostel
Schecter Hostel to Fairplay

Fairplay to Heaton Bay
Heaton Bay to Kremmling

40.9 Mini-market and café on the right.

41.2 Cross the Middle Fork South Platte River.

41.3 Turn left on Hwy. 9 and head through Fairplay, a wonderfully quaint town with several lip-smacking restaurants.

42.1 Junction 4th St.; South Park City Museum is on the left. Prior to 0.8 mile you'll pass a variety of services in this all-service town. You can choose from several motels or a bed-and-breakfast inn, or you can camp in Bonnie Edmondson's yard and use her shower. Bonnie has been hosting bicyclists since 1988. Her address is 594 4th St.; (719) 836-2573. (Make a right on 4th St. to reach Bonnie's house.)

If you want to splurge, rent a room at the Hand Hotel Bed and Breakfast. Built in the early 1930s by Jessie Rella and Jake Hand, the hotel was sold numerous times, with each new owner making his or her "improvements." Today, the hotel has been stripped back to the original walls and is representative of the 1890 to 1910 period. The rooms are decorated with antiques, most of which are for sale. There are eleven rooms to choose from, each adorned in a different theme, including the Rancher Room, the Indian Room, and the Silverheels Suite.

Fairplay to Heaton Bay Campground (35.0 miles)

This is a short day for several reasons, all fantastic ones. First, there's the climb up Hoosier Pass, the highest point on the TransAmerica Trail. The 11,542-foot pass might intimidate some, but there's no need to worry. I'm pretty slow, yet I managed to average 4 to 5 mph. Still, it takes some time and energy to get to the top, and when you do you will probably want to sit and enjoy the moment.

Next there's the hustle and bustle of Breckenridge, a town some will enjoy and others will want to avoid. The site of one of the oldest and largest historic districts in Colorado, Breckenridge is the second most popular ski mountain in North America in winter, and it's the kind of place where you can shop until you drop any time of the year. Its quaint Victorian buildings, once saloons and brothels, now house galleries, boutiques, and many tasty restaurants, including Fatty's Pizzeria, where a homemade whole wheat crust was the base for the best vegetarian pizza I have ever eaten.

Breckenridge summers are pleasant, with an average daytime temperature of 70 degrees; the streets are particularly colorful, with wildflowers lining the roadway; and special events are plentiful, including the National Festival of Music, Genuine Jazz in July, the Breckenridge Blues Festival, and the Breckenridge Festival of Film.

Outdoor activities abound: golfing, hiking, camping, horseback riding, four-wheeling, and fishing. And of course, there is biking. In fact, you can ride a 40-mile paved bike path from Breckenridge to Vail.

From Breckenridge you'll continue via a bike path to Frisco, a quaint town and a true mountain-biking mecca. Frisco offers many of the same outdoor activities as does Breckenridge, with a variety of water sports as well, including canoeing, kayaking, and sailing.

Try to be in Frisco for the town's Fantastic Fourth of July Celebration, which includes a parade, an arts and crafts fair, food booths, and a series of free concerts known as Music on Main Street. The fireworks show offers a double treat as the colorful blasts are mirrored in Dillon Reservoir.

The day ends at Heaton Bay. A Dillon Reservoir Recreation Area campground located in the heart of Summit County, it is one of Colorado's most scenic recreation areas. Embraced by the Gore, Williams Fork, and Ten Mile mountain ranges, the 25-mile shoreline is blanketed with lodgepole pines.

Traffic will probably be heavy as you climb from Fairplay, up over Hoosier Pass, and down into Breckenridge. Note that the

Downtown Breckenridge, Colorado

highway over Hoosier Pass is shoulderless, but there is a hard gravel shoulder if you need to move over due to heavy traffic. From Breckenridge to Frisco, you'll travel a bike path that can be quite busy, especially on a holiday or weekend.

MILEAGE LOG

0.0 Junction Hwy. 9 and 4th St. Continue uphill (northwest) on Hwy. 9 for 1.5 miles, then drop a little and begin another uphill; no shoulder.

1.8 Road on the left leads to the Middle Fork South Platte River and primitive camping; no facilities. Expect lots of traffic.

5.2 Enter Alma, an old mining town, which has a hotel, a mini-market, and a post office. As you exit town you'll begin the steep 4-mile climb to the summit.

11.4 Reach the top of Hoosier Pass and enjoy a moment of true pleasure before racing downhill. Watch for motorists on this busy road.

16.5 Enter Blue River; no services.

20.0 Cross the Blue River.

20.5 Shoulder begins.

21.8 Enter Breckenridge. In addition to the usual services, there are Laundromats, bike shops, and many motels. The budget-conscious will like the AYH Fireside Inn, located at 114 N. French St. in the historic district. For reservations call (907) 453-6456; email: info@firesideinn.com; www.firesideinn.com.

22.0 Visitor center on the left. Continue just past it and turn left on French St.; cross the Blue River via a bridge and make a right on the bike path. This is the Blue River Bikeway, which spans the distance from Breckenridge to Vail Pass.

26.2 Cross Hwy. 9, now traveling on the east side of the roadway.

28.0 Stop sign; there's an inn and restaurant. Cross the road and continue on the bike path. Dillon Reservoir is just ahead.

28.7 Cross Hwy. 9 again and wind up and down through the trees for roughly a mile. Anticipate some short but steep grades.

31.7 Turnoff to Main St. in downtown Frisco. Go right, then make another right on Main St., and you'll find all services as well as a Laundromat and bike shops.

32.2 Turn left onto the bike path that runs parallel to Hwy. 9. If you keep straight on Main St. you'll cross Hwy. 9 and come to the Visitor Information Building. Frisco Marina is just behind.

33.2 Bike path veers away from the road and follows the scenic shore of Dillon Reservoir.

34.6 Path on the right leads to rest rooms in 100 yards or so.

35.0 Heaton Bay Campground on the right. No showers, but there are all the usual facilities, including water.

Heaton Bay Campground to Kremmling (41.7 miles)

Another easy day grants plenty of time for enjoying Dillon Reservoir. In fact, if you're not in a hurry to get on the road in the morning, you can spend half the day at Dillon Reservoir before heading north. There are many things to do, such as fish, canoe, read a book, or just sit back and absorb the sight of the lofty mountains, which provide a splendid backdrop.

If you didn't get in enough shopping in Breckenridge, you can always stop in Silverthorne to do more of the same—only here you can hunt for bargains at one of the "top ten outlet malls in America," according to *Self* magazine.

The day's ride is less than 42 miles long and the total elevation gain is only 900 feet. While the route continues to cross some of the most magnificent high-country scenes found in the central Rockies, you can expect to spend more time watching the road after you exit the bike path near Silverthorne. Heavy truck traffic plagues portions of the roadway as you head north to Kremmling. You might want to be prepared for strong headwinds as well.

There are several options for your Kremmling stay. In this small city of just over 1,000, you can splurge and get a room (a good idea if the mosquitoes are out in droves), camp for free at the fire station, or pay a reduced rate to camp at a private campground. Kremmling has all the necessities, plus Greyhound bus service.

MILEAGE LOG

0.0 Bike path/Heaton Bay Campground entrance. As you continue along the northwest edge of Dillon Reservoir, there are many scenic viewpoints just off the path.

2.6 After crossing the Dillon Dam area, you'll see Silverthorne down in the valley to the north. Cross Dillon Dam Rd. and continue on a bike path that crosses the road and switchbacks down to US 6 in Silverthorne.

3.2 Junction US 6; head left (north) through Silverthorne, where you'll find all services, including a bike shop, a Laundromat, public showers, a pool at Silverthorne Recreation Center, and Greyhound bus service. Also, there's the Alpen Hutte (pronounced alpen HOO-ta), a hostel modeled after the alpine huts of Europe. It is located at 471 Rainbow Dr.; (907) 468-6336. Reservations are advisable.

3.6 Cross under I-70. Continue straight on Hwy. 9, a four-lane highway with a shoulder.

6.0 Road narrows to two lanes now; the shoulder is narrow or nonexistent. Anticipate heavy traffic as you continue paralleling

Scene of Dillon Reservoir between Frisco and Silverthorne, Colorado

the scenic Blue River through rural Colorado. As the day progresses you'll climb and descend, but mostly descend.

11.5 Blue River Campground on the right; gravel road leads a short distance to the national forest campground, where there are picnic facilities, outhouses, and water. Fee area.

14.4 Cross the Blue River.

17.4 Cross the Blue River.

20.6 Turnoff on the left to Heeney and the Blue Mountain Recreation Area. If you pass by in June, you might want to attend the Heeney Tick Festival, a "wacky, satirical celebration of the lowly tick held each June." Heeney is more than just a tick celebration, however; the town offers a motel, restaurant, market, and a good view of Green Mountain Reservoir, where camping, sailing, fishing, and sailboarding are popular.

20.7 Cross the Blue River again.

22.4 The Prairie Point Campground is on the left via a short gravel road. This national forest camp offers water and toilets. Fee area.

26.8 Gravel road on the left leads to Cow Creek Campground. This undeveloped national forest camp is free; toilets.

28.5 Another turnoff to Heeney, this one via Heeney Rd., which is on the left.

39.5 Cross the Colorado River.

41.4 Hwy. 9 ends at the junction of US 40. There's a post office just to the right of the junction. There's also a bakery/deli/pizza shop with excellent goodies. This segment ends at the fire station, where there is a rest room and picnic facilities but no showers. If you'd like a shower, turn right at the junction, heading less than 2 miles east via US 40 to Kremmling RV Park, which offers special rates for bicyclists, the standard amenities, and a Laundromat.

Turn left on US 40 to continue on route through Kremmling, an all-service town.

41.7 Visitor center and a park on the right. There's water in the park and a rest room and grill at the fire department. Camping is permitted behind the station, which is just behind the park. **SPECIAL NOTE:** Mosquitoes can be thick and annoying in downtown Kremmling, especially near the fire department.

Kremmling to Walden (61.7 miles)

Although traffic and winds can be unnerving at times, the route is a gorgeous one across a high plateau where sagebrush rules and the granite peaks of the high Rockies provide a fitting backdrop. Adding to the scene in the summer is a rainbow of wildflowers.

This day and the next, you traverse North Park country, land of majestic mountains, lakes and streams, wildlife refuges, forests, and abundant wildlife. It's a place with both abundant recreational opportunities and compelling historic and cultural sites.

The landscape is rural and open, with an occasional ranch dotting the land. The habitat serves the local animal life well, with moose, deer, pronghorn, and a variety of bird life sometimes visible.

The winds here are highly unpredictable, rarely doing what they are "supposed" to do. Riders going both ways confirmed that sometimes the winds blow to the northwest and other times they blow to the southeast.

The day comes to a close in the friendly community of Walden, home of the Pioneer Museum, where you can choose to camp in the city park or stay in a motel.

MILEAGE LOG

0.0 The day begins at the visitor center on US 40 in downtown Kremmling. Head north on US 40. As you continue through Colorado, the hills are rolling with an uphill trend. Shoulders are generally nonexistent, although there is a narrow one on occasion. Anticipate some traffic, including trucks, as you head through the lonely Colorado countryside.

6.0 Junction Hwy. 134 on the left. As you continue along US 40, which parallels Muddy Creek, look for pronghorn antelope, deer, and other critters. You'll also pass three sections of the Grand River Ranch.

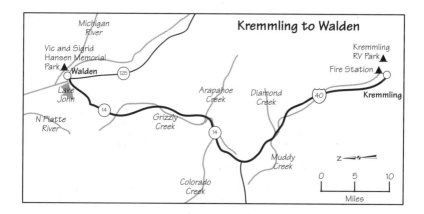

Kremmling to Walden

21.4 Cross Diamond Creek.

27.0 Cross the Continental Divide at the top of Muddy Pass, 8,772 feet above sea level. Junction Hwy. 14 is also at the crossing. Make a right and continue on Hwy. 14, a lightly traveled road. (Beware of some truck traffic, as shoulders are nonexistent.) You'll pass acres and acres of sweeping countryside as you parallel Grizzly Creek, heading mostly downhill but climbing a few times too. This is prime moose habitat; look for the big, gangly creatures as you continue.

33.2 Cross Colorado Creek.

35.6 Cross Grizzly Creek.

37.0 Arapaho Creek crossing.

44.9 Cross Grizzly Creek again.

51.5 Cross Grizzly Creek for a third time and begin climbing up Peterson Ridge.

53.3 Top of ridge. A roller-coaster-like ride with a few more descents than ascents continues.

60.1 T-junction at Hwy. 125. Turn left on Hwy. 125, which merges onto the route; there's a shoulder for a mile.

60.7 Turnoff to Lake John on the left. Cross the Illinois River soon after.

61.4 There's a Laundromat, as well as all the usual amenities as you enter Walden.

61.7 Junction 4th St. Police station to the left; the Vic and Sigrid Hanson Memorial Park is 0.2 mile to the right (east). There's a gazebo, picnic facilities, water, and rest rooms at the park; an indoor pool and showers are just a short walk away.

In my entire cross-country jaunt, this was the first town to charge bicyclists for a shower or use of the public swimming pool. No doubt about it, a shower is worth every penny, but somehow it's even more special when you get it for free.

WHY DO PEOPLE TOUR AMERICA BY BICYCLE?

"Why?" is the one question that I most often heard the summer I pedaled across America. For me, the answer was simple, maybe even corny. "It's just something I've wanted to do for a long time," I replied again and again.

I've always been intrigued by people who take the time to see the country by bike. Why do they do it? Their reasons vary as much as their personalities. Dick Davis, sixty-two years young when he rode across America, says, "I probably did it because I was told I couldn't." His favorite part? "The best part of my bike trip across the U.S. was my bike partner Earl Norman."

Sixty-seven years of age when he pedaled across, Earl Norman grins widely just thinking about bicycle touring. "I spend my winters thinking about touring in the summer," he reveals.

Carol Kaufman rides for many reasons, but mainly because she (like many of us) is addicted to the sport. After her first self-contained ride she wrote, "I loved self-contained touring because it gave me a feeling of independence, self-reliance, and freedom that I had not experienced before." And like many of us, after the ride she was "still fighting a return to my old lifestyle."

Jim Gallion had a tough time getting back into so-called "normal life." "All the things that I thought I would grow tired of are the very things that are precious to me now. Washing the little dishes, looking at the day's route, the smell of my sleeping bag, my candle lantern inside my tent, sleeping on the ground, packing and unpacking, eating pancake after pancake, and sitting on that bike— I really miss it all now!"

Randy Gonzales and Dan Hoffman are both preparing for lives serving the Lord. Last summer they rode across the country. "I went into this trip with three goals: seeing my country, experiencing the people of this nation, and making a spiritual journey to develop my relationship with God," Gonzales said. "There were times when I wanted to quit, but those goals kept me going."

The profiles of the people going coast to coast were as varied as the seasons. Some were out of school for the summer; some had just graduated from college and wanted to see the country before settling down to a regular job and family life; some were retired and had the time and money to pedal across.

A few people had such a keen desire to ride across America that they quit their jobs to do so, figuring they'd find another job after their journey ended. Dan Mauro, my biking companion off and on throughout the eastern states, did just that. He quit his job as an auto body man, cycled from his home state of New York to Yorktown, Virginia (where he met me), and then rode across the country to Wyoming before buying a car and traveling home on four wheels instead of two. When he returned, he got his job back and life went back to normal after six months on the road.

Although our reasons vary, my overall conclusion is that we pedal across the country because we know that is the best way to see it.

Bicyclists at the Colorado/Wyoming border

WYOMING

Wyoming is a Jekyll-and-Hyde-type of state for some folks, who find its southern half ugly. Indeed, it is desolate, with little more than sage and a few other scrub plants visible upon first glance. But look closer and you'll see tiny, showy wildflowers, observe prairie dogs scurrying about while others stand guard, sentry-like, atop their mounds, and watch as pronghorn scurry across the high plains, white rump hairs erect, wide nostrils flared.

As you continue north, the scenery gets more and more grand. Before you reach Lander, red cliffs begin to appear, and the scenes only improve as you continue on to Wind River country. Here the river is tucked into wide valleys, and the canyons are deep and spectacular. After climbing over the Rockies at Togwotee Pass (the second-highest summit on the TransAmerica Trail), you'll zoom down the east side and no doubt stand in awe of the Teton mountains to the west.

The Tetons are perhaps some of the greatest treasures around. And of course, north of Grand Teton National Park you'll find world-famous Yellowstone National Park. Both parks are rich in natural beauty and abundant wildlife, including moose, elk, deer, black bear, grizzly bear, and mountain lion. You might also see marmots and river otters, swans and eagles, and others too numerous to mention.

Named for a Delaware Indian word meaning "upon the great plain," Wyoming is indeed a land of plains or basins, places that are usually scant of trees and drier than the nearby mountains. You'll pedal through two of the six major Intermontane Basins—the Great Divide and Shoshone basins—which means you'll be riding "between mountains."

While you pedal across these basins, watch for wildlife. Mammals in residence include pronghorn, badgers, cottontail and jack rabbits, coyotes, foxes, and skunks. Bird life consists of wild turkeys, sage hens, pheasants, grouse, ducks, geese, and more.

Wyoming is also famous for its mountains. The Rocky Mountains tower over hundreds of clear, cold mountain lakes. In the Wind River Range alone, there are nine peaks that tower above 13,000 feet. Among them is the highest mountain in the state, 13,804-foot Gannett Peak.

Wyoming boasts the second-highest average elevation in the country, 6,700 feet. Early pioneers found the mountains a

Rocky Mountain elk calf. Elk are large members of the deer family. This calf probably weighed 25 to 40 pounds when it was born in the spring.

formidable barrier, but in the mid 1840s they found a path through at South Pass.

The California, Mormon, and Oregon trails converged at South Pass. After crossing the pass, the California and Mormon trails aimed southwest, while the Oregon Trail turned northwest. Settlers moving across southern Wyoming used the Overland or Cherokee Trail, which joined the other trails at Fort Bridger.

Although millions of people passed through the state, few stayed. Wyoming is the least populated state in the nation, with less than 500,000 residents. About 50,000 of them live in Cheyenne, the capital and the largest city in the state.

Among those who stayed were a number of influential women. Wyoming was nicknamed the Equality State because its women were the first in the nation to serve on juries, hold public office, and vote. In 1870, Esther H. Morris became the nation's first woman justice of the peace, and in 1924, Nellie Tayloe Ross was voted Wyoming's first woman governor.

Wyoming is a land of many firsts, including Devils Tower, the nation's first national monument; Shoshone National Forest, the country's first national forest; and Yellowstone National Park, the nation's largest and oldest national park.

You'll spend eight days riding 445.9 miles through the third-largest (in square miles) TransAmerica state. Traffic conditions vary throughout the state. Many of the roads offer a shoulder. You'll ride a portion of I-80 between Sinclair and Wolcott where, although traffic is heavy, a wide, smooth shoulder makes the ride bearable.

Unfortunately, the shoulders all but disappear as you head over Togwotee Pass. They're also minimal in portions of the popular

Grand Teton National Park and exist only on occasion in Yellowstone National Park. If the route is plagued with heavy summer traffic, I'd recommend that you ride early in the day. It's best to spend your afternoons on foot enjoying the parks.

Wind is one of the biggest problems in this area for some cyclists. I had but one day of harsh winds, mostly a sidewind that threatened to knock me off my bike at times, but some cyclists who rode a week ahead of me later complained of fatiguing headwinds. Some were so disenchanted that they resolved to go west to east if they ever rode cross-country again. If you're wondering which way is best, the prevailing winds are generally from the southeast, so I'd recommend sticking to the east to west route. Winds in southern Wyoming often range from 40 to 60 miles per hour.

Weather can be highly variable in the high plateaus you'll cross. Surrounded by mountain ranges, you can expect a fairly cool, semiarid climate during the day and cold weather at night. Cloudbursts, heavy hailstorms, and thunderstorms are also common.

If you go off route, note that unlike most states, Wyoming permits riding on the interstates. For information on biking in the state, contact State Bicycle Coordinator, Wyoming Department of Transportation , P.O. Box 1708, Cheyenne, WY 82003-1708; (307) 777-4719; http://wydotweb.state.wy.us; email: jmeyer@state.wy.us.

Walden to Encampment (50.5 miles)

Today's ride is a pleasant treat. Uncrowded roads continue to be the norm, gorgeous scenes may cause distraction, and best of all, you'll enter Wyoming, the seventh of ten states on your journey.

Wyoming usually offers cyclists a shoulder—a welcome blessing, to say the least, although hardly necessary, since traffic is

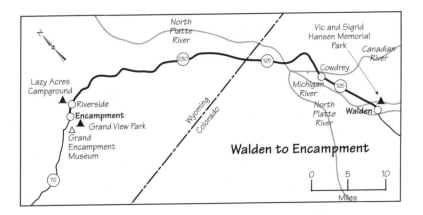

pretty much nil. No complaints from this cyclist, though, who enjoys nothing more than rolling down an uncrowded highway.

You'll find little in the way of services, since towns are scarce in this part of the country. You can stop to chat and buy goodies in Cowdrey. The next stop is near the end of the day in Riverside, a small, quiet town. When the day ends in Encampment, you'll find more services as well as an interesting museum and free camping for bicyclists.

The must-see Grand Encampment Museum is an indoor and outdoor museum, featuring a two-story outhouse that awaits your examination. Deep snow in the region forced residents to dream up the idea of a two-story toilet because drifting snow would close off the bottom half. Stairs lead about 5 to 6 feet to a second story platform just outside the privy door. Other highlights include copper-mining equipment, a folding oak bathtub, a square grand piano, vintage automobiles, a schoolhouse, and a cabin. Admission is free, though donations are welcomed.

The town of Grand Encampment and several others were born of a rich copper strike in the Sierra Madre in 1897. Amazingly, ore was transported from the mines to a smelter built along the Encampment

Grand Encampment Museum, Wyoming

River by a 16-mile-long aerial tramway, the longest in the world at that time. The smelter was powered by water delivered through a 4-foot wooden pipeline.

The S & E Railroad was built to transport the ore, but its completion came a little late. In 1908 tragedy struck, and the company that had produced $2 million in copper ore was charged with fraudulent stock sales and overcapitalization. When the mines died, so did the towns of Elwood, Battle, Rambler, Copperton, Dillon, and Rudefeha. Although Riverside and Encampment survived, the "Grand" was quietly dropped from Grand Encampment.

Once again, as you ride from one point to the next, the animal life is fun to observe. I saw coyotes, squirrels, prairie dogs, pronghorn, and deer. Avian creatures included ravens, turkey vultures, and kestrels.

MILEAGE LOG

0.0 Vic and Sigrid Hanson Memorial Park. Pedal back to Hwy. 125 in 0.2 mile. Head north (right).

0.9 Cross the Michigan River. The roadway is shoulderless and mostly level with a downhill trend as you continue.

1.4 Market on the right.

9.5 Cowdrey General Store on the left. Inside there's a café, groceries, and a high-quality selection of used books, a real surprise in this part of the country, where the scenery seemed straight out of Clint Eastwood's *High Plains Drifter* to my fellow biker Bill. In addition, the store owners allow camping behind the store; water and showers are available. There are also cabins for rent; one of the cabins houses the post office!

9.8 Cross the Canadian River.

13.5 Continue left on Hwy. 125 at the Hwy. 127 junction and climb a gradual to moderate grade up Watson Mountain.

16.7 Cross the North Platte River after a very fast downhill.

18.0 Forest Road 896 on the right; access to North Platte River in about a mile; chemical toilets. The highway is roller-coaster-like as you proceed.

22.3 Enter Wyoming, which a sign promises is "Like No Place on Earth." You are now traveling Hwy. 230 West; there is a shoulder.

33.4 Begin long uphill to the top of a pass (steepest section—about a mile long—is a 7 percent grade). Once you descend, the terrain remains a series of ups and downs with a downhill trend.

49.2 Cross the Encampment River and enter Riverside. Just across the bridge is the Lazy Acres Campground on the right, where there are cabins, tent sites, and all the other niceties. Just beyond are a mini-market and café.

49.6 Junction Hwy. 230/Hwy. 70. **SIDE TRIP:** To reach Encampment, where there is free camping at Grand View Park and the opportunity to explore the Grand Encampment Museum, go west (left) on Hwy. 70. After 0.9 mile the road T's at the junction of 6th St., where there is a post office. (Prior to and near the junction you will find all services, including a Laundromat.) Go left 3 blocks via 6th St., a gravel road.

50.5 Grand View Park; rest rooms and water, no showers. Look for "tent camping" signs. Nearby is the Grand Encampment Museum.

Encampment to Rawlins (61.1 miles)

Most of the trip from Riverside to Rawlins is pleasant—especially if the wind is either calm or at your back—although you will have a lot of traffic, including trucks, to contend with upon reaching Wolcott. You'll merge onto a busy thoroughfare at this point, but a wide shoulder makes the 13-mile stretch easier to endure.

Except for a few climbs, the trip is mainly flat or downhill. Once again, it's a journey across a high plateau, this time through an area known as North Park, where "see-forever scenes" are common and pronghorn antelope race with the wind. (Amazingly, most of the time they win the race. The fastest land mammals in North America, pronghorn can reach speeds of up to 60 mph.)

The day is relatively easy, with a total elevation gain of about 1,500 feet. If time permits, you may want to stop midway through the day for a dip in the Saratoga Hot Springs, named after a New York health resort.

The Saratoga Museum will be a must-see for some. Located in the original Union Pacific Railroad Depot building, which was built in 1915, the museum houses an assortment of railroad memorabilia as well as relics and artifacts best revealing the heritage of the Platte Valley settlers. The main exhibits consist of a pioneer home, a country store, a land office, and tie-hacking equipment. Admission is free; contributions are welcome.

The segment ends in Rawlins, center of a thriving sheep and cattle industry and a full-facility tourism center (this is the jumping-off point for those headed to Yellowstone and Grand Teton national parks). In addition to the usual amenities, you'll find bike shops and Amtrak and Greyhound service.

Rawlins, founded in 1868 when the Union Pacific Railroad laid track across this southern Wyoming landscape, is home to the old Wyoming State Penitentiary. Begun in 1898 and opened for use in 1903, it remained in operation until 1982, when a new state prison was built south of town. During the summer, tours are available.

To learn more about the history of Rawlins, visit the Carbon County Museum, where admission is free (donations are appreciated). Museum artifacts tell tales of numerous mining and ranching ventures, and relate stories about outlaws such as "Big Nose" George, an infamous train robber who was hung in downtown Rawlins after he tried to escape from jail. In addition, there are antique guns, Indian pottery, and a fine assortment of arrowheads.

MILEAGE LOG

0.0 Junction Hwy. 230/Hwy. 70. Go north on Hwy. 230; shoulder, light traffic.

10.1 Junction Hwy. 130 West; head left on Hwy. 130. There's a shoulder.

12.4 Shoulder narrows, but still exists.

16.0 Cross Spring Creek.

17.0 Motel, grocery store on left.

17.3 Saratoga Museum on the right.

17.9 Junction Walnut St. **SIDE TRIP:** To reach the clear and odorless waters of Saratoga Hot Springs, make a right on Walnut St. and pedal 0.2 mile. Pass a Laundromat and café en route. The hot springs is separate from the swimming pool and showers and is open 24 hours a day.

18.2 Downtown Saratoga; you'll find all the amenities in this all-service town.

18.5 Cross the North Platte River.

19.6 Turnoff on the right leads via gravel road to Saratoga Lake City Park in less than a mile. Facilities do not include showers, although you can use the showers at the pool/hot springs complex.

29.7 Overland Trail marker on the left. The Overland Trail was a southern alternate route to the Oregon Trail. Used by both immigrants and the stage line, the Overland Trail was preferred by some who hoped to avoid conflicts with the Indians en route. Various stage stations were set up along the trail, located at 10- to 15-mile intervals. The stage stations allowed passengers to stretch their legs for about 15 minutes while a fresh team was being hitched up. Using this method, a passenger could travel between 100 and 125 miles in a 24-hour period.

38.7 Hwy. 130 ends; cross under I-80 and head west on I-80 West/Hwy. 287 North/US 30 West to Rawlins. Just ahead are a motel, café, and mini-market in Wolcott. There's a post office in town as well. A wide shoulder makes the heavy traffic a little more bearable.

44.9 Cross the North Platte River.

45.5 Exit leads to a rest area near the river, about 0.5 mile east, and Fort Steele Historic Site. If you exit, in 0.1 mile you can turn left and reach a mini-market/restaurant.

51.7 Exit 221; leave the highway via the East Sinclair offramp.

52.1 Turn right on unsigned Hwy. 76, which also leads to Seminoe State Park. There's a restaurant/mini-market at the junction. You'll find little traffic and a narrow shoulder as you head west to Rawlins.

53.5 You can try to hold your breath as you pass stinky Sinclair Oil Corporation on the right, but I doubt if you can do it.

54.1 Downtown Sinclair; obviously a quaint little community at one time, it is now nearly a ghost town. Except for a few residences, all that remains is a post office and Su Casa, the best Mexican restaurant around.

54.3 Su Casa on the left. People come here from all over to enjoy a variety of authentic Mexican dishes. Just past the restaurant, make a left on 9th St., which is also Hwy. 76. Continue on the paved road to Rawlins; no shoulder but little traffic.

58.6 T-junction; turn left and continue to Rawlins.

58.9 Cross under I-80. There's a shoulder now.

59.7 Motels, markets, and restaurants begin as you head into the all-service town of Rawlins by staying straight on US 30 Business.

60.9 Go right on US 30/US 287/Hwy. 789 toward Lander. (This is the junction of Cedar St. and 3rd St.) Keep straight if you need a bike shop, which is located downtown.

61.1 The segment ends at this point, where US 30 heads to the left. From here you'll have to decide whether to camp or motel it. US 30 leads west for 1.2 miles to two campgrounds. The camping areas are on gravel; there are showers and Laundromats at both. As you pedal toward the campgrounds, you'll pass a large number of inexpensive motels; there are restaurants and grocery stores as well.

Rawlins to Jeffrey City (67.9 miles)

Today's ride is filled with sparse vegetation, rolling hills, abrupt ridges, and nearby mountains. Trees are rare out here, and homes are just as much an oddity. Traffic will probably be light to moderate throughout most of the day, but there's a shoulder for worry-free riding. You'll pedal across rolling terrain where the total elevation gain is about 1,400 feet. Thus the day may be long, but it won't be difficult—unless you encounter headwinds, which are, unfortunately, prevalent in this part of the country.

Along the way you can relive a bit of history; the TransAmerica Trail intersects both the Oregon Trail and the Pony Express Route near Split Rock. As you gaze into the valley below, imagine that you are standing here sometime between 1812 and 1869, when the Oregon Trail served as the main route for westward expansion. Think of an estimated 350,000 hardy immigrants traveling through here in search of a new life in the West.

Or imagine the Pony Express, which raced through here from April 4, 1860, to October 24, 1861. Covering a 1,966-mile route from St. Joseph, Missouri, to Sacramento, California, the Pony Express riders took an average of ten days to make the trip. Each participant rode about 75 miles, swapping horses every dozen miles or so.

Sign at Split Rock Historic Site, Wyoming

The sun settles over Jeffrey City at the end of this segment. I'd heard that the virtual ghost town was depressing, but a lot of bicyclists spoke of having stayed there, so I tried it. In fact, the park isn't nearly as bad as the rumors had it. It's free, and there's a shelter, outhouses, and picnic facilities. Running water can be obtained from a nearby business.

SPECIAL NOTE: If you'd rather stay elsewhere, you can spend the night at the Lamont Inn, about 33 miles northwest of Rawlins, and then make up the difference the following day when you pedal about 100 miles to Lander. Or you could stay at one of two campgrounds prior to Lander, adding extra miles to both the next day and the next day after that.

MILEAGE LOG

0.0 Junction US 30/US 287/Hwy. 789 in downtown Rawlins. (Corner of 3rd St./Cedar St.) Continue north on 3rd St. toward Lander.

0.2 Junction I-80 Business/US 30/Hwy. 789 to Rock Springs on the left. Continue north on Hwy. 789/US 287 to Lander. It's four lanes as you head out of town; no shoulder.

0.3 Look for the Wyoming State Penitentiary (Old Frontier Prison) to the left. Tours available.

1.2 Road narrows to two lanes; there's a shoulder now.

1.9 US 287 Bypass merges onto the route.

9.4 Cross the Continental Divide—elevation 7,174 feet.

16.1 Begin crossing Separation Flats.

33.3 Enter Lamont—no services except for Lamont Inn.

33.6 Junction to Bairoil on the left via Hwy. 73—no services. Gravel road on the right leads to Lamont Inn in 0.2 mile. (If you'd rather camp outside than rent a room, you can do that too.)

Sandy Cummins owns and operates the inn, purchased in 1989 for a mere $1,000. Of course, she's done a lot of "fixing up" over the years. The inn, which was once a schoolhouse, serves bicyclists, hang gliders, and hunters as well as some passersby. Sandy claims the bikers seem to appreciate her hospitality most often, calling her place "an oasis." Breakfast is served daily from June 1 through November 1 when the inn is open for business. Sandy made biscuits the day I stopped in, and they were heavenly. Phone reservations are a welcome courtesy: (307) 324-7602.

35.1 The fourth Continental Divide Crossing to date—elevation is now 6,720 feet above sea level.

43.6 Wyoming Department of Transportation Building at Muddy Gap. Green grass and trees make this a welcome oasis for many a bicyclist.

44.7 Junction Hwy. 220 straight ahead. Continue left on Hwy. 789/US 287. There's a mini-market at the junction.

53.0 Entrance to Split Rock Historic Site; rest rooms and picnic area. There's a good view of the area from the lookout, which is 0.2 mile away.

Split Rock served as a well-known landmark for the pioneers, who used the unique rock as a navigational aid. They were guided by the rock for a day of travel as they approached from the East, and it remained in view as a checkpoint for another two days as they proceeded west. (The Sweetwater Rocks were here long before the pioneers or the Pony Express; geologists say they are some of the oldest rocks in the Rocky Mountain area.)

67.5 Motel on the left. This is Jeffrey City.

67.9 Lions Club Park on the right. There's a covered area for shade and shelter, picnic tables, grill, and chemical toilets. No water. The ghost town also offers a post office, a café, and a bar.

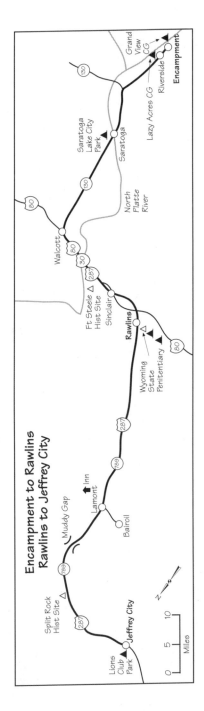

Encampment to Rawlins
Rawlins to Jeffrey City

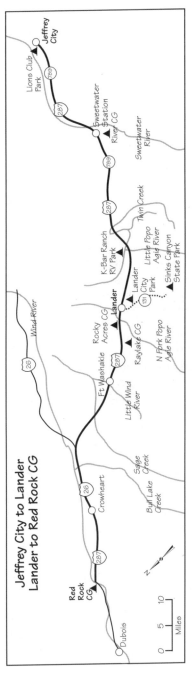

Jeffrey City to Lander
Lander to Red Rock CG

Jeffrey City to Lander (59.1 miles)

Whether you've grown accustomed to or are just plain tired of Jeffrey City, you need only get up in the morning, mount your bicycle, and head northwest through pronghorn country to see that the countryside only increases in beauty from here on. (Some of you are probably thinking that might not be too difficult to do. Take heart: it does get better!)

The terrain is similar to that of the previous segment, with lots of rolling hills and virtually traffic-free roads. As before, you should be prepared for strong winds. If the wind is fierce, I'd suggest getting an early start and covering most of your miles before midday. Sometimes the wind doesn't kick in until then; sometimes it blows all night long.

You'll pass the Sweetwater River, where you can look for the moose that live in the area. The scenes only improve as you head through red rock country en route to Lander.

Lander is a nice place for a stopover; in fact, it was recently named the fifth-nicest small town in America. Named after General F. W. Lander, government surveyor and builder of the first federally financed road in the West, Lander is one of Wyoming's oldest communities. Set along the banks of the Popo Agie River, at the base of the foothills of the southern Wind River Mountains, Lander offers Old West charm, with yearly cattle drives straight down Main St. (If you'd like to join a trail ride, cattle drive, or the like, contact Lander-based Western Encounters at (800) 572-1230.)

The first people to live in the area were native Americans. Now the Wind River Indian Reservation is a Lander neighbor and home to more than 6,000 Shoshone and Arapaho Indians.

Lander was the first permanent settlement in Wind River Country. Born as a frontier military outpost, it was later an important supply point for ranchers, Indians, and homesteaders. Its saloons were favorite watering holes for the likes of Butch Cassidy, who considered Lander home. To learn more about the region and its people, visit the free Pioneer Museum. One of Wyoming's oldest museums, it presents a fascinating collection of Indian artifacts and pioneer memorabilia.

Lander is also the gateway to Sinks Canyon State Park, located about 7 miles southwest of town. The canyon is definitely a good place to look for wildlife: deer, moose, elk, marmots, and others. One of the most fascinating mammals here is the bighorn sheep; a herd of about fifty roam the canyon and are often seen by visitors.

But the main Sinks Canyon attraction is the Sinks itself. The Middle Fork of the Popo Agie River disappears into a large cavern (the Sinks) and reappears about a quarter-mile downstream in a trout-filled pool (the Rise). Dye tests have determined that the water disappears for roughly 2 hours, emerging warmer and in greater quantities than when it vanished. Geologists don't know where the water goes for such a lengthy interval, but they speculate that there could be a myriad of channels and passages that hold the water up for an extended period as it circulates throughout—or perhaps a large underground lake slows the progress of the water.

MILEAGE LOG

0.0 Lions Club Park. The road is fairly level as you continue on Hwy. 789. I encountered construction from the 0.4-mile to the 8.9-mile mark. The highway department expects to have construction completed by 1996. Shoulders will exist at that time.

18.5 Cross the Sweetwater River and enter Sweetwater Station; River Campground (all amenities) on the left. Just ahead you'll see a mini-market (limited groceries) and a bar.

19.0 Junction Hwy. 135 on the right leads to Riverton. There's a nice rest area here, with rest rooms and picnic facilities. Begin a long, moderate climb.

25.5 Begin dropping off Beaver Ridge. It's a long, 5-mile descent with a 6 percent grade.

31.3 Bottom of ridge. You'll climb a short distance; then it's up and down for the remainder of the day.

40.5 Cross Twin Creek.

42.2 Cross Twin Creek again as you cycle through some beautiful red rock formations.

44.4 Cross Twin Creek again, then pedal through Onion Flats.

48.3 Cross the Little Popo Agie River. Just on the other side is a K-Bar Ranch RV Park, with all facilities, including a Laundromat, café, and cabins.

49.4 Junction Hwy. 28 on left leads to Rock Springs; Hwy. 789/US 287 leads right to Lander. Go right, passing a lake in less than a mile.

57.3 Enter Lander, a town of 9,000 people set in the Popo Agie Valley. There are all kinds of facilities, including a Laundromat and a bike shop, as you continue. The roadway changes to four lanes as you enter town. A shoulder still exists, but it's also a parking lane, so use caution.

57.8 Junction Hwy. 789 takes off to the right to Riverton. Continue straight on US 287, now called Main St.

58.0 Visitor center on the right.

58.2 Junction 3rd St. Turn left for 0.9 mile to Lander City Park, located at 3rd and Fremont. The park offers grassy sites, water, rest rooms, and picnic facilities. For shower, pool, and jacuzzi facilities, ride an additional 1.6 miles to Starrett Junior High, located on 9th St.

Lander to Red Rock Campground (61.3 miles)

Today's ride increases in elevation (you'll climb around 2,200 feet) and, more than that, in beauty. It begins with flat to rolling countryside through the Wind River Indian Reservation, whose people are an important part of the culture and economy of Wyoming. Eastern Shoshone and Northern Arapaho Indians live on the 2,250,000-acre reservation. The Shoshone claim the south-central, western and northern portions of the reservation, with settlements along the TransAmerica Trail at Fort Washakie, Wind River (just off route near Fort Washakie), and Crowheart. If you like pow-wows, there are much-recommended annual events at both Fort Washakie and Crowheart; beautiful Indian arts and crafts are also available at each settlement.

Teepees at Red Rock Campground east of Dubois, Wyoming

As you pedal the last portion of the ride through the Wind River Valley, you'll eventually emerge into a region of layered, sculptured cliffs and snow-capped mountains. Here the reds are like fire engines, the sculptures like those of the Grand Canyon. A campsite or room along the Wind River is one of the best ways to kiss another day good-bye.

MILEAGE LOG

0.0 Lander City Park. Head back to Main St.

0.9 Main St.; turn left and continue north through town. If you need a bike shop, turn left on 4th St. It's just off Main St.

1.1 Junction Hwy. 131 on the left leads to Sinks Canyon State Park. It'll take some effort to get there (it's about 7 miles uphill), but a local bicyclist says it's well worth the effort.

1.6 Junction 9th St. To shower, swim, or jacuzzi, turn left and go 0.3 mile to Starrett Junior High (there is an admission charge). To the right side of Main St. you'll see a bed-and-breakfast inn. There's a shoulder as you head out of town; level to rolling hills continue.

5.3 Mini-market and gift shop on the right.

5.8 Cross the North Fork Popo Agie River.

6.4 Rocky Acres Campground on the right; all amenities, including a Laundromat.

10.2 Turnoff to Raylake Campground on the left; it's 0.5 mile to the campground via Ray Lake Rd. The campground offers all facilities, including a café with native American food, snacks, and a gift shop.

11.7 Look for Ray Lake on the left.

15.3 Fort Washakie on the left; deli/market and gift shop.

17.0 Cross the Little Wind River and begin a long, moderate climb.

23.5 Cross Sage Creek.

28.6 Top of ridge.

32.6 Junction US 26 to Riverton on the right. Stay left on US 287 North/US 26 West to Dubois; shoulder. Now the highway parallels the Wind River, rising as you continue to climb to the campground.

35.0 Diversion Dam Rest Area on the left; water, rest rooms, picnic facilities. From here, there's a good view of Crowheart Butte in the distance.

36.1 Cross Bull Lake Creek.

46.3 Crowheart on the right; combination store, gift shop, and post office.

61.3 Red Rock RV Park/Campground/Motel on the right. In addition to the motel and all-service campground, which is located near the Wind River, there's a restaurant that serves lunch and dinner.

Red Rock Campground to Blackrock Campground (58.4 miles)

Today's ride is a marvelous one even though you climb about 3,700 feet. The day begins as though yesterday's never ended, with a jaunt along the Wind River and its stunning backdrop of gorgeous red rock cliffs known as the Badlands. Just east of Dubois (pronounced DO-boys), the rocks loom close for magnificent vistas and stunning photos. For the very best images, shoot early or late in the day.

The Badlands surrounding Dubois nourish more than just beauty, they radiate history as well. For instance, Crowheart Butte, which looms on the horizon about 30 miles southeast of Dubois, was the site of the Crowheart Butte Battle. The skirmish occurred in the middle 1800s, when the Crow and Shoshone Indians met here to decide who would hold claim to the Wind River Valley.

The Indians fought for three days and still the outcome was in doubt. Ultimately, the famed Shoshone chief Washakie agreed to meet Crow chief Big Robber atop the pancake-flat butte in a one-on-one fight to settle the dispute. Washakie was the victor. According to one legend, the Shoshone chief hailed his slain adversary by cutting out Big Robber's heart and carrying it on the point of his lance. Another story says that Washakie cut out the Crow chief's heart and ate it.

As you continue along, the fiery red rocks disappear, but the river remains and provides pleasant company on the ride to Dubois, a haven for about 1,000 residents. Set in the "upper country" of the Wind River region, Dubois rests at the 6,970-foot level. The Wind River Range is to the south of town, while the Absaroka (the majority say ab-SOR-uh-kuh) Mountains loom on the northern horizon.

Dubois is the jumping-off point for many activities, including fishing, camping, horseback riding, and hiking. One of the town's highlights is the National Bighorn Sheep Interpretive Center, where the primary exhibit, "Sheep Mountain," lures visitors into the world of the bighorn. This area boasts the country's largest bighorn sheep herd; if you're interested in coming back to Dubois to see the sheep in their natural habitat, you can book a winter tour to the Whiskey Mountain bighorn sheep area.

The scenery from Dubois up to Togwotee Pass is one of superb beauty. Although the shoulder all but disappears and traffic can be a bit annoying, the grade is easier than most (4 to 5 percent). Overall, this segment covers terrain that is gentle to moderate, although there are some steeper areas every now and then.

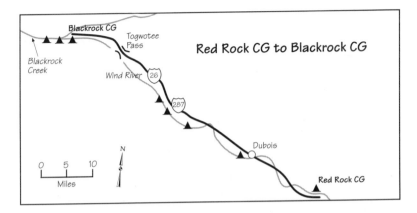

Red Rock CG to Blackrock CG

The first human trail through this region was made by Blackfoot, Crow, and Shoshone Indian hunting parties who followed the trail of elk, deer, and buffalo. Mountain men of legendary fame came next—men like Kit Carson, Jim Bridger, John Colter, and Joe Meeker.

In 1873, Captain W. A. Jones crossed these mountains with a Shoshone Indian, Togwotee, as his guide. Jones was working for the U.S. Army Corps of Engineers, on reconnaissance for a wagon road, when he made the journey. He named the 9,658-foot pass for his Shoshone guide. (Pronounced TOE-go-tee, the name means "lance thrower" in Shoshone.)

The ride up the east side is stunning, as is the ride down the west side, especially when the Grand Tetons come into view. While you're camped at Blackrock Campground, I suspect you'll be hard-pressed to think of a more spectacular place to pitch a tent than on a ridge overlooking the Tetons. (Note that water is not available at the cyclists-only campground, developed jointly by Adventure Cycling and the U.S. Forest Service. Fill up your bottles and extra containers 4 miles east before zooming down the hill to the camp.)

MILEAGE LOG

0.0 Red Rock Campground entrance. Continue northwest on US 26/US 287, a two-lane highway with a shoulder. It's a long, gradual to moderate grade along the Wind River, where red rock cliffs appear and then disappear as you pedal along.

2.0 You'll find a free spot to camp along the Wind River at this point; outhouse.

3.1 Exit the Wind River Indian Reservation.

3.3 Cross the Wind River.

5.6 Wind River access area on the left.

6.6 Wind River access area on the right.

6.7 Cross the Wind River as you parallel the Badlands.

7.6 Another Wind River access area on the right.

10.0 Cross Torrey Creek.

11.1 Wind River access area. Cross Jakeys Fork.

12.2 Motel on the right. Just ahead is a gas station with snacks.

13.4 Cross the Wind River.

14.0 Enter Dubois, "Valley of the Warm Winds." There's a hotel here and a bed-and-breakfast inn as you continue.

14.8 Bob's Bike Corral on the right, just a curb away from the TransAmerica Trail. Bob is the great-grandson of Mr. Schwinn, who began his famed business in 1895.

14.9 Road curves to the left as you head through downtown, where you'll find all services, including a Laundromat and a campground. The Circle-Up Camper Court offers all the usual amenities, including tepees to rent.

     If you're passing through in August, you might want to see if the annual Whiskey Mountain Rendezvous or the Dubois Volunteer Fire Department annual barbecue is in full swing. Another fun event is Museum Days, held in July.

15.6 National Bighorn Sheep Interpretive Center on the left. The Dubois Museum is next door.

15.8 Head out of town, passing two motels in less than a mile.

24.1 Wind River crossing.

24.3 Look for a store on the left; just past the store, begin a steep climb.

25.9 Top of hill near Hat Butte. Now the grade is easy to moderate.

29.2 Rawhide Ranch Campground on left. As of January 1995, the ranch was in the process of closing down. Enter the Shoshone National Forest, the first national forest in the United States, as you continue.

31.5 Wapiti Ridge bed-and-breakfast inn on left; Laundromat, showers, cabin rentals.

32.9 Tie Hack Memorial Wayside; rest rooms. This memorial is dedicated to "those great men, mainly of Scandinavian descent, who left their mark in the woods of the Upper Wind River Valley, the Tie Hackers." (Tie hackers were men hired to cut ties for the railroad around the turn of the century. Cut in winter, the ties—some 600,000 each year—were shipped about 100 miles downriver come spring.)

33.3 Triangle C Guest Ranch and Outfitters on the left; cabins and a campground with all services are available. There's also a Laundromat and a small restaurant. The well-known dude ranch boasts cabins from the tie-hacker days, and it was the early headquarters of tie-hack operations. Modern-day activities on the ranch include horseback riding, fishing, cookouts, and square dancing.

View of Tetons from Biker's Camp, east of Grand Teton National Park, Wyoming

34.5 Double Bar J Guest Ranch on the left. Horseback riding is available. Look for elk and moose as you continue up through the lodgepole pine and aspen forest. After a few miles, the aspens give way to Engleman spruce and some alpine fir; lodgepole pines remain.

34.9 Pinnacle Campground on the left. You'll find all amenities, including a pool and a store with limited groceries; there's also a café that is open for breakfast and dinner. From the campground, continue climbing a 4.5 percent grade.

37.7 Forest Road 515 leads to the Brooks Lake area and a campground in about 5 miles. The road is gravel and also leads to the old Brooks Lake Lodge, which is listed on the National Register of Historic Places.

38.1 Brooks Lake crossing. There is a good view of Pinnacle Butte as you head away from the Wind River. Just past the creek crossing is the turnoff to Falls Campground on the left. At this Forest Service facility, you'll find shady sites, water, toilets, and access to a very scenic waterfall.

39.6 Shoulder disappears or is narrow as you proceed.

41.0 The highway merges back along the Wind River for a short distance.

44.6 Wind River Lake/Sublett Peak to the right. You'll find good fishing and a picnic area with toilets if you're alert; it's easy to miss!

45.2 Reach Togwotee Pass and cross the Continental Divide once again. From the pass you'll see Two Ocean Mountain to the left and Breccia Peak straight ahead. There's an excellent 6 percent downhill from here, although portions of the journey consist of gently rolling hills as you descend along Blackrock Creek. On occasion expect a short climb.

52.8 If it's a clear day, this is a moment you will probably always remember: viewing the Tetons for the first time during your cross-country journey.

53.8 Scenic overlook on the right; rest rooms. The fabulous view of the Tetons from here is a must-see.

54.1 Togwotee Mountain Lodge on the right. You'll find rooms for rent, a restaurant, snacks, horseback riding, and pack trips. **SPECIAL NOTE:** If you're planning to spend the night at Blackrock Campground, be sure to load up on water here, since there isn't any at the campground.

58.4 Blackrock Campground on the left; picnic facilities and outhouses serve this cyclists-only camp. A grand view of the Tetons makes up for the lack of water.

Blackrock Campground to Grant Village (61.1 miles)

Today's ride could not be any better as the magnificent Tetons provide a rugged backdrop for the first portion of your ride. Although I ended the segment in Grant Village, making it a 61-mile day for those folks intent on generating miles, I encourage you to make this segment a two-day odyssey instead of a one-day event if you can.

Plan on taking the side trip to Jenny Lake; I doubt you'll be disappointed. The approach to the lake is magnificent, and reason enough to opt for the side trip, with the Tetons nearly close enough to touch. Mesmerized by the scene, I felt as though I could almost smell the mountains.

There's no doubt the Tetons—the result of sporadic earthquake-producing jolts—are one of the most dramatic ranges in the Rocky Mountains. Foothills are nonexistent; instead, the Tetons rise straight up from the valley known as Jackson Hole.

Twelve 12,000-foot-plus Teton peaks oversee the park. The highest—Grand Teton—spires more than a mile above the valley floor, scraping the heavens at 13,770 feet. Abode to a dozen or so mountain glaciers, the Teton Range is the youngest range in the Rocky Mountain system, yet it displays some of North America's oldest rocks.

Much of the range can be explored by hiking a network of trails, with some excellent ones accessible from Jenny Lake. While hiking or biking or simply sitting and enjoying the scenery, you should hope for and expect an array of wildlife encounters. The National Elk Refuge (located at the southeast end of the park) supports a winter population of anywhere from 7,500 to 9,000 elk, the largest herd in the world. In addition, the area also sustains bison, black bear, an occasional grizzly bear, deer, bighorn sheep, pronghorn, coyote, and many small mammals and birds.

As you head north from the Jenny Lake area you'll climb from one world of abundant animal life to another as you enter world-famous Yellowstone National Park. Think of Yellowstone and images of geysers spraying into the heavens, abundant wildlife, and breathtaking scenery probably come to mind. If geysers are your thing, you'll find plenty. In fact, more hydrothermal features exist in Yellowstone—10,000—than in the entire rest of the world.

Stunning scenes abound. Visit the park as spring blends into summer (late spring is best) and you'll see never-ending carpets of wildflowers, dainty blossoms blanketing the forest floor.

Tranquil scene of the Tetons from Oxbow Bend in Grand Teton National Park, Wyoming

And then there are the babies. A spring visit means bison calves kicking up their heels, elk calves staring at visitors with their brown, saucer-sized eyes, a newborn moose suckling, and a teddy-bear-like grizzly cub stopping to explore every little nook and cranny.

As you pedal through the park you may encounter wildlife on the roadway. The animals in the park are wild, and they can be dangerous too. Bison can injure, maim, and kill; in fact, every year about a dozen people are gored. But it's not really the bison's fault. Visitors see these big, cuddly creatures and forget that these fuzzy behemoths need their space. Most people are gored after crossing an invisible line into the bison's territory. To avoid such a tragedy, if a close-up photograph is your goal, use a telephoto lens and make images from afar.

Yellowstone is very busy in the summer; expect heavy traffic and little in the way of shoulders. Often the roads are in terrible shape. But help is on the way. A twenty-year, $300 million Federal Lands Highway Program was approved in June 1992. Although you'll still have to watch for potholes and rough road conditions, you will see an improvement in the years to come.

MILEAGE LOG

0.0 Blackrock Campground. Continue descending.

4.0 Blackrock Ranger Station is on the left just after crossing Blackrock Creek.

4.1 Hatchet Campground on the left; the national forest camp offers toilets, water, and picnic facilities.

4.4 Motel/restaurant on the left. Shoulder begins again.

6.7 Teton KOA on the left; all facilities, including a Laundromat, a mini-market, a hot tub, and a good view of the Tetons.

8.7 Cross Buffalo Fork River.

12.2 Moran Junction; post office.

12.4 Junction US 287 North, US 191, and US 89; head right toward Jackson Lake and Yellowstone. There's a narrow shoulder.

12.7 Grand Teton Entrance Station; fee area.

12.9 Fishing access (Snake River); rest rooms.

15.3 Oxbow Bend Scenic Overlook on left. This spot offers one of the best long-range views of the Tetons. It's also a great spot to look for moose, swans, pelicans, and many other species of animal life. On a clear day, the mighty Tetons are mirrored in the lazy Snake River, which meanders through the park for 27 miles. The river begins life in the wilderness, born of heavy snowpack near Yellowstone National Park, and enters Grand Teton National Park, where it integrates with Jackson Lake. The river flows out of the lake at Jackson Lake Dam, continuing past this point at Oxbow Bend.

16.6 Junction Teton Park Rd.; keep straight to continue on route. The terrain is level to rolling as you proceed; the highway sports a shoulder. **SIDE TRIP:** Teton Park Rd. leads to Jenny Lake and south to Jackson via the Teton Spur, a 35-mile one-way jaunt. See the end of this segment for further directions and information.

17.1 Wildlife overlook on left; abundant willows make this a good place to observe moose.

17.4 Cross Christian Creek.

17.7 Jackson Lake Lodge is on the left; restaurant and lodging available.

19.7 Cross Pilgrim Creek.

22.2 Colter Bay Village Entrance on left; mini-market/gift shop on the left at the junction. The village consists of a shower/Laundromat facility, a restaurant, lodging, and a market. The campground offers water, rest rooms, and hiker/biker sites.

23.0 Road on left leads to Leeks Marina/Restaurant.

30.3 Lizard Creek Campground on left; water, picnic facilities, toilets. Begin climbing a steep grade.

32.1 Top of hill; the road levels off some, then eventually descends past willows and pines.

33.1 Exit Grand Teton National Park. This is now the John D. Rockefeller Memorial Pkwy.; shoulder narrows and is non-existent on occasion. (The parkway is 82 miles long and was established on August 25, 1972, in recognition of Mr. Rockefeller's "generosity to future generations.")

37.3 Cross the Snake River.

37.4 Flagg Ranch Village on the left; lodging, restaurant, gift shop, market.

37.9 Flagg Ranch Campground entrance on the left; the usual amenities, plus showers and Laundromat. Begin climbing.

39.5 Snake River parallels road on the right.

40.0 Yellowstone National Park entrance; fee area. There are rest rooms here and a picnic area just beyond. Shoulders are rare as you continue.

41.1 Cross Crawfish Creek.

44.0 See the Lewis River Canyon on the right.

49.9 Cross Lewis River.

51.2 Entrance on the left leads to Lewis Lake Campground; water and rest rooms.

57.3 Cross the Continental Divide again, this time reaching 7,988 feet. You'll continue to climb a moderate, sometimes steep grade.

59.6 Turnoff to Grant Village on the right. **SIDE TRIP:** Make a right toward Grant Village, where there are all services. Best of all, Grant Village is located on the southwest edge of

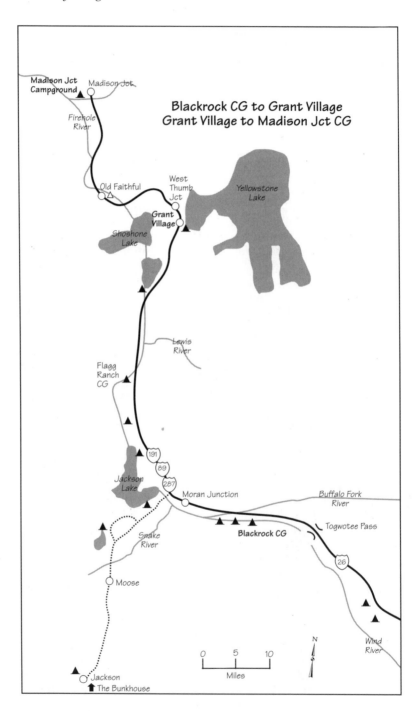

Blackrock CG to Grant Village
Grant Village to Madison Jct CG

Yellowstone Lake, the largest mountain lake in North America.

60.6 Turn left to reach the campground.

60.8 Showers/Laundromat on the left.

61.1 Registration booth for this super-large campground with hiker/biker sites, bearproof food boxes, water, and rest rooms.

Jenny Lake Side Trip

The side trip to Jenny Lake, mentioned above at the 16.6-mile mark, is no doubt one of the most beautiful jaunts across the entire country. Don't miss it!

The spur actually stretches from the junction to Jackson, descending slightly as you pass Jenny Lake en route to this artsy town. Jackson offers all the usual services, including a surprising array of bike shops considering the town's population of a mere 4,500; camping in and just outside of town; and the Bunkhouse, a hostel located at 215 N. Cache; (307) 733-3668.

Between Jenny Lake and Jackson you'll cycle through Moose, where there is a post office, a restaurant, a market, and a bike shop. In addition, there's a visitor center and the Chapel of the Transfiguration, a log chapel funded mostly through donations from a California family who summered on the dude ranches near Moose. Above the altar, a window frames the Grand Teton. It's an Episcopal church, and visitors of all faiths are most welcome.

0.0 Junction Teton Park Rd. and US 287/US 89/US 191; make a left, now riding Teton Park Rd.

1.2 Cross Jackson Lake Dam; there are rest rooms before and after the crossing.

3.1 Signal Mountain Lodge and Campground on the right; restaurant, mini-market, lodging. The campground has everything but showers.

4.2 Road on the left leads 5 miles and a total of 800 feet to Signal Mountain Summit. From the summit there's a magnificent view of the entire 40-mile Teton Range.

10.1 Jenny Lake Loop on the right; a sign promises "North Jenny Lake." Prior to this point there are several turnouts suitable for extended periods of Teton gazing.

11.7 String Lake Trailhead and parking area on the right. Now the one-way scenic road begins; bike lane.

11.9 Jenny Lake Lodge on left; restaurant and rooms where you can stay the night.

13.2 Beautiful view of Jenny Lake from this turnout.

13.8 Although the road continues to sport a bike lane, you can take the old one-way road, which is on the right. The road is now closed to motor vehicles.

Hidden Falls, Grand Teton National Park, Wyoming

14.3 Hiker/biker sites on left. There are bearproof boxes, water, picnic facilities, and rest rooms, but no showers. Continue 0.1 mile to the main parking area, where you'll find a registration box, store, and ranger station.

 Although this side trip ends here, it's easy to continue on to Jackson if you prefer. Continue south on Teton Park Rd., reaching Moose after about 8 miles and Jackson after another 13 miles.

Grant Village to Madison Junction Campground (37.2 miles)

Most of today's short ride passes through forest burned in the fire of 1988, which consumed more than one-third of Yellowstone's 2.2 million acres. Although stark and bare in some respects, the area is also filled with beauty. Is there a greater contrast than that between blackened trees and blue sky, or between scorched pine-cones and delicate wildflowers waving a rainbow hello?

One advantage to cycling through these burned areas is that it's much easier to observe wildlife. And wildlife there is, with more than 200 species of birds, a half-dozen game fish, and more than sixty species of mammals. The larger mammals include Yellowstone's famous bears—both the black bear and the grizzly—as well as moose, elk, deer, bison, pronghorn, bighorn sheep, coyote, and, on a rare occasion, mountain lion.

Mountain lions, also known as cougars, roam throughout much of western North America. Highly adaptable, the solitary animals reside mainly in mountainous regions.

Small mammals include two species of ground squirrels, three kinds of chipmunks, marmots, beavers, and porcu-pines. Bird life consists of the rare trumpeter swan, which nests there, as well as bald eagles, osprey, Canada geese, a variety of ducks, and white pelicans.

Yellowstone is the world's oldest national park. Explored in 1807 by John Colter, a former member of the Lewis and Clark expedition, it was established as a national park in 1872. The park's Old Faith-ful Inn has been around for a number of years as well; it was built in 1903–1904. With its gabled roof and Old World look, this marvelous hotel, made of hand-hewn logs, rates a visit whether or not you decide to stay overnight. Breakfast buffets are both scrumptious and reasonably priced, and rooms without baths are affordable even for the budget-minded.

The geyser Old Faithful has probably been the park's main attraction since it was first discovered. It's certainly the most famous today. At Upper Geyser Basin, where Old Faithful spouts regularly, you'll see many boiling springs. A sign at the visitor center posts approximate times of geyser eruptions.

As you continue through the park, you'll ride past several basins, all providing views of a number of different geysers.

As you travel from Grant Village to Madison Junction Campground, you'll encounter some steep grades as you pedal up Craig Pass, but the climbs are not unlike those you've experienced in recent days. In fact, the total elevation gain for the day is only about 1,500 feet. The gradual downhill to Old Faithful and then on to the campground at Madison is a real treat.

Although some cyclists proclaimed the roads the worst they had ever traveled, we had no problems. I did, however, take up most of my lane when necessary, blocking bulky RVs and speedy motorists from squeezing through when there just wasn't room. When there was ample room to pass, I moved over to the right to allow the vehicle that was tailing me to pass. My tactics worked: we got through safe and sound. Perhaps the motorists were even pleased, as no one honked in annoyance.

MILEAGE LOG

0.0 Campground fee station; head back to the main road.

1.5 Back to the main road. Turn right toward Old Faithful. There's a narrow shoulder as you continue climbing.

3.2 Junction Grand Loop Rd.; West Thumb is to the right. Keep to the left toward Old Faithful.

7.0 Divide Picnic Area on the right; rest rooms.

7.4 Continental Divide Crossing at 8,391 feet. There's a good downhill, then it's up to Craig Pass.

11.8 Delacy Creek Picnic Area on the right; rest rooms. The picnic area is just after Shoshone Point Overlook, which is on the left.

13.2 Cross the Continental Divide for the eighth time during your journey. The elevation here at Craig Pass and lily-pad-filled Isa Lake is 8,262 feet. Begin a long downhill to Old Faithful Inn.

15.4 Picnic area and rest rooms on the left.

20.9 The shoulderless roadway is now divided, with two lanes each way. **SIDE TRIP:** Offramp on the right leads to Old Faithful the geyser and Old Faithful the inn. It's 2 miles round-trip to the complex, which offers reasonably priced rooms, an excellent buffet breakfast, and, of course, Old Faithful. Actually, the Old Faithful area offers all services. Old Faithful is neither the highest, the largest, nor the most regular geyser in the park, but it's certainly consistent, and it's the most publicized as well.You can see it and several other geysers at Upper Geyser Basin.

21.4 The road shrinks to two lanes and a shoulder. Gradually descend from here to Madison Junction.

22.8 Cross the Firehole River, entering Biscuit Basin.

23.2 The shoulder disappears and the roadway is very bumpy as you make your way through Midway Geyser Basin. Use caution as you swerve to miss some tire-sucking potholes. Here the most popular attractions are Excelsior Geyser and Grand Prismatic Spring. Excelsior Geyser was once the most powerful geyser in the park; today its steam fills the entire basin at sunset. The geyser made its last appearance in 1888, when it sent a 300-foot column of water and steam heaven-bound. Grand Prismatic Spring is Yellowstone's largest hot spring, at 370 feet in diameter; it is also one of the prettiest.

27.2 Picnic area, rest rooms on the right.

27.7 Entrance to Firehole Lake Dr. on right as you continue through Lower Geyser Basin.

29.1 Enter Fountain Flats.

30.6 Nez Percé Creek crossing.

31.2 Turnoff to Fountain Flat Dr. on the left.

32.4 Picnic area on the left; rest rooms.

36.3 Exit to Firehole Canyon Rd. on the left.

36.6 Cross the Madison River as you reach the 6,806-foot level.

36.9 Junction to West Yellowstone; go left.

37.1 Exit to Madison Junction Campground; make a left.

37.2 Fee station; pop machine. Hiker/biker sites are located behind the station. Amenities include rest rooms, bearproof food boxes, and water; no showers.

MEETING "FAMOUS" BICYCLISTS

You never know who you're going to meet when you're off on a cross-country tour. I certainly never expected to meet Freddie Hoffman, the 1992 U.S. mileage champion.

My friend Carol and I had spent the second half of the day with our eyes glued on the Tetons. As we were about to enter the park we stopped off at a campground, deciding the view was too

Bicyclists chatting at Teton KOA, Wyoming

good to pass by. Besides, we desperately needed to wash our clothes, and the next night's camp was going to be primitive—in other words, no facilities!

Anyway, while we sipped diet cola and juice and munched on a snack, Freddie and another bicyclist, Jerry Augden, pulled up. Of course we started talking, and we stared in disbelief when Freddie told us he had ridden more than 200 miles on some previous days. Jerry shook his head up and down vigorously to indicate that this guy was telling the truth. Jerry admitted that Freddie could have easily blown by him, but Freddie obviously wanted company for a few days, so Jerry was trying his best to keep up.

Soon after we began chatting, I asked Freddie if he was the guy who had been written up in Bicycling magazine a few years back. He said yes and proceeded to give me a Big League Card, a baseball-like card with his picture on the front and the following information on the back. "50,000-mile-a-year Freddie: In 13 solo trips in 12 years (1979-1991) covering 42 states and totaling over 70,000 miles, Freddie's raised nearly $200,000 for 7 charities." His other hobbies include fund raising and weather watching.

I met Alan Thompson along the way, too, only this time I was in Twin Bridges, Montana. Carol and I had pitched our tents for the night before heading into town to do our laundry. En route we passed a lone touring bicyclist who didn't stop to talk. Instead, he waved, we waved, and that was that. After depositing our dirty clothes, Carol offered to finish up the process while I headed out to the fairgrounds to check out the free camping sites. On my way back through town, I encountered the lone bicyclist again. This time we stopped to talk, and I'll be forever grateful that we did.

Alan and I had actually had quite a lengthy conversation one night about nine months prior. Several reviews of my biking guidebook, Bicycling the Atlantic Coast, had appeared in a number of East Coast newspapers, and the review for a book by Alan Thompson, One Time Around, was published next to mine. After reading the review I contacted the publisher, and one night I heard from Alan himself. It seems he self-published the book, so I had inadvertently contacted him directly. We talked about riding and future plans, and I bought a copy of his book.

By the time I met Alan again in Twin Bridges, I knew something about him. He was a history teacher from Ohio, and his book and experiences had impressed me. It was a joy to have him join Carol and me for our ride into Missoula. One night we went out for Mexican food, and another night Alan prepared us the best spaghetti dinner of the entire trip. When we got to Missoula the three of us said a sad good-bye. Alan was off on a mountain-biking trip that would follow part of the route of the Lewis and Clark expedition, and Carol had to fly back to Kansas. I would dearly miss both of them.

Boothill Cemetery, Virginia City, Montana

MONTANA

I hate making enemies, so I don't want to go around saying that I think Montana is the loveliest state on the TransAmerica Trail. Instead, I'll let my bicycling companion, Carol Kaufman, say it.

"I love Montana!!" she announced again and again, to me and anyone else who would listen. No doubt about it, Carol did indeed think Montana was the prettiest state she visited during her five-week journey from Kansas to Montana.

Montana: for many folks, the state's name conjures up images of big things. Indeed, here in "Big Sky Country," the tall, rugged peaks of the Rocky Mountains search for the heavens in the western part of the state, and broad, wide plains seem to stretch to eternity in the eastern half.

Site of the last stand of Lieutenant Colonel George A. Custer and the final battles of the Nez Percé War, early Montana was Indian country. Although it has changed greatly—no longer do bison roam the plains and descendants of settlers outnumber Native Americans—the mountains, old gold-mining camps, wide, lonely places, and battlefields can still make those who visit feel close to the American frontier.

Some of my most prized moments in Montana were spent watching nesting ospreys at Earthquake Lake and absorbing a quiet sunset at Georgetown Lake. I also loved exploring Virginia City, one of the most delightful of all the small towns I encountered along my journey.

The fourth-largest state in the United States (only Alaska, Texas, and California are bigger), Montana is the largest state along the TransAmerica Trail. In addition, it is the only state in the nation drained by river systems that empty into the Pacific Ocean, Hudson Bay, and the Gulf of Mexico. The Clark Fork River drains into the Columbia River and on to the Pacific; the Belly, St. Mary's, and Waterton rivers search out Hudson Bay through the Nelson-Saskatchewan River system; and the Missouri River reaches the Gulf of Mexico via the Mississippi River.

Your six-day, 341-mile journey through Montana will allow you to explore the contrasts of the state, from the busy town of West Yellowstone to the forest setting atop the Continental Divide at Lolo Pass. As mentioned previously, I stuck to the TransAmerica Trail for most of my cross-country endeavor, although I did journey off route on several occasions. One of those occasions occurred at Twin Bridges, where I decided to go off

Old motorcycle, Virginia City, Montana

route and make my route the main route. My route offers shorter climbs, fewer miles, and captivating scenes. If you'd like to ride it, read the following segments: Virginia City to Butte, Butte to Georgetown Lake, Georgetown Lake to Chalet Bearmouth Campground, and Chalet Bearmouth Campground to Missoula. If you'd prefer sticking to the main route (which is now the alternate on my maps), use your Adventure Cycling maps for information regarding services and so on.

You can expect to ride some nice quiet roads through Montana; you can also anticipate hopping on the interstate once in a while. Wide shoulders make the interstates easier to bear, although you will still have to put up with the noise. Fortunately, you'll mostly ride through peaceful countryside. Note: Beware of heavy truck traffic on Hwy. 41 near Twin Bridges, where roads are narrow and shoulderless.

Montana's weather is as varied as its topography. Expect typical mountain weather with warm days and cold nights; be prepared for thundershowers and hailstorms, a common phenomenon on hot summer afternoons, especially in July and August.

Unlike most states, Montana permits bicyclists on the interstates. For more information, contact Carol Strizich, State Bicycle and Pedestrian Coordinator, Montana Department of Transportation, 2701 Prospect Ave., Helena, MT 59620; (406) 444-9273; email: cstrizich@state.mt.us.

Madison Junction Campground to West Fork Madison River (52.0 miles)

Today you'll enter Montana, the eighth state of your ten-state odyssey. But before doing so, you'll continue your journey through Yellowstone, paralleling the Madison River as you head out of the park.

The ride is an easy one, especially if the wind is at your back, as you'll climb a mere 900 feet and ride just over 50 miles. And you know what a short day means—plenty of time to explore the wide valleys you'll pedal through!

One or more trumpeter swans may sing you an operatic good-bye as you depart the campground, for the trumpeter, the largest swan in America, nests along the Madison River. The area west of the campground is also a good place to observe bison, although the animals move about the park and may not always be visible.

Earthquake Lake, Montana

West Yellowstone is obviously geared toward tourism, with an IMAX theater, a visitor center, a museum, two bike shops, and numerous services, including Greyhound (summers only), campgrounds, and the West Yellowstone Hostel, located at 139 W. Yellowstone Ave.; (406) 646-7745.

As you exit the town and head northwest, you're bound to remember that silence truly can be golden. Although it is not the loneliest stretch of highway across the country, it may seem so after you've spent the past few days in Yellowstone.

As you continue the mostly downward trend toward the West Fork Madison River, you'll see Hebgen Lake, where water sports are king. Several campgrounds provide access to the lake.

Later you'll pass Earthquake Lake, where snags poke out of the lake and ospreys nest close to the roadway. There are also beaver ponds and a willow-packed landscape that affords you a fine opportunity to observe moose.

I'd recommend a stop at the visitor center overlooking Earthquake Lake. Here you'll learn of the powerful earthquake that triggered a massive landslide on August 17, 1959. Amazingly, in the course of a minute over 80 million tons of rock plunged into the narrow canyon. Unfortunately, the debris blanketed more than just an open meadow; it buried some campers as well. In doing so, it completely blocked the Madison River, forming Earthquake Lake.

The Hebgen Lake Earthquake, as it is known, measured 7.5 on the Richter scale. The quake occurred when two faults—the Red Canyon and the Hebgen Lake—moved simultaneously, causing at least three blocks of the earth's crust to drop suddenly. All together, twenty-eight people lost their lives in the quake.

Astonishingly, the north shore of Hebgen Lake dropped 19 feet. As a result, lakeside cabins fell into the water, and seiches (huge waves), caused by the lake sloshing back and forth, crested over the top of Hebgen Dam.

From the visitor center, you'll continue along the West Fork Madison River, where you will spend the night in the pines, the song of the river no doubt lulling you to sleep. If you like fishing, be sure to cast out your line sometime during your stay.

MILEAGE LOG

0.0 Entrance to Madison Campground; a shoulder along the smooth, mostly downhill roadway makes the entire ride out of the park a most pleasant one.

7.9 Riverside Dr. on the right; the old, uncrowded highway parallels the new one and doesn't add any miles to the route.

This is a nice side trip along the river, although there isn't a shoulder.

8.9 Back to the main road.

11.6 Enter Montana.

13.8 Exit Yellowstone National Park and enter West Yellowstone. You'll find all services, including Laundromats and public showers.

14.0 Make a right on Canyon St., which is also US 20/US 191/US 287; four lanes, no shoulder.

14.3 US 20 takes off to the left; continue straight as you descend gradually via US 191/US 287 toward Ennis.

14.6 Hebgen Lake Ranger Station on the right. Stop here to pick up a free brochure describing the upcoming journey through the earthquake area. There's a wide shoulder now.

17.1 Baker's Hole Campground on the right. There are toilets, water, and picnic facilities.

17.7 Road on the left leads west to Madison Arm Resort and Marina in 5 miles. You'll find cabins, tent sites, all services, including a Laundromat, a store, boat rentals, and lake swimming.

18.0 Cross the Madison River.

19.1 Turnoff on the left leads 5 miles to Rainbow Point Campground; boat dock, toilets, water.

21.8 Cross Cougar Creek.

22.5 Cross Duck Creek.

22.7 Turn left on US 287 North toward Ennis. Shoulder continues, although it is not as wide. The terrain is mostly downhill for the rest of the day, although there are occasional climbs; some are moderately steep.

24.8 Cross Grayling Creek.

25.2 Good view of Hebgen Lake begins.

25.7 Enter the Madison River Canyon Earthquake Area, a 38,000-acre area set aside in 1960. As you continue, interpretive signs relate the story of the earthquake. It's time to use those brochures!

28.2 Yellowstone-Holiday Campground. You'll find cabins, tent sites, all the usual amenities, a Laundromat, and a store with limited items.

29.6 Cabins/saloon on the left.

30.9 Hebgen Lake Lodge/Motel/Café/Marina/Cabins on the left. They have hot showers too.

33.8 Motel/mini-market on the right.

36.0 Hebgen Dam on the left.

36.7 Cross Cabin Creek. Just across and on the right is Cabin Creek Campground, a Gallatin National Forest facility with toilets, water, and picnic facilities.

36.8 Campfire Lodge Resort on the left; cabins, snack items, café.

38.0 Cross Beaver Creek.

38.4 Beaver Creek Campground on the left. There are toilets, water, and picnic facilities.

39.5 Earthquake Lake (also known as Quake Lake) on the left. Look for osprey nesting atop some of the snags. The fish-eating birds are quite common in this region.

42.2 Turnoff on the right leads 0.1 mile to Earthquake Lake Visitor Center.

43.7 Leave the Madison River Canyon Earthquake Area.

43.9 Slide Inn Resort on the left; camping with all facilities, a Laundromat, and a convenience store.

44.4 There's a sign for Raynold's Pass on the left.

45.4 Junction Hwy. 87 on left leads south to Ashton, Idaho. Continue through Madison Valley.

50.9 Madison Valley Cabins on the left. Just beyond is the Grizzly Bar and Grill on the left.

51.7 Turnoff on the left leads to two West Fork Madison campgrounds. Follow the side road down to a wooden bridge and make a left, crossing the Madison River. Use caution: Some of the planks can "bite" skinny tires.

52.0 West Fork Cabin Camp. There are cabins, tent sites with all amenities, a Laundromat, and a store selling snack items. If homemade bread and cinnamon rolls sound like a breakfast winner, check out the store first thing in the morning and get them fresh out of the oven before someone else snatches them up. **SPECIAL NOTE:** There are two other campgrounds in the area, both managed by the U.S. Forest Service. To reach the Madison River Campground, head upriver for a mile via a gravel road. The closest USFS camp is very close to Cabin Camp. Just head straight for the river, which you will reach in 0.1 mile. There are tent sites, toilets, water, and picnic facilities at both campgrounds.

West Fork Madison River to Virginia City (48.5 miles)

The ride from the campground to Ennis is a downhill excursion through wide open country, where there's plenty of elbow room for the people and wildlife who live there. There's plenty of room for cyclists, too, as you pass through countryside framed by mountains and decorated with bald eagles that soar through the endless blue sky.

Be sure to enjoy the descent to Ennis, because from that point you'll face a long ascent up "the hill," as the locals call it. The

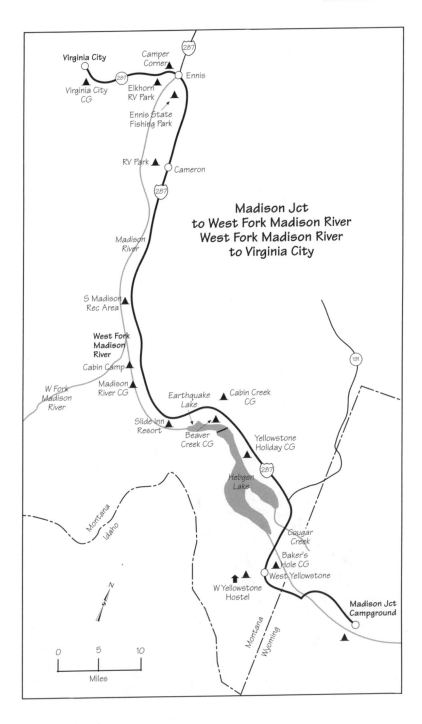

Virginia City

Camper
Corner

287

287 Ennis

Virginia City
CG

Elkhorn
RV Park

Ennis State
Fishing Park

RV Park Cameron

287

Madison Jct
to West Fork Madison River
West Fork Madison River
to Virginia City

Madison
River

191

S Madison
Rec Area

West Fork
Madison
River

Cabin Camp

W Fork
Madison
River

Madison
River CG

Earthquake
Lake

Cabin Creek
CG

Slide Inn
Resort

Beaver
Creek CG

Yellowstone
Holiday CG

287

Hebgen
Lake

Montana

Idaho

Cougar
Creek

Baker's
Hole CG

West Yellowstone

W Yellowstone
Hostel

Montana

Wyoming

Madison Jct
Campground

N

0   5   10

Miles

2,000-foot climb is steep—7 percent—and with a fully loaded bike it is definitely tough, but the descent into Virginia City is of equal gradient and perfect for those set on breaking a speed record. Although I wouldn't recommend it, I managed to clock 50.5 miles per hour, the fastest descent of my entire journey.

Whether or not you brake during the descent, you'll want to be sure to hit the brakes in downtown Virginia City, for the town is truly delightful.

Virginia City certainly made my very own top ten list of favorite small towns across the country. A blending of old and new, most of the buildings on the main streets are original, and many are furnished with thousands of authentic antiques. Just imagine a livery stable with everything but the horses, and a shoe store brimming with shoes from the 1860s.

Mosey down the boardwalk, bike shoes singing against wooden planks, and you're bound to feel as if you're back in the days of gold fever.

Bill Fairweather and his party discovered gold in nearby Alder Gulch on May 26, 1863. Although they tried to keep the find a secret, word got out and by June 6 of the same year, hundreds of

Virginia City, Montana

people were making a mad dash to claim Alder Gulch. Virginia City was born at this time, along with eight other Alder Gulch towns, and the area's population ballooned to 30,000.

Robbers arrived along with the gold miners and merchants, preying on travelers and stagecoaches on the lonely roads. The leader of the robbers was Henry Plummer, an obviously fast-talking man who got himself elected the legal sheriff of Bannack in the summer of 1863. Soon after, Plummer extended his reign to Virginia City, allowing the robbers, also known as road agents, to plunder and murder at will. Every honest citizen was at the robbers' mercy through the fall of 1863. The area's crime rate was far worse than that of today's big cities such as Los Angeles or New York.

By December 1863, however, many locals had finally had enough. They formed a group of vigilantes to clean up the problem, resulting in hangings for the sheriff, his two deputies, and five of the worst road agents. By March 1864, Virginia City was peaceful and mostly trouble-free.

The population declined in the early years of World War II, when gold production stopped. In 1944, Charles and Sue Bovey came to town as tourists. Astounded by the number of authentic, historic buildings in the town, they returned again and again and eventually ended up repairing the buildings, bringing them to life by dressing them with authentic interiors and merchandise.

Today Virginia City is the only U.S. city listed in its entirety on the National Register of Historic Places. Preserved by the Boveys, the lower end of town is celebrated by the National Park Service as being the largest group of first-construction buildings of its kind. At the present time, efforts are under way to make the city a National Historic Site, a part of the national park system.

Although the town has quieted down a lot since its rough-and-tumble days, there is still a lot to see and do. I think walking down the streets, browsing through the shops, enjoying the food, gazing at the sights, and talking to friendly folks is fun enough. But there is also the sunset from Boothill Cemetery, a blaze of dark reds and light pinks silhouetting the gravestones.

The world-famous Virginia City Players, the oldest professional acting company in the Northwest, put on summer productions of authentic melodrama in the Virginia City Opera House six days a week. Critics from Chicago and New York have acclaimed the performances here as outstanding.

MILEAGE LOG

0.0 Entrance to West Fork Madison areas. Head back across the wooden bridge over the Madison River and take the left fork.

0.2 Back to US 287; go left on US 287 North. There's a nice wide shoulder till you approach Cameron.

1.1 Rest area on the left located along the Madison River. Gentle downhill with only a rare uphill as you continue to Ennis.

8.1 South Madison Recreation Area on the left. You'll find a BLM campground via a gravel road. There's water and toilets at this fee area.

16.0 Turnoff on the left to West Madison Recreation Area. The campground (fee area) is 3 miles away; toilets, water.

16.1 Cross Indian Creek.

21.4 Shoulder disappears.

23.3 Enter Cameron; café, post office. You can also camp at the RV Park located behind the store. There are all amenities.

25.4 Road on left leads to Ennis Fish Hatchery. It's about 4 miles to the west. Here, six strains of rainbow trout produce an amazing 23 million eggs a year for stocking throughout the United States.

33.2 There's a motel on the left as you enter Ennis. A sign brags that Ennis is the home of "660 people and 11,000,000 trout."

33.5 Cross Odell Creek.

33.8 Road on the left leads to the Ennis State Fishing Park and camping area; toilets, water.

34.0 Cross the Madison River and enter downtown Ennis, where there are all services.

34.6 Fork; head left onto Hwy. 287 North. (At this point the highway forks and US 287 heads toward Helena, Hwy. 287 toward Virginia City.) There's an Antler and Wildlife Museum as you exit town.

34.7 Camper Corner on the right; all facilities, including a Laundromat.

35.1 Madison Ranger Station, Beaverhead National Forest, on the right. You'll see a Laundromat and a post office on the left as you continue. There's also the Elkhorn Store and RV Park with all amenities.

As you continue, you'll eventually begin climbing a steep grade, sometimes as much as 7 percent. The shoulder is nonexistent or narrow.

44.8 Top of pass. Now you'll zoom into Virginia City via a 7 percent grade. If you're stopping at the campground, be sure to slow down about a half-mile before town. If not, you'll just whiz by it, and you'll have to climb the hill again.

48.0 Virginia City Campground on the left; all facilities.

48.5 Downtown Virginia City, an all-service town with some groceries, although there is no actual market. If you've been camping out and would like to sleep indoors for a change, there are a couple of bed-and-breakfast inns to choose from. The Fairweather Inn, located in the middle of town, is a nice choice too.

Virginia City to Butte (74.3 miles)

Virginia City and Nevada City combine to make a twosome no one should miss. After you've thoroughly explored Virginia City, you'll descend to the equally western town of Nevada City. For a change in transportation methods, you can ride the Alder Gulch Shortline, a narrow-gauge passenger train that links the two towns.

Like Virginia City, Nevada City, which was established in the spring of 1863, is a town founded by those in search of gold. As the gold boom died, so did the town, and by 1876 Nevada City was fast becoming a real-life ghost town. A Mrs. Finney, who refused to sell the home in which she was born, was the only resident.

But once again, Charles and Sue Bovey came to the rescue, restoring the twelve original buildings that were left. In addition, Mr. Bovey moved his complete indoor village of real buildings, "Old Town," from Great Falls, where it was on exhibit at the fairgrounds, to Nevada City. He disassembled the village, which had already been taken apart and reassembled once before (the buildings were originally from Fort Benton), and moved it, weathered plank by weathered plank, to its present site in Nevada City.

Alan Thompson, round-the-world bicyclist and author of One Time Around, *standing atop Pipestone Pass, Montana*

Using a blurry photograph taken in 1866, Bovey rebuilt the front street of Nevada City to make it look as historically accurate as possible. Since 1959, additional historic buildings, some of which were originally built in Nevada City and were moved away in the 1870s, have been added to the town.

Whether or not you stroll through the town, you'll want to visit Nevada City Music Hall, one of the largest displays of its kind in the United States today. Here you'll see (and hear) an assortment of organs, player pianos, and much more. Included in the collection is a huge Gavioli organ made in Paris in the 1890s.

From Nevada City, you'll pedal north through Alder Gulch, where ugly mounds of overturned gravel stand as testament to a time of massive dredging operations. The dredges may have found millions of dollars in gold, but they left nothing but heaps of gravel in their wake.

The roadway sports little or no shoulder, and relatively light traffic, as you slowly descend through the small, pleasant towns of Alder, Sheridan, and Twin Bridges.

Twin Bridges was named for two bridges—one over the Beaverhead River, the other over the Big Hole River—built by two brothers, M. H. Lott and John T. Lott, who originally called the new town "The Bridges."

From Twin Bridges to Butte, the scenes continue to be wide and spacious—and definitely "Big Sky" impressive. At Twin Bridges, deterred by a major road construction project that had closed the road completely, I decided to go off route and make my route the main route. Adventure Cycling offered two options—one paved, one gravel. I talked to eastbounders who had ridden the gravel alternative and hated it; some fell, injuring themselves. Others rode the paved alternate route, which passes through Anaconda, Georgetown Lake, and Drummond en route to Missoula. They enjoyed it, but complained that it was certainly not the most direct route to Missoula.

Then I met an experienced, eastbound cyclist who spoke highly of a route that was similar but that angled southeast from Anaconda to Butte, then over Pipestone Pass and down to Twin Bridges. It offered shorter climbs, fewer miles, and beautiful scenery, making my decision easy. I hooked up with the main route back in Missoula.

If you'd prefer sticking to the main route (which is now the alternate on my maps), use your Adventure Cycling maps for information regarding services and so on. You can skip the next few segments, picking up on the Chalet Bearmouth Campground to Missoula segment, when my route and the main route converge at the 34.7-mile mark. From Twin Bridges to the merging point I rode a total of 178.1 miles. The main route from Twin Bridges to Missoula is approximately 224 miles; the gravel alternate is roughly 222 miles; and the paved alternate is about 246 miles.

From Twin Bridges to Butte you'll descend along Hwy. 41, which sports some truck traffic (the main route also suffers from truck traffic on Hwy. 41 in the opposite direction), then climb up Pipestone Pass, where the roads are virtually traffic-free. Scenes graced with pines and rock formations add to the climb, which is fairly easy.

From Pipestone Pass, you'll descend and occasionally climb to Butte, where authentic Mexican food at a local restaurant may force you to forgo cooking for the night. I was traveling with two other bicyclists at the time, and we all agreed it was the best Mexican food on the trip to date.

I hope the scrumptious food can make up for the view of Berkeley Pit, a 7,000-foot-long, 5,600-foot-wide, more than 1,800-foot-deep eyesore. It was the nation's largest truck-operated open-pit copper mine until 1982, when it closed. From 1955 to 1980, nearly 1.5 billion tons of material, including 290 million tons of copper ore, were removed from the pit. To learn more, visit Berkeley Pit or the World Museum of Mining, where there is a complete 1905 mining camp.

Described as "The Richest Hill on Earth," Butte began as a small mining claim and grew to booming proportions during the early 1900s. In 1917, a terrific fire killed 168 men in the worst hard rock mining tragedy in American history. Still, underground mining continued to thrive until the more cost-efficient open-pit method of extraction seized the spotlight.

Today, Butte wants visitors to have fun learning about its background while enjoying a number of activities. Highlights include the historic Uptown District, including the Copper King Mansion; and Our Lady of the Rockies, a 90-foot statue atop the Continental Divide east of the city. Begun in 1979 and completed in 1985, Our Lady was built by volunteers, is maintained by a nonprofit organization, and is visible from 100 miles away. In the summer and early fall, buses transport visitors to the top of the mountain three or more times a day.

MILEAGE LOG

0.0 Downtown Virginia City. Continue north on Hwy. 287 and descend to Nevada City; narrow or nonexistent shoulder.

0.5 Picnic area on the left.

1.3 Enter Nevada City, where in addition to the historic town there's a mining museum, a bed-and-breakfast inn, restaurants, and a music museum with the loudest organ in Montana.

2.2   Pass a sign for Adobetown, one of the Alder Gulch gold rush towns. A gradual descent continues to Sheridan.

3.5   Cross Granite Creek. From Nevada City on through Alder Gulch, you'll see a lot of evidence of mining, most notably ice-cream-scoop-like piles of gravel, some up to 50 feet high, lining the creek bed.

8.5   Alder KOA on the right; groceries and Laundromat in addition to the usual services. Enter Alder soon after. There's a mini-market, a post office, and a restaurant.

11.1   The road on the left leads 0.1 mile to a restaurant in Laurin (no other services) that is open for dinner.

11.6   Cross Alder Creek.

14.2   Sign for "Robber's Roost," an 1800s hideaway for infamous highwaymen and an assortment of thieves, on the left. Cross Ramshorn Creek just after.

19.0   Enter Sheridan. There's a Laundromat in this all-service town of 600-plus.

20.1   Cross Indian Creek, then it's a wonderful, moderate downhill to Twin Bridges.

23.1   Cross Wisconsin Creek.

28.1   A wide shoulder makes the ride more pleasant.

28.5   Enter downtown Twin Bridges. Look for a Laundromat on the right as you enter the town. You'll find all the necessities in this pleasant town.

28.7   Junction Hwy. 41. The TransAmerica Trail (now the alternate route) takes off to the left toward Dillon. **SIDE TRIP:** You can camp for free at the fairgrounds. To reach them, go left and cross the Beaverhead River in 0.1 mile. Just across the bridge is a rest area on the right; fairgrounds are on the left. There are rest rooms and water.

As mentioned in the segment introduction, I went off route due to construction and tales of an equally wonderful journey to Missoula. If you'd like to do the same, do not turn left at this point; instead, go straight on Hwy. 41 North and Hwy. 287 North toward Butte.

29.0   Stardust Country Inn and RV Park on left. They allow camping; all amenities.

29.2   The shoulder is narrow or nonexistent as you proceed through miles upon miles of vast ranchland. You should expect some truck traffic.

35.7   Cross the Jefferson River. As you go north, roller coasters begin, with emphasis on the downhills as you gradually descend.

37.5   Jefferson River Camp, located on the river, on the right; all facilities.

39.5   Enter Silver Star; a market/post office is on the right.

43.2 Junction Hwy. 55 and Hwy. 41. Hwy. 55 leads to Whitehall and I-90. Make a left and continue on Hwy. 41 North toward Butte. Climb gradually with an occasional steep grade. The road is shoulderless; traffic is light.

50.7 Reach the top of a long hill; then it's a fast descent to the next junction.

51.7 Junction Hwy. 2; head left toward Butte. The roadway is uncrowded and scenic as you travel through the pines and willows, ascending the roughly 6 percent grade. Fortunately, the slope eases up a bit before reaching the top of Pipestone Pass.

58.2 Toll Mountain Rock Shop on the left.

61.3 Pipestone Pass, elevation 6,418 feet.

64.0 Thompson Park on the left; picnic facilities, toilets.

66.0 Thompson Park (yes, they are two separate entities) on the right. Just ahead is junction CR 375. Now the road descends, with an occasional steep grade through Butte Valley.

69.2 CR 393 junction on left; keep right on Hwy. 2 West. There's a shoulder.

70.8 Wal-Mart and all other services are available as you enter the town of Butte. In addition, there are bike shops, Laundromats, a mall, and Greyhound bus service.

72.0 Visitor center on right.

72.2 Turn left on Dewey Blvd., the roadway just prior to I-90. Shoulder continues.

73.1 Post office on the right.

73.2 Turn right on City Rd., which turns into Lexington and then into Kaw.

73.7 Cross over I-90.

74.3 Butte KOA on the left; in addition to the usual amenities there is a pool, a Laundromat, cabins, groceries, and prepared foods. **SIDE TRIP:** If you like great Mexican food, continue north on Kaw for 0.3 mile. Make a right on Front St. and pedal 0.4 mile to Ranchos Los Arcos.

Butte to Georgetown Lake (43.0 miles)

Today's segment is quite short, allowing time to explore Butte if you are so inclined. Others may want to get on the road early, spending their extra time in the beautiful Georgetown Lake region.

Anaconda is your first major stop en route to the Georgetown Lake area. Founded in 1883 by Marcus Daly, one of the famous Montana Copper Kings, the historic smelter city offers a variety of things to see and do. For instance, you can tour the historic district or see the copper smelting display at the Copper Village Museum.

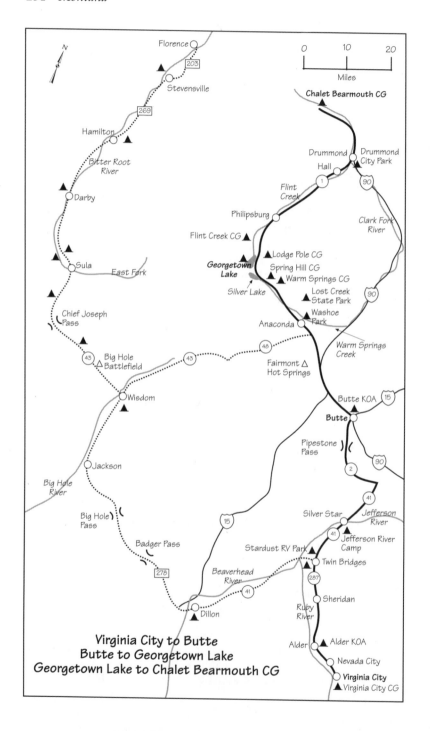

Florence

203

Stevensville

269

Hamilton

▲

Bitter Root River

0   10   20

Miles

Chalet Bearmouth CG

Drummond   Drummond City Park

Hall   90

1

Flint Creek

Clark Fork River

Darby

Philipsburg

Flint Creek CG ▲

Lodge Pole CG ▲

Georgetown Lake

Spring Hill CG

Sula   *East Fork*

Silver Lake   ▲ Warm Springs CG

Lost Creek State Park

90

Chief Joseph Pass

Washoe Park

Anaconda

Warm Springs Creek

43   Big Hole Battlefield

43   48

Fairmont △ Hot Springs

Wisdom   Butte KOA   15

Butte

Pipestone Pass

2   90

Jackson

Big Hole River

41

Silver Star   *Jefferson River*

41   Jefferson River Camp

Big Hole Pass

15

Stardust RV Park

278

Beaverhead River

▲ Twin Bridges

287   Sheridan

41   *Ruby River*

▲ Dillon

Alder   ▲ Alder KOA

Nevada City

Virginia City

▲ Virginia City CG

Virginia City to Butte
Butte to Georgetown Lake
Georgetown Lake to Chalet Bearmouth CG

The Washoe Smelter was the world's largest copper smelter. The 585-foot-tall brick smokestack and many buildings from this era are visible on the self-guided walking tour of the city. In the summer, bus tours offer an easy way to see the sights.

As you bicycle from Butte to Anaconda via the interstate, a wide shoulder and an easy downhill gradient add to the pleasure of scenery, which remains wide and open.

From Anaconda you'll pedal west and then north to Drummond by way of Hwy. 1, better known as the Pintlar Scenic Route. A high-altitude highway, it connects the copper-mining town of Anaconda with the ranching town of Drummond. Along the way you'll pass Georgetown Lake, deemed one of the best fishing lakes in North America. Lucky anglers hook brook and rainbow trout, kokanee salmon, and other species.

Nestled on top of Flint Creek Pass, Georgetown Lake is cloaked by the Flint Creek Mountain Range to the north, Flint Creek Valley to the west, and the Deer Lodge Valley and Anaconda to the east. The man-made lake comprises approximately 2,780 acres of surface area enveloped by 19 miles of shoreline.

The climb up Georgetown Mountain is a long, mostly gradual climb except for the last 3 miles to Silver Lake, where the grade is a bit steep but not thigh-busting. Both lakes are gorgeous, the mountain backdrops stunning. Here rock hounds have found everything from garnets and sapphires to fossils, crystals, and gold. As you explore this pine- and willow-covered region, look for moose and other animal life.

MILEAGE LOG

0.0 KOA Entrance; continue north on Kaw St.

0.3 Make a left on Front St.; shoulder.

0.5 Make a right on Montana St. There's a motel, restaurant, and market here.

0.8 Great Divide Cyclery on the left. Just past the bike shop, turn left on Iron St. which becomes I-15; shoulder. **SIDE TRIP:** The historic downtown area is straight up Montana St. Ride up the hill for a mile or so and explore Park, Broadway, Granite, and Quartz streets.

2.4 Merge onto what is now I-15 and I-90. There's a wide shoulder except for a bridge crossing in 0.9 mile. Terrain is mostly downhill, with an occasional uphill.

4.3 Restaurant, motel.

5.2 Exit to Dillon and Idaho Falls via I-15 South on the right.

12.8 Junction Hwy. 441 to Fairmont on the right.

16.0 Pintlar Scenic Route/Hwy. 1 West Exit 208 on the right. After exiting, turn left toward Anaconda and Georgetown Lake Recreation Area.

Flowers at Georgetown Lake, Montana

18.2 Road on the right leads to Opportunity.

19.3 Fairmont Hot Springs turnoff on the left.

20.9 Road on the left leads to Wisdom in 50 miles. (One of the alternates merges with my route at this point.)

22.1 Turnoff on the right via Hwy. 48 leads to Lost Creek State Park. **SIDE TRIP:** Located about 8 miles away, Lost Creek State Park offers camping with water, toilets, and picnic facilities available. Highlights include spectacular limestone cliffs that rise 1,200 feet above the canyon floor, a waterfall, and the opportunity to observe Rocky Mountain bighorn sheep and Rocky Mountain goats.

23.4 Gas station/mini-market on the right as you enter Anaconda. Continue past all services, including a Laundromat.

24.7 Visitor center on the left via Cherry St. The visitor center is housed in a replica of a railroad depot and features a train display.

24.8 Turn right on Main St.

25.0 T-junction; turn left on N. Pennsylvania St.

25.3 Washoe Park Fish Hatchery on the right.

25.4 Washoe Park and Pool on the right. Bicyclists camp and shower for free. Check in with Washoe Park Director Bill Hill, 563-3408, before camping. If you'd prefer staying at a campground where there are laundry facilities, try nearby Big Sky RV Park at 200 N. Locust.

25.7 Make a left on unsigned street (Sycamore St.).

25.8 Make a right on Park Ave. (Hwy. 1). Hwy. 1 was called Commercial St. when you first entered Anaconda. Continue past a market as you head out of town.

26.7 Road narrows from four lanes to two; shoulder remains. Road climbs gradually for the first 10 miles out of town; then the grade gets steeper as you pedal up the mountain.

26.8 Restaurant on the left.

27.1 Cross Warm Springs Creek.

35.6 Spring Hill Picnic Area exit on the left. It's 0.2 mile via a gravel road.

35.7 Road to Warm Springs Campground and Picnic Area on the right. It's gravel for 2.5 miles by way of Forest Road 170. Water, toilet, no fee.

36.0 Spring Hill Campground on the right; water and toilets.

38.6 Silver Lake on the left. The roadway is level or slightly downhill now.

40.7 Motel/restaurant on the right.

40.8 Denton's Point Rd. on the left leads to motels, campgrounds, and cafés. The campgrounds offer all services; some also provide a Laundromat and store.

41.0 Shoulder disappears.

41.2 Georgetown Lake on the left.

41.6 Grassy Point Boat Launch on the left; restaurant, picnic area. The road on the right leads to Seven Gables in 0.1 mile, where you'll find a motel/bar.

43.0 Lodgepole Campground on the right; toilets, water, fee area.

Georgetown Lake to Chalet Bearmouth Campground (54.6 miles)

This segment continues through what is known as Gold West Country. You'll enjoy superb scenes, the quaint town of Philipsburg, the cattle-ranching town of Drummond, where some structures date back to the 1880s, and your home for the night, the Chalet Bearmouth Campground.

You'll head mostly downhill today, a real treat to say the least, with a 3,000-foot descent in just over 54 miles. Be prepared for a little climbing, however, as you'll ascend a total of about 500 feet. Most of the roads sport a shoulder. From Drummond to the campground you'll parallel the interstate by way of a lightly traveled frontage road that winds along the Clark Fork River to day's end.

The delightful little town of Philipsburg is definitely worth a stop. Known for its wildlife, winter snow sports, and many historic buildings, Philipsburg is located in the heart of Granite County. Prior to the silver crash in the 1890s, it was a booming mining town. Today it could be called Sapphire City.

Montana is well-known for its sapphires, and Granite County is one of the best places in the world to find them. If you don't have time to hunt for the precious stones, however, you can "hunt" in the Sapphire Gallery instead. Housed inside one of Philipsburg's historic buildings—Huffman Grocery—the Sapphire Gallery is a real gem, with one of the largest selections of sapphire jewelry in the western United States. And if you can't afford the finished product, you can always buy a bag of gravel and search for your own gemstone in the indoor mining room, the only such room in the world.

MILEAGE LOG

0.0 Campground entrance. Continue north on Hwy. 1.

0.4 Georgetown Lake Rd. and dam on the left. Begin steep descent through a scenic canyon with steep walls, a cascading river, and a thick blanket of pines.

3.4 Turnoff to Flint Creek Campground on the left. The campground is a mile southeast on gravel Forest Road 1090; toilets, water.

  The grade lessens to a gentle downhill with an occasional climb as you continue. There are willows in the area as you descend through Flint Creek Valley to Drummond.

3.8 Shoulder begins again.

4.7 Hwy. 38 on the left leads to Skalkaho Pass and Falls and on to Hamilton. Stay straight to Philipsburg.

8.4 Fred Burr Creek crossing.

9.2 Philipsburg turnoff. Turn right and head into town via a road that will get you back to the highway without backtracking. (You can skip the town, but I wouldn't recommend it.)

10.0 Philipsburg Ranger Station, Deerlodge National Forest, on the left.

10.6 Philipsburg Park on the left with picnic facilities, rest rooms, water.

11.2 Junction Broadway Ave. in downtown Philipsburg. Make a left to continue on route. Philipsburg offers a museum, a visitor center, a post office, the Sapphire Gallery, a market, restaurants, and shops.

Farm scene off Hwy. 1, south of Philipsburg, Montana

11.8 Motel and Burg Camper Park on the right.
12.0 Grocery store on the left.
12.1 Back to Hwy. 1; make a right toward Drummond. Soon after turning you'll pass the junction for CR 348.
22.3 Shoulder disappears.

22.5 Turnoff on right to Maxville. A gravel road leads 0.1 mile to a bar and nothing else.

23.0 Boulder Creek crossing.

27.3 Cross Flint Creek.

31.6 Junction Hwy. 513 on the left and Hwy. 512 on the right in downtown Hall, where there is a post office, market, bar, and combination auto parts/convenience store.

36.5 There's a shoulder once again.

37.1 Turn right at the "Camping" sign and head into Drummond. You'll see the interstate just ahead before turning.

37.5 Drummond City Park on the right. Located near the Clark Fork River, the park has picnic facilities, water, rest rooms.

37.9 T-junction in downtown Drummond, billed as the "Bull Shipper's Capital of the World." If you go to the right, you'll find a motel, restaurant, market, and post office within 0.3 mile.

To continue on route head left, passing a Laundromat, restaurant, and motel.

38.4 T-junction; make a right and head under I-90. Do not ride onto the interstate unless you want to; a frontage road offers a splendid ride through the river valley. The road is level or descends along the river, although there are some short, steep climbs.

54.6 Chalet Bearmouth Campground on the left, along the Clark Fork River. You'll find all facilities, including a gift shop with snacks, a restaurant/bar, a Laundromat, and a motel and lodge.

Chalet Bearmouth Campground to Missoula (35.4 miles)

Missoula, home of Adventure Cycling Association, is a special treat for most of the cyclists riding the TransAmerica Trail, for a variety of reasons. Many of us have heard of the free cookies the staff so willingly gives out, some of us need more maps or other supplies, and some of us just want Greg Siple, the association's art director, to take our picture, hopeful that we'll appear in a future issue of *Adventure Cyclist* magazine.

This segment is a short one, with plenty of time for exploring the university town of Missoula, with its fun downtown area and friendly hostel. If you're in town on a Saturday morning or a Tuesday night, be sure to visit the farmers market at the end of Higgins St. Fresh produce and delicious, mouth-watering baked goods satisfy the hungriest of tummies.

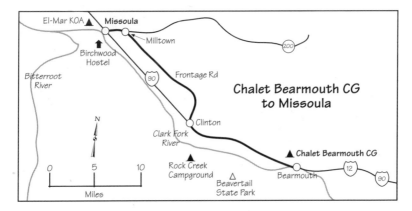

Located along the banks of the Clark Fork River, the area was explored by Lewis and Clark in the early 1800s and was named Nemissodatakoo by explorer David Thompson in 1812. The name is fitting, for it is a Flathead Indian name meaning "by or near the cold chilling waters."

Missoula, the Garden City, is and has always been a major commercial center in western Montana. Nestled near the head of five valley systems—the Missoula Valley to the west, the Hellgate and Blackfoot valleys to the east, the Bitterroot Valley to the south, and the Flathead-Jocko Valley to the north—the first settlement was established in 1860 at the Hellgate Trading Post.

There's a lot to do in Missoula. Many of the buildings are listed on the National Register of Historic Places (pick up a free "Historic Missoula" map for specifics). In addition, you'll find a cultural treat on every corner, with art galleries, theaters, and live music options ranging from the Missoula Symphony and Chorale to bands playing in local bars.

The ride to Missoula, where there are all amenities, including bike shops and Greyhound bus service, is nearly as fun as the city itself. It's a true downhill pleasure along the Clark Fork River, where pines, aspens, and a variety of other trees hug the valley. You'll experience little traffic save on the interstate, where there is a wide shoulder.

MILEAGE LOG

0.0 Campground entrance. Continue left on Frontage Rd. No shoulder.

0.5 Road curves over the Clark Fork River and merges with I-90 in 0.1 mile. Head right onto I-90 West/US 12 West; wide shoulder. It's mostly downhill to Missoula, with an occasional short ascent. You'll climb a measly 500 feet today.

1.2 Cross the Clark Fork River.

8.1 Beavertail exit. This road leads to Beavertail State Park in 0.7 mile; toilets, water, fee area.

12.5 Rock Creek Rd. exit. **SIDE TRIP:** In 0.2 mile head left over I-90. Pedal another 0.1 mile to Rock Creek Lodge/Restaurant/ Bar/Gift Shop/Campground and free Wild West Museum. This is the home of the annual Testicle Festival, held in late September. In 1993, over 7,000 people attended the wild and raunchy eleventh annual event.

17.4 Exit to Clinton. To hop back on Frontage Rd., exit I-90 at this point.

Testicle Festival signs at Rock Creek Lodge, east of Missoula, Montana

17.5 A bridge leads to the left over I-90 to Clinton, where there is a market.

17.6 Turn right, then make a quick left on Frontage Rd. No shoulder, little traffic.

24.5 Steak house/casino on right.

27.7 T-junction at Hwy. 200; make a left onto Hwy. 200 West; shoulder.

27.9 Enter Milltown, where there's a mini-market and a post office.

28.1 Cross the Blackfoot River. Hwy. 200 curves to the right. To the left is I-90. You can keep right on Hwy. 200, a shoulderless road bearing more traffic, or continue on shoulder-blessed I-90. I rode Hwy. 200, but I think that it might have been better to hop on I-90. Hwy. 200 merges with I-90 in about 4 miles.

29.3 Restaurant on the right.

32.0 There's a motel and a couple of restaurants.

32.4 Merge onto I-90.

33.9 Exit Van Buren St. (Business Loop I-90 and US 12) and head into downtown Missoula.

34.1 Stop sign. Make a left on US 12 West.

34.2 Junction Broadway. A visitor center and the University of Montana are straight ahead. Make a right to continue on route.

34.6 Junction Pattee St. Adventure Cycling is to the right in 1 block, at the corner of Pine.

34.7 Junction Higgins St.; turn left on Higgins St., merging back onto the TransAmerica Trail.

If you'd rather camp than stay at the upcoming hostel, the Missoula El-Mar KOA has tent sites. It's about 3 miles west on Broadway, then 0.2 mile south on Reserve St. to Tina Ave., where you'll go northwest about 0.5 mile. You'll find all facilities, including a Laundromat and store.

35.0 Cross the Clark Fork River.

35.1 Turn right on S. 4th St. W.

35.4 Birchwood Hostel on the left at the corner of 4th and Orange. Excellent accommodations include a kitchen and Laundromat; grocery store nearby. Staying overnight requires performing one chore a day. Contact Ernie Franceschi, (406) 728-9799, for reservations.

Snake River at Oxbow Dam, Idaho

IDAHO

Cycling through the eastern part of Idaho may lead you to believe that the state contains nothing but mountains and forests and rivers. Not that one should complain! Idaho is a skier's paradise and a land of mountain ranges, steep canyons, plunging gorges, numerous lakes, and roller-coaster-like whitewater rapids. But the state is also famous for its potatoes; it leads the nation in spud production. (Its other crops include sugar beets and wheat.)

Idaho was first known, however, for its gold. The valuable metal was discovered here in the 1860s, sending thousands of gold dreamers flocking into the area. Farmers and ranchers emerged on the scene as well. When the mines were worked out, the miners moved on, but the farmers and ranchers remained and founded a state.

Idaho is a potpourri of geographical regions, with the Rocky Mountains forming the state's largest land region. (About fifty peaks soar above the 10,000-foot level in the Bitterroot Range.) Fortunately for bicyclists, an assortment of plateaus and valleys lies among the mountains, providing for fairly easy riding.

You'll spend five days and 283.4 miles pedaling through the Gem State, crossing the Bitterroot Range, the Clearwater Mountains, and the Salmon River Mountains en route to Hells Canyon. Fortunately, more than half of those days are spent hugging the banks of one gorgeous river after another. And you'll spend nights one and two at scenic campgrounds where the river massages tired muscles, washes off road grime, and eventually sings tired campers to sleep. (These same rivers probably helped ease the worries of the Lewis and Clark expedition when they passed through the region in 1805 and 1806. The TransAmerica Trail parallels a small portion of their historic path.)

As you continue southwest through the state, you'll cross a high plateau area en route to Grangeville. Next, you'll ride up and over White Bird Hill traveling through sections of the Nez Percé National Historic Park. From that point you'll descend a 7 percent grade to the Salmon River, which you'll parallel until reaching the whitewater-rafting mecca known as Riggins.

The Salmon River, a branch of the Snake River that drains most of the state, is often referred to as the "River of No Return." The term came about because early-day travelers could not maneuver upstream against its violent current and rapids.

Adventure Cycling Association gives an extra warning to those cycling US 12 from Lolo, Montana, to Kooskia. Although I experienced

Farm scene south of Council, Idaho

little traffic for the entire distance, you should be prepared for heavy traffic, especially truck traffic. The road is narrow and often shoulderless, so use caution and stop at the side of the road to let passing trucks and RVs by if necessary.

Your ride through Idaho will likely be fraught with high temperatures, especially along the Snake River canyon, where daytime temperatures in excess of 100 degrees are not uncommon. Fortunately, the nights are usually cool and the humidity is low, making it nice for sleeping. Mountains block the moist Pacific winds, so you can expect a relatively dry journey through Idaho.

As in Montana, you can ride the interstate if you are so inclined. For more information on bicycling in Idaho, contact Bicycle Planner, Idaho Department of Transportation, P.O. Box 7129, Boise, ID 83707; (208) 334-8272; website: www.idoc.state.id.us/itd/bike.html.

Missoula to Whitehouse Campground (61.0 miles)

Today's ride begins in Missoula, a university town of 40,000, and ends at Whitehouse Campground, a quiet, scenic spot with a river playing along its banks and pines providing shade. Best of all, you'll continue to more or less follow a portion of the Lewis and Clark Trail and the Nez Percé Trail as you enter Idaho, the ninth state in your journey.

Amazingly, Meriwether Lewis and William Clark, the first white men to enter Idaho, traveled almost twice the miles that you'll cover in your cross-country quest. In just over twenty-eight months—from May 1804 to September 1806—the two explorers chocked up more than 8,000 miles on their expedition, which established U.S. claims and paved the way for future settlement of the West. Traveling by foot, on horseback, and by boat, the pair began their journey in St. Louis, Missouri, and reached the Pacific at the mouth of the Columbia River, the present-day dividing line between Oregon and Washington. More than a quarter of their momentous journey was spent in Montana.

As the two brave, tireless men searched for a water route to the Pacific Ocean, they kept detailed journals of the people and natural wonders of the West. In their travels they discovered 122 animals and 178 plants, including Montana's state tree, the ponderosa pine. They also wrote of Montana's state fish, state bird, state grass, and state flower: the cutthroat trout, the western meadowlark, bluebunch wheatgrass, and the bitterroot, respectively.

From Missoula you'll travel south to Lolo, then west as you haul your belongings up Lolo Pass via US 12. US 12 parallels the historic Lolo Trail, which was used by the Nez Percé Indians as a buffalo trail and by the Lewis and Clark expedition en route to the sea. Interpretive signs along the way help to describe this grand adventure. An excellent map, "Lewis and Clark Across the Lolo Trail," is available by contacting the U.S. Forest Service, Clearwater National Forest, 12730 Hwy. 12, Orofino, ID 83544. Write to the same address for more information regarding the Nez Percé National Historic Trail.

The Nez Percé, or Nee-Me-Poo as they called themselves, were a generous people and were longtime friends of the whites, including missionaries, fur trappers, and Lewis and Clark. Unfortunately, like all native Americans, they were forced from their homeland. Those who didn't surrender were hunted down by the Army, which is how the Nez Percé War began.

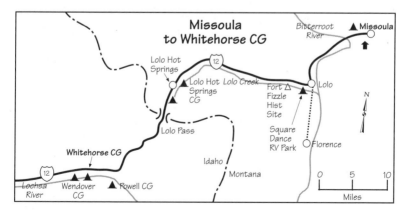

A band of some 750 Nez Percé Indians—250 of them warriors, the rest women, children, and old or sick people—fled from Wallowa Lake in northeast Oregon, traveling more than 1,100 miles in their quest to reach freedom in Canada. En route, the Nez Percé defended themselves against more than 2,000 soldiers, Indians of other tribes, and civilian volunteers. All told, the Nez Percé were involved in some twenty battles and skirmishes.

To escape the Army, the Indians traveled what is today a National Historic Trail known as the Nez Percé, or Nee-Me-Poo, Trail. The Indians linked various trails, such as the Lolo Trail, with virgin paths as they fled through four states. Sadly, they were captured at Montana's Bears Paw Mountains, 42 miles short of the Canadian border, nearly four months later.

This segment of the ride is mostly level or slightly downhill to Lolo; then it's a gradual climb as you ride US 12, a two-lane highway with a moderate shoulder. The traffic isn't too bad, although it is a major thoroughfare, so watch for trucks and RVs. Lolo Hot Springs will be a must-stop for some. From there you'll climb a 5 percent grade to the top of Lolo Pass; then you'll descend to the Lochsa River for a night along its banks.

MILEAGE LOG

0.0 Birchwood Hostel. Continue on S. 4th St. W. No shoulders, but there's little traffic as you ride through a residential area.

1.3 Reach the second-to-last stop sign and turn left on Kemp.

1.5 Go right on S. 7th St. W.

1.7 Turn left on Eaton.

3.1 Eaton merges right onto Harve St.

3.2 T-junction at stop sign; turn left on Clark St.

3.5 Clark St. ends; make a right on Old US 93.

3.6 Cross Reserve St., a major thoroughfare near Kmart and other services.

4.4 Merge onto US 93 South/US 12 West; make a right. Wide shoulder; four lanes.

4.7 Cross the Bitterroot River.

10.9 Enter Lolo; cafés, motel, restaurant, Laundromat, post office. Lewis and Clark named this spot "Traveller's Rest" and camped here, resting for two days before starting their trek over the Bitterroot Mountains. As you head up over the pass, look for interpretive signs that point out various expedition campsites.

11.6 Head right on US 12 West. A narrow to moderate shoulder exists as you begin a gradual climb to the mountain. Later the shoulder narrows; sometimes it is nonexistent.

14.3 Square Dance RV Park on left; all facilities, including trout fishing.

14.7 Café/motel on the left.

16.2 Fort Fizzle Historic Site and picnic area on left; toilets. The road climbs through forest as you continue.

18.3 Country store on the left.

18.9 Good view of Lolo Peak (9,096 feet) off to the left.

27.3 Lewis and Clark Picnic Area on the left; toilets, water.

28.2 Turnoff on Graves Creek Rd. (to the right on gravel). A sign indicates there's a Lumberjack Saloon, RV Park, camping, cabins, and restaurant.

30.5 Howard Creek Picnic Area on the right.

35.4 Lewis and Clark camped near here on the night of September 12, 1805. They stayed to the more open north side of Lolo Creek as they proceeded west. About the area, Clark wrote (words are misspelled as Clark wrote them), "The road through this hilley countrey is verry bad passing over hills and thro-steep hollows, over fallen timber . . . crossed a mountain 8 miles with out water and encamped on a hill side on the creek after decending a long steep mountain. Some of our party did not get up until 10 p.m. . . . party and horses much fatigued."

36.7 Lolo Hot Springs Campground on the left; all amenities. Across the street is Lolo Hot Springs and a restaurant/gift shop.

Lewis and Clark passed by this spot the next morning, September 13, 1805. Clark wrote, "I tasted this water and found it hot and not bad tasting . . . in further examonation I found this water nearly boiling hot at the places it spouted from the rocks . . . I put my finger in the water at first could not bare it in a second." The Lewis and Clark expedition camped here on their return journey as well, enjoying four deer for supper (their first fresh meat in five days) and a hot bath on June 29, 1806.

38.9 Lee Creek Campground; national forest campground with water, toilets, fee area.

41.4 Grade increases to 5 percent as you continue up.

44.9 Lolo Pass and Visitor Center. More than just the top of a 5,235-foot pass, it's also the place where the Lewis and Clark party camped on September 13, 1805. In addition, Lolo Pass marks your entry into Idaho. The Lolo Pass Visitor Center offers information and toilets. The shoulder is narrow or nonexistent as you continue, descending via a 6 percent grade. Expect some truck traffic.

49.7 Cross Crooked Fork Creek.

56.0 White Sands Elk Summit turnoff on the left.

57.7 Turnoff to Lochsa Lodge and Powell Campground. Reach the complex in 0.2 mile; all facilities, including horseback riding, cabins, groceries, and a café.

60.0 Cross Papoose Creek.

61.0 Whitehouse Campground entrance on the left; national forest facility set along the Lochsa River. Toilets and water; fee area.

Whitehouse Campground to Wild Goose Campground (63.7 miles)

A bicyclist's dream is in store for you: the downhill descent through the forest to the Wild Goose Campground is pure pleasure. And nowhere else on the entire journey does the day's ride consist of nothing more than hugging a gorgeous river.

The Lochsa River only widens and intensifies in beauty as you descend. Its name, a Salish Indian term meaning "rough water," is certainly appropriate for the rocky, swift river. It had to be bypassed by the Lewis and Clark expedition and other settlers who followed; in fact, the wildness of the Lochsa wasn't exposed to the traveler until the highway was completed in 1962.

Whitewater enthusiasts will be happy to learn that the river lives up to its name, with forty rapids that rate class 4 or above on the European rating system. The whitewater season generally extends from May to August. Note that expert boatsmen consider the Lochsa hazardous; if you have minimal experience and cannot handle extremely difficult water conditions, do not even attempt a run down this river.

Wildlife is abundant, especially bird life, with osprey nesting along the river and kingfishers, gray jays, and Steller's jays enchanting all who stop. Mammals are plentiful as well, but are usually not as easily seen. In the early morning and late evening, look for elk, mule and white-tailed deer, coyotes, and porcupines.

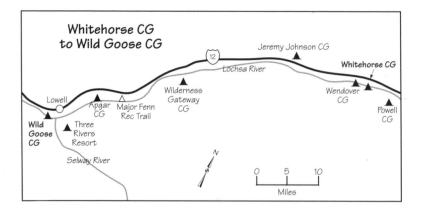

A quiet moment along the Lochsa River, Idaho

The only downside to the day's segment is some truck traffic and a narrow or nonexistent shoulder.

MILEAGE LOG

0.0 Whitehouse Campground entrance. Just past the entrance is Whitehouse Pond on the right. The westward-bound Lewis and Clark party crossed here on September 15, 1805, after camping 4 miles upstream at Powell. From near this point the expedition headed north, climbing the very steep Wendover Ridge and leaving present-day US 12.

0.2 Wendover Campground on the left; a national forest facility with water, toilets, fee area.

4.7 Cross Squaw Creek.

8.2 Jerry Johnson, a national forest campground, is on the right; toilets, water, fee area.

11.0 Free camping area along the river; toilet.

13.9 Cross Post Office Creek.

29.5 Rest rooms on the right.

30.3 Cross Bald Mountain Creek.

36.2 Wilderness Gateway Campground on the left. The national forest campground is across the river about a mile via a paved road. Toilets, water, fee area.

37.4 Lochsa Historical Ranger Station and Visitor Center on the right.

38.7 Cross Fish Creek.

43.5 Shoestring Falls Creek on the left.

51.2 Major Fenn Picnic Area on the left; toilets. Water is available on occasion, when it passes a monthly test. Major Fenn Recreation Trail leads 0.5 mile through a unique ecosystem along the Lower Lochsa and Selway rivers. Some fifteen plant species normally found west, not east, of the Cascades thrive here. Climate and geological forces have joined to create an ecological niche totally distinct from the surrounding area. Here you'll find Pacific dogwood, western sword fern, Pacific yew, and snowberry, to name a few.

52.3 Cross Deadman Creek. There's a free place to camp on the right; outhouse.

54.7 Apgar Campground on the left. This national forest facility asks for a fee; water, toilets, Lochsa River nearby.

61.7 Lowell; café and country store on the right.

62.1 A bridge on the left spans the Lochsa River and leads to Three Rivers Resort, where there is a motel, cabins, a campground with all amenities and a pool, and a café. Three Rivers also offers float trips down the Lochsa, Selway, and Clearwater rivers.

At this point the Lochsa merges with the Middle Fork Clearwater River, which you will now follow.

63.7 Wild Goose Campground on the left. Located on the banks of the Middle Fork Clearwater River, this national forest campground has toilets and water; fee area.

Wild Goose Campground to Grangeville (46.8 miles)

You'll continue riding through forest before entering the Nez Percé Indian Reservation. As in previous days, the highway parallels a river, this time to Harpster. First you'll ride along the Middle Fork Clearwater River; later, the South Fork Clearwater River.

It's an easy ride for the first portion of the day, with a gradual descent to Kooskia, which you'll reach a little less than halfway through the day. A good place to stop for lunch, Kooskia is a well-known jumping-off point for hikers, fishermen, and floaters. Nestled at the mouth of two beautiful rivers—the South Fork and the Middle Fork of the Clearwater River—Kooskia was born in 1899 when a railroad line was constructed up the river.

Before entering Kooskia, you'll pedal through a portion of the Nez Percé Indian Reservation. Ancestors of the Nez Percé people lived in this area for more than 10,000 years. The earliest ancestors were nomadic hunters and gatherers who lived beneath rock over-hangs. Later, about 2,500 years ago, they began living in semi-subterranean pit houses usually nestled along riverbanks. Still later, above-ground dwellings appeared.

It's a gradual uphill climb from Kooskia to Harpster, where the true test begins as you climb out of the canyon of the South Fork Clearwater and up onto the high prairie. (Total elevation gain for the day is about 2,200 feet.) The sweeping view and open ranch-land are mesmerizing, a dramatic change from the forest and rivers of the past days.

Unfortunately, the ride to Grangeville may be a bit stressful due to an increase in traffic and the lack of shoulders. Fortunately, at times a narrow shoulder does exist.

I've chosen to end the segment in the middle of Grangeville. You can decide whether you want to camp at either Lions Club Park or Mount View Park, a private campground, or splurge on a motel room.

Grangeville snuggles up to the base of the Bitterroot Mountain foothills and is Idaho County's largest town. Overlooking lovely Camas Prairie, the town of about 3,500 offers an array of outdoor activities, including access to six national Wild and Scenic Rivers with gorgeous views and exciting whitewater rafting.

Annual events include Border Days, held over the Fourth of July holiday, and Oktubberfest, the first weekend of October. Border Days combines three rodeo shows with three parades, dancing, food, and fun. Oktubberfest consists of townsfolk who compete in tub races along Main St. In addition, there's an art show, a street dance, and a festival with food booths and games.

If you'd like to explore the town and region further, visit the Bi-centennial Historical Museum or the Country Memories Museum. The Bicentennial Museum houses an array of Nez Percé Indian items

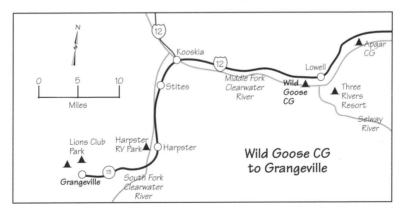

that is one of the largest displays of its kind, with seventy-five items ranging from native dresses to tools and corn-husk bags. Country Memories preserves the life-style of the Depression era. You'll see a living room, kitchen, bedroom, schoolroom, blacksmith shop, and so on. In addition, a display of antique machinery and old cars is available for viewing.

MILEAGE LOG

0.0 Wild Goose Campground entrance. Continue on US 12, following the Middle Fork Clearwater River.

1.0 Three Devils Picnic Area on the left, located along the river; toilets.

5.2 Café to the right.

7.9 Leaving Clearwater National Forest. Private homes are scattered about as you proceed past lots of blackberry bushes.

10.7 Lookingglass Lodge bed-and-breakfast inn on the right.

14.5 Bear Hollow bed-and-breakfast inn on the right.

16.4 Entering Nez Percé Indian Reservation.

18.7 Cross Maggie Creek.

19.2 Tukaytesp'e "Skipping Stones" Picnic Area on the left; toilets. Like most of the other picnic areas in the region, it is located along the river.

20.3 Turn left and cross the river. A sign points the way to Kooskia City Center. After crossing the bridge, you'll see a T-junction; head right on Hwy. 13 (Broadway Ave.). No shoulders; little traffic.

21.1 Kooskia Ranger Station, Clearwater National Forest, on the right. You'll reach junction Hwy. 13 and access to US 12 at the same point; head left on Hwy. 13 South; shoulder.

21.4 Enter Kooskia, where there are all services, including a Laundromat.

21.7 Shoulder ends as you head out of town, now paralleling the South Fork Clearwater River.

24.8 Enter Stites; market, café, post office, and site of the Oldtimers Picnic, usually held the second Sunday in June.

26.1 Clearwater Battlefield marker on the right. The Nez Percé War was only a few weeks old when General O. O. Howard and his troops crossed the Clearwater, hoping to surprise the Nez Percé. His plan failed, and the fighting ended with the Nez Percé withdrawing.

32.2 Cross Sally Ann Creek.

33.6 Leaving Nez Percé Indian Reservation.

33.9 Enter Harpster.

34.3 Harpster RV Park on the right; tent camping along the river; all amenities, including a market, Laundromat, and some hot food items.

35.9 Cross the South Fork Clearwater River.

36.1 Junction Hwy. 14 on the left leads to Elk City; keep right on Hwy. 13 toward Grangeville. Begin climbing a 5 to 6 percent grade. The shoulder continues to be narrow or nonexistent, but wherever you find new construction you'll find a shoulder.

41.3 Reach top of first long grade; then it's a climb with an occasional descent as you cross the high prairie, where trees and ranch houses dot the land.

46.0 Clearwater Ranger Station on the right.

46.2 Reach the junction of Myrtle St. If you want to camp, head right on N. Myrtle St. to Lions Club Park in 0.1 mile. There are rest rooms and water.

46.6 City park to the left has showers and a pool.

46.8 Holiday Sports Bike Shop on the left. The all-service town of Grangeville also offers a Laundromat, and Greyhound services the area as well.

Grangeville to Riggins (44.7 miles)

If it's a typical hot summer day when you ride this segment, you can expect it to be sweltering. On a more positive note, if you have the time and cash you just might want to cool off by floating the Salmon River.

The Shoshone Indians called the river "Tom-Agit-Pah," or "big fish water." Anglers do hook big fish in the Salmon, but the river is more than just a fishing mecca. It's also enjoyed by thousands of visitors who come each year to float it, camp by it, photograph it, or simply relax by it.

After ascending White Bird Hill, you'll pass the White Bird Battlefield Site, where the first battle of the famous Nez Percé War was fought on June 17, 1877; the Nez Percé fought bravely, killing thirty-four soldiers while losing not a single warrior. From the battlefield, you'll descend by means of a 7 percent grade. Although there's usually a shoulder, beware of side winds during your rapid

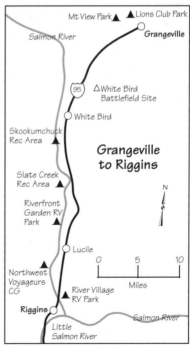

Rafters float the Salmon River near Riggins, Idaho

descent. Once down in the valley, you'll closely parallel the Salmon River via US 95, a shoulder-blessed road, until entering Riggins, "Idaho's Whitewater Capital."

Riggins boasts one of the mildest climates in Idaho, reason enough for the town's status as an "outdoor lover's paradise." The small town with the western feel lies deep in a T-shaped canyon where the Salmon and the Little Salmon rivers join forces. As you may have guessed, it is the base for several river outfitters.

If you like rodeos and you're in town the first full weekend in May, you'll want to attend the famous Riggins Rodeo. Be sure to get a campsite or motel early, as the town swells from a few hundred people to about 3,000 folks. Other annual events include the Old-Fashioned Fourth of July, with a barbecue and much more; the

Old-Time Fiddlers Jamboree; and the Salmon River Art Guild's Arts and Crafts Show the last weekend in October.

MILEAGE LOG

0.0 Holiday Sports in downtown Grangeville.

0.5 T-junction as Hwy. 13 ends at the US 95 junction. Head left on US 95 South, a two-lane road. There's a nice shoulder as you gradually ascend (expect a few downhills) along the outskirts of beautiful Camas Prairie, where the average wheat harvest is 100 bushels per acre.

6.7 You lose the shoulder but gain a second lane as you begin climbing a steep grade.

7.4 Road narrows to two lanes; shoulder returns.

9.0 Top of White Bird Hill—elevation 4,245 feet. Descend a speedy (if you're going downhill) 7 percent grade into the Salmon River Valley.

10.4 White Bird Auto Tour Route on the left. Although you can descend via the old road, you'll have to suffer through countless switchbacks. But if you're going to be stopping at every curve to enjoy the sights, then it won't be much of a problem. Although I preferred descending via the new road, the old road would have been great for an uphill climb. Nearly traffic-free, the old road, which was completed in 1915 and which served as Idaho's only north-south highway for sixty years, climbs about 2,300 feet in roughly 11.6 miles. The new road, which replaced the old one in 1975, gains the same number of feet in only 7.6 miles.

13.4 White Bird Battlefield Shelter on the left. From here, there's a panoramic view of the battlefield area, allowing you to get a better idea of the tactics used by the Nez Percé to defeat the U.S. Army in the first battle of the Nez Percé War.

16.6 Cross White Bird Creek.

16.8 Exit leads to the all-service town of White Bird, about 0.5 mile off route. In addition to the usual facilities, there's a Laundromat.

17.9 Café on the left as you descend to the Salmon River, where you will once again begin a gradual uphill.

21.2 Skookumchuck Recreation Area on the right; the free BLM camp is located along the river and offers water and toilets. Note that automatic sprinklers come on nightly.

21.4 Cross Skookumchuck Creek.

24.1 Cross the Salmon River.

24.4 Cross the Salmon River again.

25.7 Slate Creek Recreation Area on the right. This BLM area, located along the river, charges a fee. There are toilets and water.

26.3   Cross Slate Creek.

26.5   Slate Creek Historical Museum on the left, as well as the Slate Creek Ranger Station, Nez Percé National Forest. The log cabin museum, built in 1909, was originally located 5 miles up Slate Creek. Filled with many historic items, the building served as district headquarters until 1917; fire, trail, and road crews used it until 1959.

30.2   Riverfront Garden RV Park on the right, on the banks of the Salmon River; all amenities.

32.2   Cross John Day Creek.

35.9   Turnoff to Lucile on the right; post office.

36.2   Northwest Voyageurs Campground on the right. The riverfront campground offers water and rest rooms; no showers. Float trips are available here; the most popular such trips in Idaho drift from this point down to Riggins.

37.2   Lucile Recreation Site on the right. Toilets, no water, no fee.

39.8   Fruit stand on the left; snacks, fruit, cold drinks.

43.4   Cross the Salmon River and enter the Mountain Time Zone. Shoulder disappears.

44.7   River Village RV Park on the left. Tents are allowed at this all-facility park with a Laundromat. If you'd rather stay at a motel in the all-service town of Riggins, continue south for another 0.3 mile, where there's a motel. Go a mile or so farther and you'll find a Laundromat and various other shops.

Riggins to Council (61.3 miles)

Today you'll continue through Riggins, pass through New Meadows, and spend the night in Council, all of which are located in "Idaho's Heartland." And tomorrow you'll continue through several other west-central Idaho towns that offer whitewater delights, fishing, water skiing, biking, hang gliding, and other outdoor activities.

Today's ride is a steady, nearly all-day climb up, up, and up again (you'll climb about 2,900 feet) to Tamarack, then down (with one uphill) to Council. Most of the roads are okay, but you should watch for broken-up and disheveled areas from about Tamarack to Council.

Council was a favored gathering place for native American tribes, who met here to play tribal games, gather around the council fires, and, most importantly, to make peace. In 1878, while in search of grand homesteading opportunities, pioneers discovered abundant wildlife and fertile soil, so they stopped and formed a community. Today Council, the oldest community in the area, is home to about 1,000 people.

The people of Council delight in attending a multitude of annual events. These include the Heartland Quilt Exhibit, which opens for six weeks in mid-June and is touted as the best show of its kind in the state. Rodeo Bible Camp occurs in June, and there's a county fair and rodeo the third full week in July. The Fourth of July Celebration is also popular, with a parade, a jam session, a barbecue, fireworks, and the famous porcupine race.

Before rolling into Council, you'll pass through New Meadows, not only the crossroads between northern and southern Idaho but a place where the forty-fifth parallel bisects the valley floor.

The small community of about 500 offers a fun Labor Day weekend celebration, their

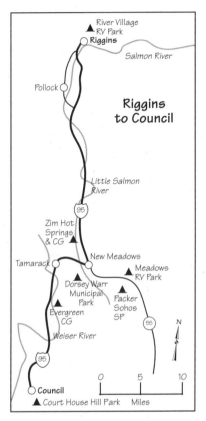

biggest festivity of the year. Hundreds of visitors come to see an amateur logging show and an antique car display, and to pig out on beef at the barbecue. Of course, most don't want to miss the Monday morning Hillbilly Breakfast either!

MILEAGE LOG

0.0 River Village RV Park entrance. Continue south on US 95.

0.1 There's a shoulder once again as you head through downtown Riggins.

0.5 Cleo H. Patterson Memorial Park on left. You'll find picnic facilities and toilets along the Salmon River.

1.3 You lose the shoulder (although there is an occasional one) as you near the south edge of town, where there is a Laundromat. The Salmon River heads east as you begin following the Little Salmon River.

1.8 Riggins Office of the Hells Canyon National Recreation Area on the right.

5.0 Cross the Rapid River; there's a shoulder as you climb through the pines.

6.2 Cross the Little Salmon River.

7.3 Rest area on the right; water, toilets. Camping is allowed, but not on the grass due to automatic sprinklers, which have surprised more than one sleepy cyclist.

13.9 Cross the Little Salmon River.

14.3 Enter Pinehurst, a pretty river community with cabins for rent, an antique store, and a combination café/grocery store.

15.3 Shoulder disappears.

19.6 Shoulder reappears.

19.9 Cross the Little Salmon River near Hazard Creek Rd. area. Willow trees mix with an abundance of other deciduous trees as you proceed upward.

22.1 Lose the shoulder again.

22.4 Cross the Little Salmon River again.

24.6 Shoulder again; on the right is Smokey Boulder Rd. The road flattens out as you travel, passing expansive meadowlike areas and open plains.

31.2 Zims Rd. turnoff leads about 0.8 mile west to Zims Hot Springs. A gravel road leads to the campground, which has a pool and all the usual amenities.

33.3 Forty-fifth parallel; this spot is halfway between the equator and the North Pole.

35.7 Enter New Meadows, the "Center of Idaho's Heartland." In town are all the standard facilities in addition to a Laundromat.

Junction US 95 and Hwy. 55; make a right and continue on US 95. Hwy. 55 leads to the left (east) to two campgrounds. Meadows RV Park is 2.5 miles away, and has all amenities, including a Laundromat. Packer John's Cabin is a state park facility with toilets and water.

36.0 Dorsey Warr Municipal Park on the left; bicyclists can camp for free; facilities include water and toilets. The roadway is shoulderless as you head out of town.

36.5 Cross the Little Salmon River and begin climbing again. It's a mostly moderate climb, although there are occasional steep areas as you continue through the forest.

42.7 Tamarack, a sawmill town with no services.

43.4 Begin downhill. Watch for trucks and RVs on this windy highway. Use caution.

44.2 Café on the right; they sell snack items too.

Bicycle camp at Court House Hill Park in Council, Idaho

45.1 Enter Payette National Forest.
47.9 Evergreen Campground on the left. Located along the Weiser River, this national forest facility offers water and toilets.
51.0 Cross the Weiser River.
52.1 Exit Payette National Forest. Begin climbing a steep grade.
53.7 Crest the hill, then begin dropping into more of Idaho's Heartland.
56.6 Level off and proceed across wide, open ranchland.
60.5 Convenience store on the left as you enter Council. As you continue there's a Laundromat and all the standard amenities, including a visitor information center.
61.1 Make a left on S. Galena St.
61.3 Court House Hill Park. A post office, library, and police station are nearby. The rest rooms are located just past the library, in the city park, which is at the corner of Illinois Ave. and US 95. Check in with the sheriff at 253-4227 for more information.

The author climbing McKenzie Pass, Oregon (Photo: Diego C. Rueda)

OREGON

Cycling through Oregon will be a special experience for all bicyclists, regardless of whether they are ending or embarking upon their cross-country journey across the USA. After riding more than 4,000 miles, those who began their journey in Yorktown will at last be able to touch the Pacific surf with their front tire! And those who are beginning their cross-country odyssey will ride through the state with visions of dipping their front tires in the Atlantic.

Whether your trip is ending or just beginning, a 499.8-mile, nine-day ride through my favorite state of Oregon (a 661.5-mile, thirteen-day ride if you're bound for Astoria) is a real treat. Nicknamed the Beaver State because the region yielded thousands of beaver skins during fur-trading days, today it is also called the Pacific Wonderland because it offers an assortment of outstanding natural wonders such as Crater Lake, the Columbia River Gorge, Hells Canyon, the Oregon Caves, and the state's highest peaks, Mounts Hood and Jefferson.

Although Oregon is probably best known for its scenic, 300-mile-long coast, its green, rain-soaked valleys, and the mighty Cascade Mountains, the country on the east side of the Cascades is hardly lush and green; rather, it is dry, with a climate ranging from very hot in the summer to very cold in the winter. Eastern Oregon supports the largest livestock ranches in the state, as well as farms where you'll find everything from potatoes and sugar beets to a variety of other crops, including wheat, Oregon's most valuable food crop.

Just outside Baker City lies the National Historic Oregon Trail Interpretive Center, where numerous volunteers will give you the facts about what really happened on the trail. The center, located atop Flagstaff Hill, has a full-size replica of a wagon train, informative exhibits, and wagon ruts. Although you might expect the wagon train to be the highlight for most visitors, the wagon ruts are actually the most popular feature. (Several miles of footpaths allow visitors to explore the ruts.)

From the interpretive center you'll head west to Baker City. Known as the "Queen City of the Mines" at the turn of the century, it was the first town established along the Oregon Trail in northeastern Oregon. Boasting a population of 6,663 in 1890, the town was a major trading center, a regular frontier metropolis. Here the wealthy abounded, and it shows in the downtown's unique architecture, including carpenter Gothic, Victorian, and Italianate classic revival styles.

Llama ranches near Sisters, Oregon

As you head through central Oregon, you'll have the opportunity to take a side trip to the John Day Fossil Beds National Monument. Once home to a lush subtropical paradise of dense, tangled vines, palms, sycamores, avocados and marshland, the region is now decorated with sagebrush and juniper trees. Why the change? Today the mighty Cascades block moisture-laden clouds streaming in from the Pacific, but millions of years ago they did not. Though annual precipitation is limited in the high desert environment, at one time clouds annually dumped more than 100 inches of rain on the area.

An assortment of exotic animals—including aquatic rhinos and alligators—ranged upon the once rain-soaked land. But there was trouble in paradise. Rain combined with volcanic ash from the volcanic eruptions that were common at that time. Mud formed, swallowing leaves, nuts, and mammals, wiping out all life but preserving it through fossilization.

Short, self-guided trails lead past actual fossil specimens. You can see an ancient hackberry tree, which thrived 40 million years ago. In addition, there are countless leaf and tree limb imprints to examine.

The Painted Hills is one of the most beautiful regions in the preserve, a place where many claim nothing ever looks the same twice. Barren and beautiful, smooth and stunning, the rounded hills are decorated with a variety of hues such as red to gold, and bronze to buff and black.

The next major Oregon attraction is the Cascade Mountains, a magnificent range stretching more than 600 miles from Canada to northern California. The Cascade Range abounds with lakes, glaciers, and lofty peaks, some of which are volcanic cones. The route passes over picturesque McKenzie Pass, which offers a commanding view of volcanic activity.

Both the Three Sisters and Mount Washington wilderness areas are accessible from various points along the highway. The Three Sisters Wilderness is Oregon's busiest preserve, a place where more than 350 azure lakes dot the land and flowers carpet the landscape.

Once named Faith, Hope, and Charity (by pioneer missionaries), the Three Sisters dominate the landscape. Despite their name, researchers believe they are by no means "sisters." Some say they should be called the Mother and Two Daughters, for the North Sister is much older than the Middle Sister and the South Sister.

It's obvious that Mother Nature has been hard at work in the Mount Washington Wilderness. Hardened lava flows blanket much of the preserve—so much so that it is often called the "Black Wilderness." If you enjoy lava's rugged, sharp texture and like to imagine the flows of long ago, you're in luck. Lava must have been a problem for early travelers, but their determination proved tougher.

As you continue on you'll head down the west side of the Cascades. And if you're ending your ride in Florence, you'll cross the Willamette Valley, climb the Coast Range, and then zip down to the sea, perhaps saving the best for last.

In my nearly ten years of seeing the country by bicycle, Oregon's coast remains my favorite ride. It was the site of my very first tour and has been the object of many tours since. I don't know if it has something to do with my being a transplanted Oregonian, but prejudice aside, I can't help but be enamored with Oregon's rugged coast.

The weather varies widely from Hells Canyon to the coast. In the eastern part of the state, expect hot temperatures in the summer; low humidity and cold nights make the temperatures more bearable. Thunderstorms and hailstorms are not uncommon, so be prepared. The same is true for the valleys west of the Cascades, although heavy rainfall is common in all seasons but summer. Along the coast you can be assured of cool weather, including fog and heavy precipitation, even during midsummer. On occasion the coast secures a hot, dry day with temperatures in the 90s. However, this is a rare occurrence.

As you ride through the state, you'll ride lightly traveled to busy roads, many of them shoulder-blessed but some of them narrow or shoulderless. Use caution, especially around Baker City, on Hwy. 126 as you near the town of Springfield, and from Eugene to Florence, where the highway is very busy and the road often provides only a narrow shoulder.

Along the coastline—especially during the summer, weekends, and holidays—US 101 bears an abundance of traffic. Wear bright clothing, watch for RVs and logging trucks, and enjoy some of the quieter back roads that you'll ride as an alternative to US 101.

If you decide to go off route, note that interstate riding is allowed on I-5, I-84, I-205, and I-405, except in metropolitan Portland, and for 1 mile through Medford. For more information on biking in Oregon, contact Michael Ronkin, Bicycle/Pedestrian Program Manager, Oregon Department of Transportation, 355 Capitol St. NE, 5th Floor, Salem, OR 97301; (503) 986-3554; website: www.odot.state.or.us; email: michael.p.ronkin@odot.state.or.us.

Council to Hells Canyon (62.2 miles)

Beautiful farmland and big scenery will escort bicyclists to the small town of Cambridge, population 300-plus. Hardly just another town in the "Idaho's Heartland" clique, Cambridge began its existence in January 1900 after the Pacific & Idaho Northern Railroad completed a line to the area.

While in Cambridge, don't miss the award-winning Cambridge Museum. And if you're in town for the first weekend in June or the first week in August, don't miss the town's major annual events: Hells Canyon Days in June and the Washington County Fair and Cambridge Rodeo in August.

Cambridge touts itself as the town with the most convenient and best access to the rugged Hells Canyon area. In any case, it provides entry to cyclists, who will indeed climb out of Cambridge via the Pine Creek drainage. It's a moderate to steep (sometimes very steep) climb, then down to Brownlee

Dam and the depths of Hells Canyon. (I had to pedal straight into a headwind the day I climbed the drainage, so the grade may not be as tough as it seemed to me.)

The Snake River in Hells Canyon divides Idaho and Oregon, flowing through North America's deepest river canyon. (Yes, it is deeper than the Grand Canyon!) More than 67 miles of Wild and Scenic River corridor pass through Hells Canyon Wilderness, although the river itself is not designated wilderness. Thus, nonmotorized and motorized access is permissible. The largest rapids are located in the wild section, which boasts several Class IV rapids. The scenic section offers less challenging Class II to III rapids and spectacular canyon vistas.

Dwarfed by Idaho's lofty Seven Devils Mountains and Oregon's Wallowa Mountains (often referred to as the "Alps of North America") Hells Canyon is more than just a place to run the rapids. It also provides refuge for many species of animal life and is a mecca for many birds of prey, including bald and golden eagles, peregrine falcons, and an assortment of hawks. Other bird species include crows and great blue herons.

Hwy. 71 along the Snake River, Hells Canyon, Idaho

Humans have enjoyed exploring Hells Canyon for at least 7,100 years, with modern trekkers doing so by bicycle, jet boat, kayak, raft, horseback, and on foot. Day hikes and backpacking trips are very popular in this region.

MILEAGE LOG

0.0 Corner of US 95 and Galena St. Continue through town. Road curves to the left at the city park, which has rest rooms.

0.8 Restaurant on the left.

4.1 Shoulder begins as you head up a short hill, then a longer one. Afterwards the terrain is nearly level to Cambridge.

5.2 Cross Middle Fork Weiser River.

7.7 Mesa turnoff on the right; post office.

11.2 Market on the right.

11.3 Café on the left.

11.7 Shoulder shrinks, sometimes disappearing altogether.

21.3 Cross the Weiser River.

21.7 US 95 curves to the left in downtown Cambridge, an all-service town that also offers a Laundromat and the Cambridge Museum. If you need a post office, before turning left turn right.

21.8 Turn right on Hwy. 71 West, a two-lane highway with no shoulder. **SIDE TRIP:** If you'd like a shower, continue straight on US 95 for 0.2 to the Frontier Motel and RV Park; all amenities and a Laundromat.

22.0 Water Tower Park on the left. You can camp here for free; toilets, water.

As you head up the canyon along Pine Creek, you'll see aspens, cottonwoods, and a variety of other trees. Sagebrush and other Great-Basin-type plants are scattered about the hillsides.

34.1 Mill Creek Rd. on the left.

36.0 Enter Payette National Forest. Just beyond is Seid Creek Rd. on the right.

37.5 Top of summit at 4,131 feet. Head downhill to Brownlee Dam with a couple of short steep climbs now and again.

38.6 Brownlee Campground to the right via gravel road. This national forest camp is over a mile away and offers water and toilets for a fee.

40.1 Leave Payette National Forest and descend from the trees to steep, dry slopes.

44.5 Café/groceries/motel on the right.

46.8 Woodhead Park Campground on the left; all amenities at this facility, managed by Idaho Power.

50.6 Brownlee Dam on the left.

50.8 Hwy. 71 ends here. **SIDE TRIP:** The road on the right leads to McCormick Ranch Park, another Idaho Power facility. It's 0.5 mile via a gravel road to the all-amenities campground.

Cross the Snake River into Oregon! Now you'll travel via a private road. Set your clocks back an hour; you are now in the Pacific Time Zone. Look for plums growing along the roadway as you travel a gradual downhill.

54.4 Carters Landing on the right; there's free tent camping, toilets, and picnic facilities.

59.1 Outhouses on the right.

61.0 Begin short, very steep grade up over a ridge.

61.4 Top of hill.

62.0 Junction Hwy. 86 leads left to Halfway. You'll return to this point tomorrow to continue on across Oregon. Keep right to the campground and post office.

62.2 Copperfield Park. Run by Idaho Power, this scenic park is inexpensive and provides all the necessities of camp life.

Hells Canyon to Baker City (72.0 miles)

Today's ride is a tough one, to say the least. Add heat and a headwind, and the day will seem even tougher. Add a nice tailwind and it will be easier, although you'll still have to climb more than 4,000 feet in elevation during the 72-mile ride.

On the plus side, there's a nice shoulder-clad highway to ride, with access to the quaint town of Halfway and a direct link through the cow-blessed (or should I say cursed?) town of Richland. The highway leads through the high desert, where sagebrush is king and the Eagle Cap Wilderness struts its stuff to the north. (If you ever have the time to hike into a wilderness, I'd recommend

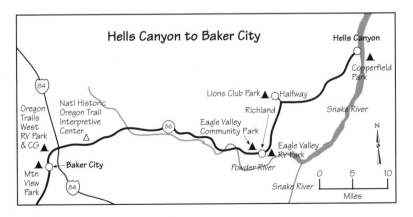

Eagle Cap, with its high granite peaks and gem-like alpine lakes.)

A few miles before Baker City you'll pass the National Historic Oregon Trail Interpretive Center, a definite must-see. In fact, if you want to spend a day at the center, you can continue into town to camp or motel it, and ride back out the next day to explore the center. (For more information about the center, see the introduction to this chapter.)

Baker City is your home for the night. Located at the southern end of the Powder River Valley, the town was founded in 1862 when gold was discovered a few miles to the west. Upon reaching town you'll have to decide whether a campground or a motel is more suited to your tastes. A couple of campgrounds are located just out of town, while a number of motels and bed-and-breakfast inns are located in town.

While you're out exploring the town, be sure to notice Baker City's unique architecture (see the introduction to this chapter for more information), and don't forget to visit the Oregon Trail Regional Museum, once a natatorium (an indoor swimming pool), where you'll be able to examine many antiques as well as a vast rock, mineral, and fossil collection.

MILEAGE LOG

0.0   Entrance to Copperfield Park. Begin a moderate climb out of the canyon via Hwy. 86. The road is two lanes with a shoulder and climbs through the pines.

2.1   Cabins/Laundromat on the left.

2.3   Market/café on the right.

7.0   Cross North Pine Creek.

7.2   Road on the right leads to Imnaha and Joseph.

12.4   Junction Buchanan Rd. on the right. Now you'll head out into open country where sagebrush and quail are abundant. There are also grand views of the Wallowa Mountains and the Eagle Cap Wilderness.

14.5   Another junction to Buchanan Rd. on the right. You'll climb gradually now.

14.9   Cross E. Pine Creek.

16.4   Make a right toward Halfway via the business loop. If you'd rather skip the town, stay left on Hwy. 86.

16.9   Cross Pine Creek.

17.3   Downtown Halfway; all services, including a Laundromat and free camping at the Lions Club Park. No rest rooms at the park.

18.5   Back to Hwy. 86 at this point; head right and climb a steep, 7 percent grade.

Scene from Hwy. 86 between Oxbow Dam and Baker City, Oregon

- **23.3** Top of hill—elevation 3,653 feet; zoom down via an equally steep grade.
- **29.3** Bottom of hill; now it's nearly level across acres of farmland to Richland.
- **29.9** Enter Richland, another all-service community. In addition, there's camping with all amenities, including a Laundromat, at Eagle Valley RV Park, which you'll pass as you enter town.
- **30.4** Eagle Valley Community Park on the right as you head out of town; toilets, water.
- **30.9** Cross Eagle Creek.
- **35.8** Climb, then descend to the Powder River, which is on the left.
- **40.2** Cross the Powder River, then climb above it.
- **41.3** Cross the Powder River again, then head back down along the river. It's a gradual uphill climb.
- **49.3** Pop machine on the right at a private home. Begin steeper climb, with some breaks in between.
- **50.7** Cross the Powder River again.
- **55.3** Ritter Rd. on the right.
- **57.3** Cross Ruckles Creek.

64.3 National Historic Oregon Trail Interpretive Center on the right. It's uphill to the center, but well worth the climb.

65.6 Top of Flagstaff Hill Pass at 3,684 feet. Head down the hill, then level off across ranchland.

69.5 Cross over I-84.

69.8 T-junction; head left on Cedar St., which becomes Clark St. Oregon Trails West RV Park and Campground at junction; all amenities, including a Laundromat and grocery items. Continue on toward town via a bike lane.

70.3 Junction Hughes Lane. **SIDE TRIP:** Head right via Hughes Lane for a mile to Mountain View Holiday Trav-l-Park; all services as well as a Laundromat.

71.3 Turn right on Campbell St./Hwy. 7, a four-lane highway.

71.7 Turn left and continue on Hwy. 7 (called Main St. through downtown Baker City).

72.0 Junction Broadway in downtown Baker City, where there are all services, including bike shops, Amtrak, and Greyhound. I've ended the segment here, giving you the choice of a campground or motel. **SPECIAL NOTE:** Want to sample the local cuisine? If you love Mexican food, try El Erradero—on Broadway near Main St. You won't be sorry. If you crave sweets, visit the Donut Factory, where the Bulldawg brownie is featured. It's a brownie on a stick that has been dipped in baking chocolate and covered with sprinkles. If pizza is more to your liking, venture over to Pizza a' fetta, where pizza is sold by the slice. A variety of toppings, from pancetta (Italian-style bacon) to Montrachet chèvre (goat cheese), blanket the homemade crusts, which are truly scrumptious.

Baker City to Dixie Summit (58.4 miles)

Today's ride is certainly pleasant, since Hwy. 7 sports little traffic and offers a shoulder most of the way. The most difficult part of the ride will be the triple summits—Sumpter at 5,082 feet, Tipton at 5,124 feet, and Dixie at 5,277 feet—which encompass about half of the route. (You'll climb about 3,800 feet by the end of the day.) Before the day is over you'll roll into the Dixie Summit Campground, where you can pitch your tent amid the pines.

You'll travel a portion of the Elkhorn Scenic Route, a 106-mile loop comprising of lovely scenes and great fishing, camping, hiking, boating, and picnicking opportunities. As you follow the byway, which circles the Elkhorn Mountains, you'll pass a road leading a few miles to Sumpter.

Although gold was discovered in Sumpter in 1862, the town didn't boom until thirty years later, with the arrival of the railroad and the opening of hard rock mines. Prior to entering town,

today's visitors see one of the old dredges that mined the valley. Last used in 1954, the humongous dredge is located on private property. Please view it from the highway.

Once home to an opera house, three newspapers, and fifteen saloons, Sumpter, population 140, is a great spot for a layover day. You'll find all services in the historic town, as well as the Sumpter Valley Railroad, a must-ride for some.

Built between 1890 and 1910, the railroad stretched from Baker to Prairie City, a total of some 80 miles. During the gold rush the railroad delivered supplies to miners and returned with loads of gold and lumber. Today the restored narrow-gauge railroad (36 inches between the rails instead of 56 inches for standard-gauge) carries passengers from Sumpter Depot to Dredge Depot, a round trip of 10 miles, on weekends and holidays from Memorial Day through September.

Be sure to carry extra supplies, since it is 60 miles from Baker City to the next town, Prairie City. If you're heading off route to Sumpter, where you'll find all services, then you won't have a problem. If you are not going off route, however, you can always stop for a snack at McEwen Country Store after riding more than 23 miles, and carry food from there to the campground.

MILEAGE LOG

0.0 Corner of Broadway and Main St./Hwy. 7. Continue south on Hwy. 7 through downtown Baker City.

0.2 Junction US 30 to Ontario. Keep straight on Hwy. 7 South; two lanes, shoulder. This route is also known as Elkhorn Dr. Scenic Route.

1.7 Powder River bed-and-breakfast inn on the right. There are a number of other inns in town. Climb gradually as you parallel the Powder River through vast ranchland.

9.0 Cross the Powder River.

McEwen Country Store off Hwy. 7, Oregon

9.5 Junction Hwy. 245 on left; shoulder disappears.

10.2 Cross the Powder River.

14.1 Enter the Wallowa-Whitman National Forest as you head up through the pines.

16.1 Forest Road 150 on the left leads to Mason Dam Picnic Area, where there are toilets but no water. A good, level gravel road leads about a mile to the picnic site.

Begin climbing; shoulder reappears.

17.3 Top of hill and a good view of Phillips Lake.

19.2 Union Creek Recreation Area on the left. This Forest Service campground offers all services and is located on Phillips Lake. Formed by damming the Powder River at Mason Dam, when completely full the lake is 5 miles long. Fishing and swimming are popular pastimes.

21.0 Cross Deer Creek.

21.2 Mowich Loop Picnic Grounds on left; toilets, picnic tables.

22.5 Leaving the Wallowa-Whitman National Forest. Lose the shoulder once again.

23.5 McEwen Country Store on the right. Camping is available; water and toilets are the amenities. In addition to grocery items, you'll be able to visit with the owner's exotic Tibetan yaks.

24.1 Turnoff to Baker County Dredge Depot Park on the left. You'll find a picnic area, toilets, and nature trails where you can observe the valley's animal life. Fortunate visitors may observe beavers, deer, cranes, ducks, and more.

26.3 Shoulder again.

26.5 Turnoff to Sumpter on the right as Hwy. 7 curves left; begin a steep climb. **SIDE TRIP:** Sumpter is 3 miles northwest of this junction; McCulley Fork, a free national forest campground, is another 3 miles northwest of town. Toilets only.

27.0 Cross the Powder River.

27.2 Leave Sumpter Valley and enter the Wallowa-Whitman National Forest again.

30.2 Top of hill at Sumpter Summit.

36.3 You'll see the old town of Whitney on the left. In 1901 the railroad greeted townsfolk, and by 1911 a sawmill was born. Unfortunately, the town is now closed to visitors.

40.9 Cross North Fork Burnt River. Begin another uphill jaunt that's a little easier than the last.

44.3 Enter Malheur National Forest.

44.4 Tipton Summit—elevation 5,124 feet. Begin a long, fun downhill.

50.1 Turnoff on the right to Austin, where there are no services. Austin was once a stage stop; later it became a railroad center. Climb again.

50.9 CR 20 on the right leads to Bates (no services) in 19 miles.

51.1 Cross Clear Creek.

52.0 T-junction at US 26 West. Turn right on US 26; two lanes. Austin Junction is for sale, so everything is closed except the post office and a telephone. Begin a moderately steep climb.

53.4 Cross Bridge Creek and continue to follow it as it parallels the highway.

56.6 North Fork Bridge Creek Rd. on the right.

56.9 Grade increases in intensity as you proceed.

58.1 Entrance to Dixie Summit Campground; make a right.

58.4 Reach the Forest Service campground, where there are toilets and water. Note that the water was not safe to drink in August 1994. To inquire about current water conditions, call the Forest Service at 575-2110.

Dixie Summit to Dayville Hostel (54.3 miles)

After some really tough segments, this one is a real treat. Except for the first half-mile and a couple of very short hills, it's all downhill to Dayville.

The ride through the John Day River valley is pleasant and truly beautiful. En route you'll pedal through the gold rush town of Prairie City, gateway to the Strawberry Mountain Wilderness. If

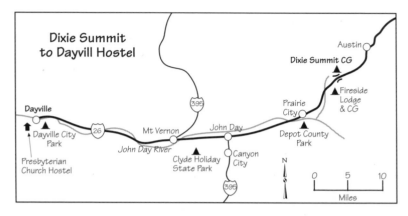

Dixie Summit
to Dayvill Hostel

Austin

Dixie Summit CG

Fireside
Lodge
& CG

Prairie
City

Dayville

Dayville City
Park

Mt Vernon

John Day

Depot County
Park

John Day River

Clyde Holiday
State Park

Canyon
City

Presbyterian
Church Hostel

N

0   5   10

Miles

you're touring by mountain bike, I'd recommend riding up to the wilderness. Bikes aren't allowed in the preserve, but you can camp at the trailhead, then hike the trail of your choice.

The day ends in Dayville, where you have three choices; bed-and-breakfast inn pampering, camping, or staying in the church hostel, where there's a shower. It's the only church hostel with a shower that I happened upon during my journey.

MILEAGE LOG

0.0 Entrance to Dixie Summit Campground. Continue up US 26 West; shoulder.

0.5 Dixie Summit—elevation 5,277 feet. Descend through open ranchland, where there is a spectacular view of the Strawberry Mountains.

1.4 Leave the Malheur National Forest.

1.6 Fireside Lodge and Campground on the left; all amenities, including a restaurant. Cabins may or may not be open. A projected completion date wasn't available.

6.6 Motel on the right.

9.5 Junction Main St. in downtown Prairie City. The town has all services, including a Laundromat. There's also camping (all facilities) at Depot County Park, located 0.5 mile south on Main St.

9.7 Prairie City Ranger Station, Malheur National Forest. Parallel the John Day River as you gradually descend through the valley.

9.8 Cross Dixie Creek.

14.2 Cross the John Day River.

14.3 Cross Indian Creek.

22.1 You'll see the Long Creek/Bear Valley ranger stations for the Malheur National Forest as you enter the east end of John Day.

22.6 Junction US 395 South to Canyon City on the left; US 395 North merges onto US 26 at this point. Continue west through the all-service town of John Day.

22.9 John Day Fossil Beds Headquarters on the left.

23.0 Bike shop on the right.

23.2 Market and miscellaneous shops on the right.

29.3 Cross the John Day River.

29.5 Clyde Holliday State Park on the left. You'll find hiker/biker sites in this campground with all facilities.

31.1 US 395 takes off to the right; keep straight on US 26.

31.2 Enter Mount Vernon, an all-service town. As you continue, there's an intermittent shoulder.

32.8 Cross the John Day River.

40.9 Cross Fields Creek.

41.3 Fields Creek Rd. on the left.

42.0 Cross the John Day River; you'll cross it again in about 9 miles.

54.0 Cross the South Fork John Day River.

54.1 Dayville City Park on the right; toilets, water. Across the road via CR 42 is the Presbyterian Church Hostel, managed since 1976 by Millie Grindstaff, who lives next door. You'll find the usual amenities, including a shower; donations are welcome. Call Millie at (503) 987-2586 for more information.

54.3 Downtown Dayville. The friendly little town offers a bed-and-breakfast inn with campsites available for those who'd rather rough it. Facilities are semiprimitive with toilets and water. In addition, there's a post office, a market, and a café.

Dayville Hostel to Ochoco Divide Campground (54.7 miles)

I hope you enjoyed the previous segment, because it was an easy ride; this segment is anything but. Actually, the roads are wonderful, the traffic is relatively light, and the scenery remains wide open. Even the wildlife seems abundant, with quail, swallows, kestrels, and coyotes out in force. The only difficult part is the nearly 5,000 feet in elevation gain.

Fortunately, you don't have to grin and bear it; instead, you can split this portion of the ride in half, thereby cutting the elevation gain in half too. If you decide to split the ride, you can camp for free in the friendly little community of Mitchell and while away your spare time at the Painted Hills and Sheep Rock units of John Day Fossil Beds National Monument, an intriguing place formed millions of years ago.

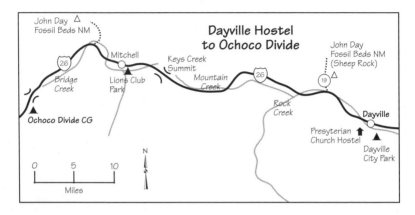

Three separate units—Clarno, Sheep Rock, and Painted Hills—make up the 14,000-acre preserve. A visitor center with exhibits and helpful personnel makes the prehistory of the John Day Basin a bit easier to understand. Hiking is also a good way to see the monument. (For more information on John Day Fossil Beds National Monument, see the introduction to this chapter.)

MILEAGE LOG

0.0 Downtown Dayville. Continue west on US 26; no shoulder. You'll proceed through a maze of ranchland as you continue the slight descent.

5.3 Cross Rattlesnake Creek.

5.6 Enter Picture Gorge, a gorgeous narrow canyon in the John Day Fossil Beds Sheep Rock Unit.

6.9 Junction Hwy. 19 on the right. Begin climbing through a narrow canyon for 2 miles while paralleling Rock Creek, then head out into an open valley. There's a narrow, intermittent shoulder. **SIDE TRIP:** The highway leads to the John Day Fossil Beds Visitor Center in 2 miles. If you're up for a hike, try the Blue Basin Overlook Trail, which is another 3.2 miles on the other side of the visitor center.

11.2 Cross Rock Creek. There's a couple of short downhills as you continue, but most of the ride is up a moderate, sometimes steep grade. Now the road parallels Mountain Creek.

25.5 Junction Forest Road 12 on the left. The shoulder improves about 2 miles prior to this point.

32.0 Reach Keyes Creek Summit—elevation 4,369 feet—then head down to Mitchell.

37.9 Turn left at the sign reading "Mitchell Business Loop."

38.2 Downtown Mitchell. Just prior (0.1 mile) is Lions Club Park, where free camping is available; water, toilets. In town you'll find all services and a Laundromat.

38.3 Back to US 26 West; shoulder continues. Head left past the Blueberry Café as you exit town, traveling slightly downhill through ranchland and sagebrush country.

38.5 Hwy. 207 on the right leads to Fossil.

38.6 Cross Bridge Creek.

39.5 Cross Bridge Creek again.

41.3 Cross Bridge Creek again.

42.0 Junction to the Painted Hills Unit as you begin climbing. **SIDE TRIP:** The paved road on the right leads to the Painted Hills Unit in 6 miles. Upon entering the unit, however, the road turns to gravel. There's a picnic area with water and toilets, and access to the Carroll Rim Trail. If you are interested, see the end of this segment.

42.9 Cross West Branch Bridge Creek.

54.7 Enter Ochoco National Forest before reaching Ochoco Pass at 4,720 feet. Ochoco Divide Campground is just ahead on the left. A paved road leads to this national forest campground; water and toilets.

Sheep Rock, John Day Fossil Beds National Monument, Oregon

Ochoco Divide Campground to Sisters (72.3 miles)

As you continue across central Oregon, you'll get a rare break from climbing, gaining a mere 1,000 feet or so in more than 70 miles of riding. It's virtually downhill to Redmond; then you'll climb a gradual grade to Sisters, with one major uphill en route. Traffic is fairly light to Redmond and heavy from there to Sisters. However, a bike lane from Redmond to Sisters makes the ride a good one.

Along the way, be sure to stop in Prineville, central Oregon's first city. To learn more about the region, stop in at the A. R. Bowman Museum, where you'll find two floors of exhibits. The museum is free and is included on the National Register of Historic Places.

Prineville is worth a visit. Engulfed by high rimrock cliffs, it is the only city in the nation that owns and operates its own railroad. The City of Prineville Railroad serves the area's agriculture and timber industries. In addition, it is a favorite for rock hounds, who join together for the annual Rockhound Pow Wow held in late June. Other annual events include the Central Oregon Timber Carnival in June, the Crook County Fair in August, and the Crooked River Roundup in early July.

The day ends in Sisters, a lively town where hordes of cars have replaced the horses and buggies of long ago. If you can ignore the crowds, though, you can still enjoy Sisters' western storefronts and the boardwalk. Browse through antique shops, admire the art displayed in various galleries, and relish a real, old-fashioned milkshake served in a stainless steel tumbler.

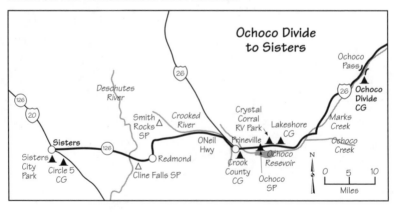

If you visit in June, you may want to attend the annual Sisters Rodeo, dubbed "the biggest little show on earth." The second Saturday in July hosts another big draw—the Sisters Quilt Show. Celebrating its twentieth season in 1995, the show boasts hundreds of quilts, hung inside retail stores during the week prior to the show and decorating all the porches, buildings, and fences in Sisters the day of the show. It's a sight you won't want to miss!

Greyhound services all three towns—Prineville, Redmond, and Sisters—in this segment.

MILEAGE LOG

0.0 Entrance to the Ochoco Divide Campground and US 26 West. There's a nice shoulder as you descend along Marks Creek.

1.2 Bandit Springs Rest Area on the right; toilets.

10.6 Cross Marks Creek.

12.6 Leaving the Ochoco National Forest.

15.3 Junction Ochoco Creek Rd. on the left.

16.1 Cross Marks Creek; shoulder is intermittent now.

22.0 Cross Mill Creek. You'll see Ochoco Reservoir off to the left as you continue through the Crooked River valley.

23.5 Lakeshore Campground on the right; all amenities plus a Laundromat. On the left is a convenience store and restaurant.

24.0 Crystal Corral Restaurant and RV Park on the right; Laundromat and the usual amenities. On the left is Ochoco State Park; hiker/biker sites available with water and toilets.

26.0 Shoulder improves. As you continue across the pancake-flat valley, look for the Cascade Mountains in the distance.

29.6 Ochoco National Forest Headquarters on the left as you enter Prineville, "Central Oregon's Oldest City." Prineville offers all services, including a Laundromat, a bike shop, and a campground.

30.2 Road Top Bike Shop on the left. If you need repairs or supplies, this is the place to go. In 1994, Rod and Camie Bachmeier celebrated their fourth year of doing labor-free repair work for long-distance cyclists.

31.7 Junction Main St. **SIDE TRIP:** To reach the Crook County Campground, turn left on S. Main St. There's a bike lane. Look for a market on the left in 0.6 mile. The all-service campground is 0.1 mile past the market.

32.3 Reach the west edge of town at the Hwy. 126 junction. As US 26 takes off to the right, bear left on Hwy. 126.

32.5 Cross the Crooked River, then make a right on unsigned O'Neil Hwy., a quiet, two-lane, shoulderless road. A sign

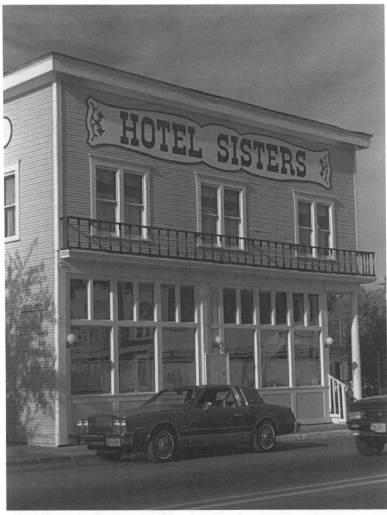

Hotel Sisters, Sisters, Oregon

does point the way to "O'Neil" and "Terrebonne." The terrain is flat except for one short hill, and the scenery is quite nice, with views of Mount Jefferson, Oregon's second-highest peak, in the background.

45.3 Junction Lone Pine Rd. Keep straight, climbing over the rimrock ridge. Lone Pine Rd. leads to Terrebonne as well as Smith Rocks State Park, a well-known rock-climbing mecca.

A scenic canyon and colorful igneous rock formations challenge the best of climbers.

46.1 Reach the top of the ridge for a fantastic view of the Cascade Mountains, including (from south to north) Mount Bachelor, the Three Sisters, Mount Washington, and Mount Jefferson.

46.5 Cross Main Canal.

49.5 O'Neil Hwy. curves and becomes N.E. 5th St.; bear left.

49.9 Stop sign. Road curves to the right as you cross five sets of railroad tracks.

50.2 Cross the canal and turn left on N. Canal Blvd. There's a "76 Bike Route" sign here, just prior to reaching US 97.

52.0 Bike lane begins.

52.7 T-junction at Antler Ave.; turn right following "76 Bike Route" signs. Go one block and turn left on S. 2nd St.

53.2 Delicious Pietro's Pizza is on the right as you reach the W. Highland Ave. junction in Redmond. Head through the stoplight, following signs for Sisters and Eugene via Hwy. 126. If you need anything in Redmond, head right on US 97. You'll find all facilities, including Laundromats and a bike shop. You'll also pass a Laundromat and various restaurants as you head out of town.

53.8 A bike lane begins as you pass a scattering of juniper trees through rolling hill country. There is one steeper grade, but it's not too long.

55.6 Operation Santa Claus on the right. Admission to the world's largest commercial reindeer ranch (home to more than 100 domesticated reindeer) and gift shop is free.

57.4 Turnoff on the left to Cline Falls State Park, a day use picnic area.

57.5 Cross the Deschutes River. Just beyond is Cline Falls Rd. A resort and restaurant are located to the left about a mile.

72.3 Junction US 20. Although the route continues to the right, go left 0.1 mile to reach Sisters City Park, which is on the right. Facilities include toilets and water. If you need a shower and Laundromat, continue straight for another 0.2 mile to Circle 5 Campground on the left. If you need supplies or just want to check out the town of Sisters, it is less than a mile to the west (right) on US 20.

Sisters to McKenzie Bridge (43.6 miles)

Today is a short day, with good reason: the magnificent Cascade Range. After you finish your tour of Sisters, you'll begin climbing the Cascades, which stretch more than 600 miles from Canada to northern California.

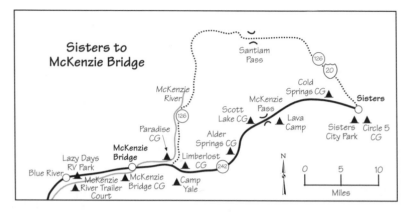

Thirty to 80 miles wide, the Cascade Range is blessed with thousands of lakes, approximately 900 glaciers, and hundreds of lofty peaks. In fact, the Cascades boast more volcanic cones than any other range in the United States—eighteen in all. Two of them—Lassen Peak and Mount St. Helens—have erupted in this century.

It's a nice, although steep, climb over the Cascades. Soon you'll be atop picturesque McKenzie Pass, which offers one of the most striking views of volcanic activity in the continental United States. Climb the stairs to the top of the Dee Wright Observatory and you'll see from Mount Hood to the Three Sisters, counting eleven mountain peaks on a clear day. Atop the pass are trails to hike and enormous lava fields to explore.

From the top of McKenzie Pass you'll continue your ride via the scenic highway, descending a number of switchbacks before zooming through the trees and ending your day along the McKenzie River, which will sing you to sleep.

MILEAGE LOG

0.0 Junction Sisters City Park entrance/US 20/Hwy. 126. Go left into Sisters, a quaint all-service town.

0.8 Junction Hwy. 242 (McKenzie Pass Scenic Route) is on the left as US 20/Hwy. 126 takes off to the right. Make a left on Hwy. 242, a two-lane roadway with a bike lane, and ride past the largest llama breeding ranch in the world. (The Sisters Ranger Station for the Deschutes National Forest is on the right just prior to the junction.)

Note that Hwy. 242 is closed in the winter due to heavy snow. If you find it closed, use the alternate route via Hwy. 126 described in the Adventure Cycling maps.

1.6 Bike lane ends; shoulder is nonexistent as you climb through a forest filled with aspens, pines, and mahogany. Fortunately, traffic is usually light.

2.0 Enter the Deschutes National Forest.

4.8 Cold Springs Campground on the right. The national forest campground provides toilets and water.

6.5 Begin climbing a 6 percent grade.

9.1 Historic Highway Site begins and continues for the next 17 miles.

12.5 Black Crater Trailhead on the left. Windy Point is just ahead. Stop for a grand view of the lava flow, Mounts Washington and Jefferson, and beyond.

15.4 Lava Camp Lake Rd. on the left. **SIDE TRIP:** A Forest Service camp is to the left in about 0.5 mile via a gravel road. This is a free national forest campground with toilets, no water.

15.8 Enter the Willamette National Forest.

15.9 McKenzie Pass—elevation 5,325 feet. From the observatory you'll see north as far as Mount Hood. Also, there's a close-up view of the mighty Three Sisters. In addition, there are rest rooms and hiking trails.

22.0 Turnoff to Scott Lake Campground on the right. **SIDE TRIP:** A sign points the way to Scott Lake Trailhead. A gravel road leads about a mile to the free Forest Service campground with toilets.

    A trail leading to Scott Mountain begins at the campground.

22.6 Obsidian Trailhead Rd. on the left.

23.7 From the pass, the highway rolls, with emphasis on the downhill. At this point it descends rapidly through dense forest.

27.6 Alder Springs Campground on the right. This national forest campground is free and provides toilets.

29.5 Trailhead on the left leads to Proxy Falls. **SIDE TRIP:** Enter the Three Sisters Wilderness by hiking Proxy Falls Trail 3532 for a mere 0.6 mile.

36.8 Limberlost Campground on the right. Again, there are toilets at this free national forest campground located along White Branch Creek.

37.8 Camp Yale on the left; all amenities.

38.3 T-junction at junction Hwy. 126, a two-lane road with a shoulder. Head left toward Blue River and Eugene.

39.1 Paradise Campground on the right; you'll find water and toilets at this national forest campground located along the beautiful McKenzie River.

The author at McKenzie Pass, Oregon, with Mt. Washington in background (Photo: Diego C. Rueda)

40.5 McKenzie Ranger Station, Willamette National Forest, on the left.
42.0 Leaving Willamette National Forest.
42.3 Lolo Mountain Lodge on the right; riverfront cottages are available.
42.5 Jennie B. Harris Rest Area on the right; toilets.
42.7 Cedarwood Lodge on the right. Just past is the Historic Log Cabin Inn and Restaurant.
42.9 Cross the McKenzie River.
43.0 McKenzie Bridge; general store on the left.
43.6 Turnoff to the McKenzie Bridge Campground on the left. Situated on the banks of the scenic McKenzie River, this national forest campground provides toilets and water.

McKenzie Bridge to Coburg (56.3 miles)

Today's task of riding 56 miles to Coburg is easy on the thighs and eyes as you continue a slight descent along the McKenzie River, passing several rural communities en route to a campground for the night.

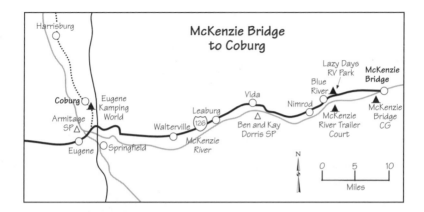

Deciding where to end your cross-country ride might not be as easy a task. I struggled with the question of where to end my ride for many days before reaching McKenzie Bridge. But in the end, like many westbounders, I opted for Florence. If you read the introduction to this book, you know my reasons for choosing Florence. If you'd rather continue on to Astoria, daily mileage plans follow for the 200-plus miles to this historic city.

Regardless of where you decide to end your ride, this segment ends in Coburg. Westbounders destined for Astoria, and all eastbounders who began their ride in Astoria, will veer a mere 0.5 mile off route to the campground. Westbound riders heading directly for Florence will end up going about 2 miles off route to spend the night in Coburg. Those who'd rather spend the night at a motel will find plenty to choose from in the all-service towns of Eugene and Springfield. In addition to bike shops and the usual facilities, there is also airline, bus, and train service.

MILEAGE LOG

0.0 Entrance to McKenzie Bridge Campground. Continue west on Hwy. 126, gradually descending (with a slight uphill once in a while) along the scenic McKenzie River. Shoulders remain, although they tend to be narrow at times. Watch for trucks and RVs, which are plentiful en route to Walterville.

2.3 Mini-market on the left.

2.5 Motel/restaurant on the right.

4.4 Junction Forest Road 19 on the left leads to Cougar Reservoir.

7.2 Lazy Days RV Park on the right. On the left is the McKenzie River Trailer Court. Both provide water and toilets.

8.7 Restaurant at junction of Blue River Dr., which leads to the town of Blue River. Named for the hue the stones give the water of Blue River as it integrates with the McKenzie, Blue River offers a post office, restaurant, and groceries. If you need supplies, make a right onto the spur loop.

8.9 Cross the Blue River.

10.0 Blue River Dr. loop merges onto the highway.

11.7 Finn Rock General Store on the left.

13.1 Cottages on the right.

13.8 Motel on the right.

13.9 "Mom's Delicious Homemade Pies" (café) on the right. The pies are indeed wonderful!

15.2 Nimrod; there's a mini-market here. Also, whitewater raft excursions are available at McKenzie River Guide Trips.

18.4 Cross Bear Creek.

20.6 Ben and Kay Dorris State Park on the left. Located along some of the wildest water on the lower McKenzie River, this is a popular "take-out" spot for rafters and kayakers. A paved road leads to a boat launch and picnic grounds.

23.2 Cross Gate Creek and enter Vida. There's a motel, restaurant, mini-market, and post office. Just west of Vida, look for the Goodpasture Covered Bridge. Built in 1938, the bridge was restored in 1986. At 165 feet, it is Oregon's second-longest covered bridge. It is also one of the most photographed of the many covered bridges in Oregon.

27.2 Cross Leaburg Canal.

29.9 Leaburg; market, post office.

33.4 Cross Lane Creek.

36.8 Cross the Walterville Canal.

37.1 Turn right on Camp Creek Rd. at Walterville and head away from the McKenzie River and busy Hwy. 126. There's a market, restaurant, and post office at the junction. The roadway sports a shoulder as you wind along this quiet backcountry road, descending slightly with an occasional short, steep uphill. You'll pass plenty of berry bushes along the way.

40.8 Mini-market on the right at junction Upper Camp Creek Rd.

42.7 Head back near the McKenzie River, then drift away from it again.

45.7 Stop sign at Marcola Rd. Continue straight on what is now called Old Mohawk Rd. As you continue, the hills are rolling, the scenes rural. (If you need groceries, turn left on Marcola Rd. and go 100 yards or so to a mini-market. If you need other supplies, head into Springfield, which is a couple of miles down the road.)

47.2 Road forks; Mohawk takes off to the right. Stay straight on Hill Rd.

47.5 Turn left on McKenzie View Dr. No shoulder; scenery remains rolling and rural; very little traffic.

51.7 The McKenzie River makes another appearance.

53.5 Cross under I-5.

53.6 Junction Coburg Rd.; bike lane. Go left to reach the cities of Eugene and Florence, right to continue to Astoria. If you're going to Florence but want to spend the night in Coburg, make a right onto Coburg Rd. Note that you will be going a couple of miles off route. There's a bike lane.

55.6 Enter historic Coburg, founded in 1847. There's a country store and a café in the downtown area. To reach Eugene Kamping World and RV Park, turn right on E. Pearl St.

56.0 Make a right on Stuart Way.

56.3 Reach the campground, which offers all facilities, including a Laundromat.

River otters are playful animals with webbed feet. They live mostly along rivers, ponds, and lakes in wooded areas.

Coburg to Florence (76.8 miles)

The last day's ride is long in mileage, although it doesn't have to be. If you'd rather spend two days bicycling to the coast, you can call the Archie Knowles Campground home for the night. This national forest campground is about 59 miles from Coburg.

The segment is an easy one, climbing roughly 900 feet in more than 70 miles. Although you won't face many uphill climbs, you may have to strain against headwinds, so be prepared.

The scenes from Coburg to Florence are certainly lovely. You'll pass open fields and the McKenzie River before entering Eugene, the largest city on the TransAmerica Trail and one that boasts many festivals and much cultural diversity. Some may want to spend an extra day visiting Eugene's numerous galleries and museums, while others may want to play in the parks or ride the many biking paths that wind along the Willamette River. Bike lanes are also laced throughout the community and can lead you to such affairs as the Saturday Market, a festival of crafts and food held downtown every Saturday.

Eugene is Oregon's second-largest city, rated by *Bicycling* magazine as one of the top ten cycling communities in the country. Home of the University of Oregon's Fighting Ducks, Eugene is a sports-oriented city, known as the track-and-

Raccoon

field capital of America. Here you can shop at the quaint 5th St. Public Market, whitewater raft down the McKenzie River, hear a symphony, absorb the beauty of a ballet, and enjoy a wild time at the annual Eugene Celebration, billed as the biggest bash of the year and held the third weekend in September.

The neighboring city of Springfield is the gateway to the McKenzie River Recreation Area. It is also the home of the annual Oregon Filbert Festival, held in late August.

As you leave the rush-rush of city life behind, you'll pedal quiet country lanes through lush countryside, where it rains a lot and it shows. About midway into the ride, however, you'll merge onto Hwy. 126, a popular route to the coast. Be prepared for an abundance of motorists and truck traffic, especially on weekends. A shoulder makes the ride more bearable.

The sights along Hwy. 126 certainly make up for any increase in traffic. You'll ride over the Coast Range, then down to the little community of Mapleton, which is located on the banks of the beautiful Siuslaw River. From there, you'll parallel the river before dipping your front tire in the Pacific Ocean at Florence.

Whenever I think of Florence, I remember its proximity to an array of dramatic sand dunes. I also think of Old Town, where you can browse through quaint shops or eat at a number of fine restaurants; the restored storefronts make the day that much more enjoyable. If you'd like to learn more about the history of the area, visit the Siuslaw Pioneer Museum, which emphasizes early Indian and pioneer history.

I will always remember the day I finally rolled into Florence. I was alone (my boyfriend met me with dry clothes about 10 minutes later), but the thrill of finishing was divine. I ended my ride soaking wet on the outside (it rained for half the day) but bright and sunny inside because I finished the day knowing I had bicycled more than 4,600 miles across the USA. (My total mileage includes side trips.)

MILEAGE LOG

0.0 Campground entrance. Head back to Coburg Rd.

0.7 Coburg; pedal left (south) toward Eugene.

2.7 Back to the McKenzie View Dr./Coburg Rd. junction. Keep straight on Coburg Rd., a two-lane road with a bike lane.

2.8 Cross the McKenzie River.

3.2 Entrance to Armitage State Park on the right. Located on the banks of the McKenzie River, this day use area supplies picnic facilities, water, and toilets.

4.5 Coburg Rd. turns from two lanes to four; the bike lane remains. You'll find all services, including bike shops and Laundromats, as you pedal through Eugene. Greyhound, Amtrak, and a number of airlines also service the area.

6.9 Junction I-105. Head left, following the bike lane along Coburg Rd. Be sure to follow the signs, as the bike path consists of a sidewalk for a short way.

7.3 Cross the Willamette River via a sidewalk that is a bike and pedestrian path. As you exit the bridge, turn right toward downtown on 2nd Ave E.

7.6 Stop sign; turn left on High St.

7.8 Turn right on 5th St. E.

7.9 Turn left on Pearl St., a one-way street with a bike lane.

8.9 Make a right on 18th Ave. E., a four-lane road with a bike lane.

9.0 Junction Willamette St. Keep straight on what is now 18th Ave. W.

11.0 Stop sign at Bertelsen Ave. Keep straight on 18th Ave. W., which is now two lanes instead of four. The bike lane ends, but the road isn't crowded; businesses succumb to residences at this point.

13.3 18th Ave. W. merges into Willow Creek Rd. You'll find plenty of berries throughout this rural area.

13.5 Keep right on Willow Creek Rd.

14.1 T-junction; turn left on 11th Ave. W. (Hwy. 126). The highway is two lanes with a shoulder; expect lots of traffic.

15.6 Turn left onto Greenhill Rd. There's a mini-market at the junction. Greenhill Rd. turns into Crow Rd. as you continue along the shoulder-blessed street through rolling hills and glorious countryside.

23.8 T-junction. Make a right on Territorial Hwy. toward the town of Crow. The road is shoulderless and truck traffic can be a problem, so use caution.

24.8 Go left on Vaughn Rd.; mini-market/deli at the junction. The roadway lacks a shoulder for the first few miles; then there is an intermittent one. Fortunately, traffic is usually light.

34.7 T-junction at Noti; make a left on Hwy. 126, a two-lane, shoulder-blessed road that winds over the Coast Range. Expect heavy traffic. There's a post office and mini-market at the junction.

39.8 Begin a short climb and gain about 200 feet. You'll lose the shoulder to the top, but there's a passing lane, so you'll still have some space.

40.5 Top of hill. When crossing bridges, use caution—most are virtually shoulderless.

43.9 Walton; post office, café.

52.3 Lane County Park located on the right along the Siuslaw River; toilets.

53.6 Camp Lane Group Camp, a reservation-only campground, is on the right.

56.2 Begin climbing.

56.6 Reach the top of the hill and, just beyond, a tunnel. Be sure to push the button before entering; flashing lights will serve to warn motorists of your presence. Enjoy a nice, mile-long 6 percent downhill.

58.1 Cross Knowles Creek.

59.1 Archie Knowles Campground on the left; water and toilets. Now the highway slightly descends to the coast.

60.9 Restaurant on the left.

61.0 Cross Knowles Creek.

62.0 Junction E. Mapleton Rd. **SIDE TRIP:** City pool at Mapleton School District is to the right about 0.1 mile. Camping is free. Showers, therapy spa, and fitness room are available for a fee. Call Diane Saubert at 268-4289 to check in.
Cross the Siuslaw River just beyond.

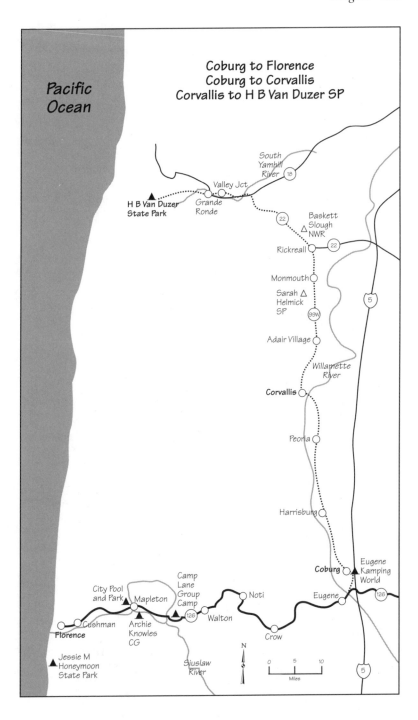

62.3 Road curves to the left as you enter Mapleton, where there is a restaurant, store/deli, and post office. The highway parallels the Siuslaw River as you leave the forest and head toward the Pacific.

73.7 Cushman Store on the left.

74.1 Blue Heron bed-and-breakfast inn on the right.

75.5 Cross the North Fork Siuslaw River.

76.8 Junction US 101 in downtown Florence. Camping is available in town, as well as both north and south of town approximately 3 miles in each direction. Jessie M. Honeymoon State Park, south of town, offers hiker/biker sites with all amenities, including a store and restaurant. Motels and other services, including a bike shop and Greyhound bus service, are also available.

There are many fine eating establishments in Florence. My favorite is the Blue Hen Café, where they serve the biggest, most scrumptious biscuits I have ever tasted.

Coburg to Corvallis (Alternate Route) (37.1 miles)

The ride to Corvallis is basically flat with a downhill tendency. Best of all, it's filled with scenes from a bicyclist's wishbook. You'll encounter wide open farm scenes, tiny towns, and basically uncrowded roads as you pedal through Oregon's lush Willamette Valley.

Corvallis has a lot to offer. Named America's second most livable city in one survey, it also boasts one of the best bicycling systems in the nation. After reaching town, pick up a "Corvallis Area Bikeways" map for further exploration.

With a population of 45,000, Corvallis is the seventh-largest city in Oregon and the home of Oregon State University, the state's oldest state-supported education facility.

Corvallis-area events are many. In June you can join in the Oregon Folklife Festival, or in July you can participate in the da Vinci Days Celebration, where world-renowned explorers, scientists, artists, and musical performers pay tribute to Leonardo da Vinci, whose best-known works are the *Mona Lisa* and *The Last Supper*. One of the greatest painters of the Italian Renaissance, da Vinci also studied anatomy, botany, astronomy, and geology, and he drew plans for hundreds of inventions.

If you're in town the first week of August, be sure to attend the Benton County Fair, featuring top musical performers, a rodeo, sheepdog trials, animals, jugglers, food, and fun. In late September, look for the Corvallis Fall Festival in Central Park. A Corvallis tradition for more than twenty years, the festival features arts and crafts, food booths, and live music.

MILEAGE LOG

0.0 Campground entrance; head back to Coburg Rd.

0.7 Historic Coburg. Pedal right (north) toward Albany; there's a shoulder as you continue, but you'll lose it after about 7 miles. You'll pass quite a few farms as you pedal through a rural area with little traffic.

12.2 Turn left on La Salle St. as you enter Harrisburg.

12.5 Stop sign; turn right on 3rd St. Signs point the way to Hailey and Albany. There's a bike lane now.

12.7 Look for a market on the right and another just beyond. There are also two cafés.

13.1 Turn left on Peoria Rd. toward Peoria. Traffic continues to be light and farmland plentiful. There's a narrow shoulder.

22.7 Mini-market. The shoulder is off again, on again.

26.0 Enter Peoria, a no-service town.

26.5 Peoria Park/Rest Area on the left, located along the Willamette River; water, toilets.

35.3 T-junction at Hwy. 34 West; turn left toward Corvallis. Shoulder now.

36.3 Cross the Willamette River and enter Corvallis.

36.5 Just past the bridge, reach a signal and turn right on N.W. 2nd St. (Hwy. 20 East) toward Albany. In one block, turn left on N.W. Tyler Ave. and head through a lightly traveled residential area.

37.1 Stop sign; turn right on N.W. 10th St., which turns into N.W. Highland Dr. as you proceed farther north. There's a bike lane now.

This segment ends here. You'll find all services in Corvallis (including bike shops, Laundromats, and Greyhound service), most of which are to the left of the route, on Van Buren and Harrison. There are also services on Hwy. 20. Campgrounds are nonexistent, so you'll have to opt for a motel or ask permission to camp in someone's yard.

Corvallis to H. B. Van Duzer State Park (Alternate Route) (62.5 miles)

Today's journey gets you more than 60 miles closer to your goal—Astoria, Oregon. And it does so in a nice way, gaining a total of about 2,000 feet in elevation as you pedal from Corvallis to H. B.

Van Duzer State Park, where there are hiker/biker sites in a noncampground environment. This segment heads north from Corvallis, passing through several small towns along the way: Adair Village, Monmouth, Rickreall, and Grande Ronde.

You'll pass through Baskett Slough National Wildlife Refuge in your quest for the sea. Named for George J. Baskett, an early thoroughbred horse breeder in the valley, the 2,492-acre refuge is composed of farmed fields, shallow wetlands, and rolling, oak-covered hills. It is home to the dusky Canada goose, the largest remaining population of Fender's blue butterfly, and a small number of wintering bald eagles.

En route you'll travel either quiet lanes or Hwys. 22 and 18, but a shoulder on the busier highways makes the entire ride quite pleasant.

MILEAGE LOG

0.0 Corner of N.W. Tyler Ave. and N.W. 10th St. in Corvallis. Head north on N.W. 10th St., which turns into N.W. Highland Dr. as you proceed north.

0.6 Market on the right.

2.1 Begin a steep climb.

2.7 Downhill begins.

4.3 T-junction at Lewisburg; make a right on N.W. Lewisburg Ave.; bike lane.

5.3 Stoplight in Lewisburg. You'll find a mini-market at this point. Go left on Scenic Hwy. 99W, which is not signed. Rolling hills continue as you ride north.

8.5 Enter Adair Village; market on the right.

8.7 Adair Village entrance on the right. Adair County Park, Benton County's newest and largest park, is near here.

10.8 Camp Adair sign on the right. Camp Adair was a World War II army cantonment, chosen by the U.S. War Department as a training site for Triangular Divisions. Interestingly, to mimic genuine conditions, full-scale models of European towns were constructed in the area and used for training maneuvers. Later used as a prisoner-of-war camp for Italians and Germans, the camp was often called "Swamp Adair," named for Oregon's intense rains. Today a few buildings and foundations remain, and an exhibit tells the history of Camp Adair.

13.8 Airlie Rd. junction. There's a snack shop and a gift shop at the crossroads.

14.0 Bear left on an unsigned road that now parallels Hwy. 99W. The road is narrow and minus a shoulder, but it passes through dense trees and farmland and isn't crowded at all. Flat to rolling terrain continues as you pass numerous berry bushes and some fruit trees.

16.7 Sarah Helmick State Park on the left. Water and toilets are available in addition to the usual facilities. Quail frequent the area, so watch for them.

21.3 The road curves at this point; take the right fork via Knox St.

21.6 Turn right on Main St. E. in downtown Monmouth, where there are all services, including a bike shop and Laundromat. Pass a market and a café as you head out of town.

21.9 Turn left on Hwy. 99W. A sidewalk on the southbound side of the highway leads to a nice, wide bike lane.

27.2 The designated bike lane ends at the junction of Hwy. 223 in Rickreall. There's a restaurant at the junction. Hwy. 223 leads to Dallas. Continue straight on the highway, which bears a shoulder.

28.0 Turn left on Hwy. 22 West, following the sign reading "Ocean Beaches." Hwy. 22 is a busy, shoulder-blessed highway through the countryside.

29.4 Enter Baskett Slough National Wildlife Refuge.

35.8 Country store on the left.

36.1 Cross Sale Creek.

36.8 Begin climbing.

37.9 Top of the hill and a winery on the right.

40.5 Cross Gooseneck Creek. Continue pedaling through rolling hills.

44.7 Hwy. 18 West joins the route. Continue straight.

48.1 Restaurant/mini-market on the right.

48.2 Cross the South Yamhill River.

48.7 Country store on the left.

48.8 Cross South Yamhill River again at Valley Junction. Hwy. 22 leaves the route; continue straight on Hwy. 18.

49.3 Fruit stand on the left.

50.5 Cross the South Yamhill River once again. Just beyond, enter the small community of Grande Ronde.

50.8 Market and restaurant on the right.

53.4 Enter the Van Duzer Forest corridor, where there are lovely trees and the terrain continues to roll.

57.0 Café/bakery on the left.

62.5 H. B. Van Duzer State Park on the right. You'll find toilets and water (boil before drinking because sometimes the water doesn't pass inspection) at this facility, which offers hiker/biker sites for a fee.

H. B. Van Duzer State Park to Cape Lookout State Park (Alternate Route) (44.8 miles)

For those who chose the alternate route instead of the more direct path to Florence, this will be a special day. Why? Because, for the first time in your cross-country quest, your eyes will gaze upon the deep blue Pacific. Its shimmering waters are bound to bring tears to some eyes.

Before reaching the coast, however, you'll pedal up and down Old Scenic US 101, a wonderful route through thick forest. Next you'll reach the beach at Neskowin, one of the coast's oldest beach towns. From there, US 101 is your guide north to Pacific City, Cape Kiwanda, and on to Cape Lookout State Park, part of the Three Capes Scenic Route majesty.

The Three Capes—Cape Kiwanda, Cape Lookout, and Cape Meares—are a definite treat and certainly worthy of a layover day. At Cape Kiwanda State Park, smashing surf, delightful views, critter-filled tide pools, and quiet beaches await all who visit. Some visitors watch as fishermen launch their dories in the surf, others observe hang gliders soaring from the cape, and still others embrace the view as gigantic waves crash against unique sandstone cliffs.

North of there, Cape Lookout offers wide, stunning views of the coastline as well as intimate looks at the coastal rain forest. A 0.25-mile self-guided nature trail boasts nearly twenty interpretive stations where typical vegetation is pointed out and described. Other popular activities here include clamming, crabbing, and searching the beach for Japanese fishing floats, driftwood, jaspers, and agates.

Named for the rocky headland that extends nearly 2 miles into the ocean, Cape Lookout State Park embodies virtually every natural and geologic feature found along the Oregon coast. The coastal rain forest consists of Sitka spruce, western hemlock, salmonberry, sword fern, skunk cabbage, and wildflowers such as trillium and lily-of-the-valley.

If you're hoping Cape Lookout State Park will be your home for the night, you're in luck. This segment is relatively short, spanning about 45 miles with a total elevation gain of 1,900 feet or so, allowing you plenty of time to explore.

MILEAGE LOG

0.0 Entrance to H. B. Van Duzer State Park. Continue west on Hwy. 18; expect some traffic. However, a shoulder is usually sufficient.

1.2 Leave the Van Duzer Forest Corridor.

2.9 Enter Alder Brook as you pedal through a relatively flat, rural valley that hosts the Salmon River.

3.3 Restaurant on the left.

3.6 Cross the Salmon River.

3.8 Salmon River RV Park on the right. Located along the river, the park has all services, including a Laundromat.

4.7 Cross Slick Rock Creek. Just beyond is Rose Lodge Store on the right. Between the two is North Bank Rd.; make a right.

8.9 Stop sign. Turn right on unsigned Old Scenic US 101.

9.1 The shoulderless road curves to the right as you head up the highway. Fortunately, vehicles are few as you ride up the steep grade.

13.1 Top of hill.

18.8 T-junction; make a right (go north) onto shoulder-blessed US 101.

20.0 Neskowin Beach Wayside on the left. Rest rooms, water. Nearby is the family resort of Neskowin, where you'll find restaurants, motels, a post office, and two golf courses. There's also a stable where you can rent horses to ride on the beach.

23.1 There's a wonderful view of the ocean from this overlook, which is near the top of a hill.

24.2 Enter Oretown; no services.

25.2 Cross the Little Nestucca River.

26.7 A sign points the way to the Cape Kiwanda Area and Pacific City. Go left on Brooten Rd., following the sign. This scenic road is shoulderless; use caution.

29.0 Bike route begins as you enter Pacific City, a quaint town with all services. There are two excellent bakeries in town.

Pacific City is famous for its flat-bottomed dory fishing boats. You can observe the boats from shore or join the fleet on a charter trip. If you'd rather hook a steelhead in the Nestucca River, or go crabbing and clamming in the bay, you'll find information and gear in town.

29.5 Stop sign at Pacific Ave. in downtown Pacific City. Go left, following signs for the Three Capes Scenic Area. (You'll continue to follow the signs until reaching Tillamook.)

29.7 Cross the Nestucca River and make a right at the stop sign.

30.6 Cape Kiwanda RV Park on the right. In addition to the usual amenities, there are groceries, a Laundromat, and special hiker/biker sites. Restaurants nearby.

30.7 RV Park on the right; you'll find deli/groceries as well as the usual. The road also leads to Webb Park, a Tillamook County Park with hiker/biker sites, water, and toilets. Across from the RV park, there's a beach access area with rest rooms.

From this point you'll continue to climb up and down the shoulderless road. Anticipate some steep grades.

35.1 **SIDE TRIP:** Turnoff on left leads to Whalen Island Park, a Tillamook County park. A gravel road leads 0.3 mile to hiker/biker sites, water, and toilets.

37.6 Look for a store on the left and the junction to Sand Lake Recreation Area. You'll find a campground at the Forest Service facility.

38.7 T-junction; make a left.

39.5 Ride through the sand dunes, a popular all-terrain vehicle area.

40.6 Begin climbing.

42.2 Top of hill and turnoff to a wonderful overlook.

43.7 Scenic overlook—Cape Lookout area.

44.8 Turnoff to Cape Lookout State Park on the left. The park is located in a typical coastal rain forest and includes the usual facilities, including hiker/biker sites.There's also a 2.5-mile hiking trail to the tip of the cape, which affords one of the most commanding views of the entire Oregon coast.

Cape Lookout State Park to Nehalem Bay State Park (Alternate Route) (47.9 miles)

Another relatively short day (less than 48 miles and about 1,500 feet in elevation gain) allows time to complete your exploration of the Three Capes Scenic Area. This time you'll visit Cape Meares State Park, site of the 40-foot-tall Cape Meares Lighthouse. First lit on about January 1, 1890, the tower is the shortest on the Oregon coast, standing 217 feet above the ocean. If you visit the lighthouse area, you'll be rewarded with excellent views of the animal life that frequents Cape Meares Rocks.

A state park and migratory bird sanctuary, Cape Meares State Park is the setting for the "Octopus Tree," an unusually large Sitka spruce with a diameter of over 10 feet at its base. Unlike most spruce trees, it has no central trunk; instead, limbs about 3 to 5 feet thick branch out close to the ground, lending it its name. A path leading to the tree offers several fine viewpoints of the Three Arches National Wildlife Refuge, home to sea lions and migratory birds.

As you head north from the Three Capes, you'll ride through historic Tillamook, named after an Indian term meaning "land of many waters" and home of Oregon's largest cheese plant. Amazingly, more than 800,000 people a year visit the Tillamook Cheese Factory, located just north of town. The factory also boasts a gift

Boats and dock, Nehalem Bay, Oregon

shop, a cheese museum, an ice cream bar and deli, and a videotape showing the cheese-making process.

If you like Brie, look for the Blue Heron French Cheese Company, just south of the Tillamook Cheese Factory. Here folks invite you to take a look and a taste, with free samples of cheese and wine available in an old Dutch barn.

The Tillamook County Pioneer Museum presents the history of the area, displaying more than 35,000 artifacts in the 1905 county courthouse. The historic and wildlife exhibits are exceptional.

As you ride from the Three Capes to Tillamook and north to Nehalem Bay State Park for the night, you'll travel a number of roads, most of which are quiet and uncrowded but usually shoulderless. You should expect heavy traffic for the 9 miles from Tillamook to Bay City. Fortunately, US 101 offers a bike lane. Also, watch for motorists along the Three Capes Scenic Route, as it can be quite busy.

MILEAGE LOG

0.0 Entrance to Cape Lookout State Park. Continue north following the Three Capes Scenic Route, climbing and descending the hilly terrain en route.

0.4 Leave the state park, now pedaling along beautiful Netarts Bay.

2.6 Whiskey Creek bed-and-breakfast inn on the left.

3.0 Café on the left.

4.1 Fork in the road; turn left toward Oceanside, staying on the Three Capes Scenic Route. The road on the right leads to Tillamook.

5.4 Rest rooms, market, and jetty area on the left.

5.7 T-junction; turn left and continue on the Three Capes Scenic Route.

5.9 Store/motel on the left. Begin climbing a steeper hill.

7.1 Top of hill.

8.0 Enter Oceanside, which boasts a beach that is a magnet for agate hunters.

8.1 Road forks; go right toward Tillamook via the Three Capes Scenic Route and climb again. **SIDE TRIP:** If you want to explore Oceanside, head left for 0.2 mile. You'll find a post office, motels, and restaurants.There's is beach access at Oceanside Beach Wayside; rest rooms too.

8.9 Top of hill; now the terrain is rolling once again.

10.7 Lighthouse State Park at Cape Meares on the left. **SIDE TRIP:** Ride 0.6 mile to the parking area. There's a gift shop, picnic facilities, interpretive center, scenic overlook, and, of course, the "Octopus Tree." It's all downhill to the parking area.

11.5 Top of hill.

12.7 T-junction; go right toward Tillamook.

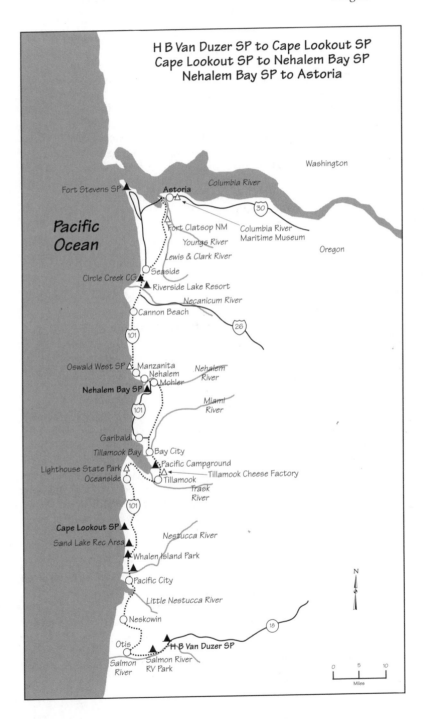

H B Van Duzer SP to Cape Lookout SP
Cape Lookout SP to Nehalem Bay SP
Nehalem Bay SP to Astoria

Washington

Columbia River

Fort Stevens SP

Astoria

30

**Pacific
Ocean**

Fort Clatsop NM

Columbia River
Maritime Museum

Younus River

Lewis & Clark River

Oregon

Circle Creek CG

Seaside

Riverside Lake Resort

Necanicum River

Cannon Beach

101

26

Oswald West SP

Manzanita

Nehalem

Nehalem
River

Mohler

Nehalem Bay SP

101

Miami
River

Garibaldi

Tillamook Bay

Bay City

Pacific Campground

Tillamook Cheese Factory

Lighthouse State Park

Oceanside

Tillamook

Trask
River

101

Cape Lookout SP

Nestucca River

Sand Lake Rec Area

Whalen Island Park

Pacific City

Little Nestucca River

Neskowin

18

N

Otis

H B Van Duzer SP

Salmon
River

Salmon River
RV Park

0   5   10

Miles

13.1 The road on the left leads a mile or so out onto Bay Ocean Peninsula. Now the main roadway hugs Tillamook Bay, where fishing seems to be the most popular pastime.

18.2 T-junction; continue left to Tillamook. Now there's a shoulder.

19.2 Cross the Trask River.

20.1 Junction US 101 in downtown Tillamook. Go left on US 101, a four-lane, divided highway without a shoulder. **SIDE TRIP:** A WWII blimp hangar is about 2 miles south on US 101 and a mile east. You can't miss the hangar, as it is the world's largest clear-span wood building. Inside, you'll find an array of World War II fighter planes, blimps, balloons, and other exhibits. Bicycle parking, a gift shop, and rest rooms are available.

20.3 Cross Hoquarton Slough.

20.7 The highway shrinks to two lanes and gains a shoulder. As you head north there are many services, including a Laundromat; look for the Blue Heron French Cheese Company on the right.

21.9 Cross the Wilson River.

22.2 You'll find a visitor center and the Tillamook Cheese Factory on the right.

22.5 Pacific Campground on the left; all amenities.

23.2 Cross the Kilchis River.

25.5 Market/deli on the right. Watch for a sign leading to the all-service town of Bay City, which is just off the highway. Continue riding along Tillamook Bay.

29.1 Cross the Miami River.

29.3 Make a right on Miami River Rd. No shoulder, but traffic is light. The terrain rolls as you travel through an area butchered with clear-cuts.

    Although staying on the coast may subject you to more winds, it is certainly more scenic. If you'd rather ride the coast, stay on US 101, traveling about the same number of miles through Garibaldi, Rockaway Beach, and Wheeler en route to the 43.7-mile mark. At this point you'll join the main route.

41.3 Cross the Nehalem River.

42.3 T-junction; turn left on Hwy. 53, a shoulderless road with some traffic, and head toward Mohler. Cross the Nehalem River again just after turning.

42.6 Mohler; groceries on the right.

43.7 Junction US 101; turn right to Nehalem. There's a shoulder now. (Had you stayed on US 101, you would merge onto the route at this point.)

44.3 Nehalem Boat Launch and rest rooms on the left.

44.6 Cross the Nehalem River.

45.0 Enter the quaint town of Nehalem, where there are all services and plenty of shops.

45.4 Downtown Nehalem; US 101 curves to the left. Begin climbing a short, steep hill. The shoulder shrinks or is nonexistent at times as you proceed.

45.7 Top of hill.

46.3 Restaurant/motel on the left.

46.6 Necarney City Rd. leads to Nehalem Bay State Park on the left. If you need food, there's a mini-market at the junction and a restaurant nearby. You'll climb and descend en route to the campground. Follow the signs and use caution on the narrow, winding road.

47.9 Entrance to Nehalem Bay State Park. The park has all services, including hiker/biker campsites, and a 1.5-mile bike trail.

Nehalem Bay State Park to Astoria (Alternate Route) (46.2 miles)

Today is either the starting point or the finishing point for cross-country cyclists pedaling the popular TransAmerica Trail. Bicyclists headed east will no doubt be excited, maybe even nervous, about the prospect of such an undertaking. And bicyclists finishing up their journey in Astoria, Oregon, will no doubt jump for joy; some might even cry.

For me the end of a trip is always somewhat bittersweet. After months on the road, I am happy to be off my bike for a while. In fact, I usually can't wait to grab my pack and go hiking. Yet, once I'm off, I can barely think of anything else but getting back on. And so today you can either breathe a sigh of relief and put the maps away, or you can grab an atlas and start planning your next tour.

Although you may have to battle hefty headwinds en route to Astoria, I'm hoping the scenery will more than make up for any drudgery. Note, however, that the winds do blow from the northwest and can be mighty alarming. I've ridden the coast on many occasions, always from north to south, and I've regularly felt great empathy for those few individuals who were headed north. They never look as though they are having any fun.

Along the way you'll pass Oswald West State Park and beautiful Cannon Beach—home to the famous Haystack Rock, one of the most photographed monoliths on the Oregon coast. Haystack Rock is also home to several bird species that nest there during the summer, the most popular one being the tufted puffin. Although the puffins nest on the rock from April through July, they are best seen during June and July.

Seaside, Oregon

In addition, Cannon Beach visitors will discover 7 miles of beautiful, walkable beach, and extensive tide pools. In late spring you can join in the annual Sandcastle Contest celebration, which attracts 15,000 to 35,000 spectators and about 1,000 contestants.

From Cannon Beach you'll want to spend time in busy Seaside Beach, the westernmost end of the Lewis and Clark trail, before rolling past Fort Clatsop National Memorial. Lewis and Clark led expedition members here in 1805 and built a stockade for winter quarters. Moving in on Christmas Day, the team spent the next three months replacing their worn-out clothing with handmade moccasins and buckskins. They also put up game and made other preparations for the long journey home. Although the original fort quickly deteriorated, a replica was built in 1955, and in 1958 the unit became part of the National Park Service.

The day ends in the lovely town of Astoria, a hamlet nestled along the mighty Columbia River. In addition to the usual services, the town offers Laundromats, a bike shop, a wonderful maritime museum, and a side trip to the Astoria Column for a gorgeous bird's-eye view of Astoria and surrounding areas from atop 635-foot Coscomb Hill.

Built in 1926 by the Great Northern Railway, the Astoria Column was fashioned after Trajan's Column (erected in Rome by Emperor Trajan in 114 A.D.). The history of the area is represented by a dozen events depicted in murals on a pictorial frieze. The murals, by Italian artist Atillio Pusterla, spiral up to near the top of the 123-foot column. After bicycling to the monument, be sure to climb the 166-step circular stairway to the top for a breathtaking view of the region.

If you'd rather camp out than stay in a motel, there are several places to camp, all off route. Fort Stevens State Park is about 10 miles west of Astoria and provides all the usual amenities, including hiker/biker sites.

This ride is less than 50 miles and gains about 1,700 feet in elevation, allowing you ample time to visit the various sites en route. If you have the time and the wind is blowing, perhaps you'd rather take two or three days to get to Astoria. The option is yours.

By the way—congratulations on having ridden across the country! SPECIAL NOTE: Access from Astoria to Portland, where you'll find the Portland International Airport, Amtrak, and Greyhound, is available by riding 95 miles southeast. Or you can contact the Portland Visitor Association regarding occasional bus service between Portland and Astoria; (877) 678-5263; email: info@pova.com.

MILEAGE LOG

0.0 Entrance to Nehalem Bay State Park. Ride back to US 101.

1.3 Junction US 101; make a left and continue north on US 101. The terrain is mostly rolling, with some steep climbs.

2.0 Manzanita; this resort community offers all services and 7 miles of sandy beaches.

2.3 Neahkanie Beach turnoff on the left.

3.9 Enter Oswald West State Park.

5.7 Cross Necarney Creek.

5.9 Parking area for Oswald West Campground. This is a foot-access-only campground with wheelbarrows for walk-in campers. Toilets and water are available at the campground, which is about 0.5 mile away. Also, there are trails through a rain forest thick with massive spruce and cedar trees, with paths leading to Cape Falcon and Smuggler's Cove.

6.9 Cross Short Sand Creek. Shoulder improves.

10.2 Arch Cape Tunnel. Descend through the tunnel, where flashing lights warn motorists of your presence. (Be sure to push the flasher button before entering the tunnel.) Exit Oswald West State Park just beyond.

10.6 Cross Arch Cape Creek. Enter Arch Cape.

11.0 Deli/post office on the left.

12.5 Hug Point State Park entrance on the left; rest rooms, water. Those who visit the park, located just north of Arch Cape, at low tide will thrill to tidal caves and a waterfall.

13.7 Arcadia Beach State Park on the left; rest rooms, water. If you like rock formations and tide-pool exploring, this is the place. **SPECIAL NOTE:** The shoulder was narrow or nonexistent for about 3 miles prior to this point.

14.5 Cannon Beach exit on the left. Named after a piece of artillery that drifted ashore in 1846, Cannon Beach hosts an annual sand-castle building contest in addition to a Puffin Kite Festival and Sunday Concerts in the Park.

This exit also leads to Ecola State Park, where there's a hike-in-only campground at Indian Creek. The park offers some of Oregon's finest coastal scenery, with breathtaking views of Cannon Beach. Other highlights include observing the sea lions that bask on surf-drenched rocks and hiking to Tillamook Head.

17.6 Cross Ecola Creek; climb again.

19.0 Top of hill.

20.9 US 26 joins the route.

21.4 A restaurant is on the right; another is on the left just beyond.

22.2 Entrance to Riverside Lake Resort on the right. All amenities are available. Cross the Necanicum River just after.

23.3 Circle Creek Campground on the left. You'll find all services, including a Laundromat.

23.7 Enter Seaside, an all-service community boasting art-filled galleries, delightful boutiques, and fine restaurants.

25.3 Junction Broadway. Make a right on Broadway toward the city park. **SIDE TRIP:** Go left 0.5 mile to the beach, a 2-mile-long promenade, and the famous Seaside Turnaround, the end of the historic Lewis and Clark trail.

25.6 City park/rest rooms on the left; cross the river just beyond.

25.7 Stop sign; go left on Wehana Rd., a shoulderless road. Use caution, as you'll find moderate traffic.

26.9 T-junction; turn right on Lewis and Clark Rd.

29.0 Climb to this point. The roadway is often windy and, except for a couple of steep climbs, fairly rolling.

29.5 Water treatment facility on the left. Continue straight.

32.0 Begin cycling along the river.

33.8 Fork in road; go left and up the short, steep hill.

34.4 Junction; continue straight.

36.2 Road on the right leads across the river; don't take it. Instead, continue left on Fort Clatsop Rd.

36.9 Road curves to the right.

38.8 Enter Fort Clatsop National Monument, where you'll learn about Oregon's earliest history.

39.4 **SIDE TRIP:** The road on the right leads to the monument, which you will reach in 0.3 mile. The monument consists of a replica of the fort where Lewis and Clark wintered in 1805–1806. During the summer, rangers adorned in buckskin demonstrate frontier survival skills.

40.0 Stop sign; turn right on Business 101 to Astoria. No shoulder. Mostly level now.

41.1 Cross the Lewis and Clark River.

42.1 Road curves to the left toward Astoria. There's a deli/mini-market here.

43.1 Cross Youngs Bay.

43.4 Road forks; head left and continue on Business 101 to Astoria. There's a shoulder now.

44.9 Merge onto US 101 and enter Astoria, site of the first permanent European-American settlement on the Pacific coast.

Haystack Rock, Cannon Beach, Oregon

46.2 Road merges onto Hwy. 30 East. If you continue through town you'll pass the Columbia River Maritime Museum, featuring one of the country's finest exhibits of ship models and nautical artifacts. **SIDE TRIP:** To reach the Astoria Column, continue straight up 8th St. via a very steep grade. After 0.6 mile turn left at the top of the hill, now riding Niagara Ave. Ride another 0.4 mile and turn left on 15th St. Pedal 0.1 mile and go right on Coxcomb Dr., climbing another very steep grade. After 1.0 more mile, reach the parking area for the column.

GERD LEMBECK—CROSS-COUNTRY BICYCLIST

I'll never forget the first time I saw Gerd Lembeck. I had already made camp at a city park in Chester, Illinois, when I decided to go into town to explore. When I returned "home" I found Gerd camped nearby.

Right from the start I knew that Gerd was different, but different in a special way. For one thing, he shunned Lycra shorts of any sort, even the padded variety. And he abhorred special biking shoes—and, regrettably, helmets too. In addition, he disdained panniers and all other "fancy" trappings.

Instead, he sat at the picnic table in big, baggy shorts, a shapeless tank top, and sandals, his typical riding attire. When I asked if he wore sandals even when it was cold, he said that if the weather turned bad he'd just put on his hiking boots!

Next to Gerd himself, his bike impressed me most. Nowadays most people have a fancy, lightweight bike—the kind that costs lots and lots of money. Not Gerd! The sixty-four-year-old was riding a Rixe, a standard German bike that was designed with multiple types of riding in mind. When asked how many gears the heavy, old-fashioned bike sported, Gerd proudly reported in broken German, "It has seven speeds; the eighth is when I push it up hills."

The forty-year-old bike (Gerd has owned it for half of those years) is no lightweight. It weighs 20 kilos unloaded, 40 kilos loaded. Instead of a regular handlebar bag, Gerd carries his "kitchen" in a wicker basket tied to the front of his bike. And although Gerd did use one pannier of sorts, most of his gear was carried in a huge duffel bag that he had strapped onto a back bike rack.

Gerd is a dedicated bicyclist and hiker who has spent his entire life traveling in the summer, either on two wheels or on foot. He has pedaled (and pushed) a lot of miles in recent years. Gerd rode from Canada to Mexico in the summer of 1992, and in 1993 he pedaled throughout Germany, riding north to south, following the line between what used to be East and West Germany. Of course, Gerd observed a lot of changes. "It was enormous," he said, "like being in another world."

This husband and father of four pulled ahead of me the next morning when I stayed on to explore Chester and Fort Kaskaskia. Gerd had a schedule to meet: he planned to ride 70 miles a day for ten weeks, allowing himself one day off per week.

As I continued west, I asked about, and often heard of, the cute little German man on the big, cumbersome bike. The night Gerd and I camped together he told me, "I figured I must do it." As far as I know, he did!

RECOMMENDED READING

Accommodations

Hostelling North America: The Official Guide to Hostels in Canada and the United States. Washington, DC: Hostelling International–American Youth Hostels, 1995.

Bicycle Maintenance/Touring

Bridge, Raymond. *Bike Touring: The Sierra Club Guide to Outings on Wheels.* San Francisco, CA: Sierra Club, 1979.

Butterman, Steve. *Bicycle Touring: How to Prepare for Long Rides.* Berkeley, CA: Wilderness Press, 1994.

Cuthbertson, Tom. *Anybody's Bike Book.* Berkeley, CA: Ten Speed Press, 1990.

Editors of *Bicycling*. *600 Tips for Better Bicycling.* Emmaus, PA: Rodale Press, 1991.

Toyoshima, Tim. *Mountain Bike Emergency Repair.* Seattle, WA: The Mountaineers, 1995.

Van der Plas, Bob. *Roadside Bicycle Repairs.* Mill Valley, CA: Bicycle Books, Inc., 1990.

Cooking

Hefferon, Lauren. *Cycle Food: A Guide to Satisfying Your Inner Tube.* Berkeley, CA: Ten Speed Press, 1983.

Wilkerson, James A., M.D. *Medicine for Mountaineering and Other Wilderness Activities.* 4th ed. Seattle, WA: The Mountaineers, 1992.

First Aid

Gill Jr., Paul G. *Simon & Schuster's Pocket Guide to Wilderness Medicine.* Atlanta, GA: Simon & Schuster, 1991.

General Interest

Ballantine, Richard, and Richard Grant. *Richard's Ultimate Bicycle Book.* New York: Dorling Kindersley, 1992.

Health and Fitness

Editors of *Bicycling*. *Training for Fitness and Endurance.* Emmaus, PA: Rodale Press, 1990.

Rafoth, Richard. *Bicycling Fuel: Nutrition for Bicycle Riders.* Mill Valley, CA: Bicycle Books, 1993.

Tour Accounts

Retallick, Martha J. *Discovering America: Bicycling Adventures in All 50 States*. Tucson, AZ: Lone Rider, 1993.

Savage, Barbara. *Miles from Nowhere*. Seattle, WA: The Mountaineers, 1985.

Skillman, Don, and Lolly Skillman. *Pedaling Across America*. Ashland, OR: Author. (Available from Don and Lolly Skillman, P.O. Box 381, Ashland, OR 97529; (503) 482-0309.)

Thompson, Alan. *One Time Around: A Solo World Bicycle Journey*. Toledo, OH: Author, 1991. (Available from Alan Thompson (APT), 6103 Reo St., Toledo, OH 43615; (419) 865-1556.)

INDEX

About the Author

Donna Lynn Ikenberry is a full-time photojournalist with a passion for travel. And while any method of travel can suffice, hiking and biking are her favorites.

Donna sold her southern California home and most of her belongings in 1983, choosing life on the road instead. After traveling full-time for 16 years, she married Mike Vining and now has a home base in South Fork, Colorado.

Donna has published more than 500 magazine articles and 3,000 photographs and is the author of 11 hiking and biking guidebooks, including *Bicycling the Atlantic Coast* (Mountaineers, 1993), *Hiking Oregon* (Falcon Press, 1997) and *Hiking Colorado's Weminuche Wilderness* (Falcon Press, 1999).

THE MOUNTAINEERS, founded in 1906, is a nonprofit outdoor activity and conservation club, whose mission is "to explore, study, preserve, and enjoy the natural beauty of the outdoors. . . . " Based in Seattle, Washington, the club is now the third-largest such organization in the United States, with 15,000 members and five branches throughout Washington State.

The Mountaineers sponsors both classes and year-round outdoor activities in the Pacific Northwest, which include hiking, mountain climbing, ski-touring, snowshoeing, bicycling, camping, kayaking and canoeing, nature study, sailing, and adventure travel. The club's conservation division supports environmental causes through educational activities, sponsoring legislation, and presenting informational programs. All club activities are led by skilled, experienced volunteers, who are dedicated to promoting safe and responsible enjoyment and preservation of the outdoors.

If you would like to participate in these organized outdoor activities or the club's programs, consider a membership in The Mountaineers. For information and an application, write or call The Mountaineers, Club Headquarters, 300 Third Avenue West, Seattle, WA 98119; (206) 284-6310

The Mountaineers Books, an active, nonprofit publishing program of the club, produces guidebooks, instructional texts, historical works, natural history guides, and works on environmental conservation. All books produced by The Mountaineers are aimed at fulfilling the club's mission.

Send or call for our catalog of more than 300 outdoor titles:

The Mountaineers Books
1001 SW Klickitat Way, Suite 201
Seattle, WA 98134
1-800-553-4453

Other books you may enjoy from The Mountaineers:

Bicycling the Atlantic Coast: A Complete Route Guide, Florida to Maine, Donna Lynn Ikenberry. 0-89886-303-1. $14.95.

Bicycling the Pacific Coast, 3d Ed.: *A Complete Route Guide, Canada to Mexico,* Tom Kirkendall & Vicky Spring. 0-89886-232-9. $14.95.

Mountain Bike Emergency Repair, Tim Toyoshima. 0-89886-422-4. $7.95.

Biking the Great Northwest: 20 Tours in Washington, Oregon, Idaho, and Montana, Jean Henderson. 0-89886-425-9. $14.95.

China by Bike: Taiwan, Hong Kong, China's East Coast, Roger Grigsby. 0-89886-410-0. $14.95.

England by Bike: 18 Tours Geared for Discovery, Les Woodland. 0-89886-275-2. $14.95.

Europe by Bike, 2d Ed.: *18 Tours Geared for Discovery,* Karen and Terry Whitehill. 0-89886-317-1. $14.95.

Hawaii by Bike: 20 Tours Geared for Discovery, Nadine Slavinski. 0-89886-432-1. $14.95.

Ireland by Bike, 2d Ed.: *21 Tours Geared for Discovery,* Robin Krause. 0-89886-366-X. $14.95.

Latin America by Bike: A Complete Touring Guide, Walter Sienko. 0-89886-365-1. $14.95.

Miles From Nowhere: A Round-the-World Bicycle Adventure, Barbara Savage. 0-89886-109-8. $14.95.

MAP ORDER FORM

Extensively detailed maps to the cycle touring route described in this book may be ordered directly from their publisher, Adventure Cycling Association. The "TransAmerica Trail," 4,250 miles from Williamsburg, Virginia, to Portland, Oregon, is represented by a set of 12 maps, each sized to fit a handlebar bag and waterproof. The maps are complete with turn-by-turn directions, detailed blow-ups of the tricky sections, and elevation profiles in the high country. Adventure Cycling is the organization that developed the TransAmerica Trail route, and these unique maps are an important part of the cycle-tourer's kit of information.

Adventure Cycling also publishes map series on two other cross-country cycling routes: the "Northern Tier" (4,415 miles, 10 maps) from Anacortes, Washington, to Bar Harbor, Maine, and the "Southern Tier" (3,135 miles, 7 maps) from San Diego, California, to St. Augustine, Florida.

Use the coupon below to send for your maps or a catalog of other Adventure Cycling maps and literature.

Mail to:
Adventure Cycling Association, P. O. Box 8308-PT, Missoula, MT 59807 (800) 721-8719

Adventure Cycling Association
P. O. Box 8308-PT
Missoula, MT 59807   (800) 721-8719

❏ Please send me a catalog of all Adventure Cycling maps and other literature.

Please send me the following sets of your detailed cycle touring maps:
TransAmerica Trail (BCP-15) 12 maps/set
_____sets   ❏ ACA member $78,   ❏ non member $114   Total $_____
Northern Tier Route (BCP-10) 10 maps/set
_____sets   ❏ ACA member $65,   ❏ non member $99.50   Total $_____
Southern Tier Route (BCP-17) 7 maps/set)
_____sets   ❏ ACA member $45.50, ❏ non member $66.50   Total $_____
For each set of maps add $5.00 for shipping/handling   S/H $_____
                                    Amount enclosed: TOTAL $_____

Credit card orders: Call toll free 800-721-8719, or use order form:
❏ Check enclosed   ❏ VISA   ❏ Mastercard

Account number _____ Expiration date _____

Name _____

Address _____

City _____ State _____ Zip _____

Signature _____
(required for credit card orders)

ACA member number _____ Daytime phone (___) _____